THE SPINACH KING

Seabrook family outing, August 1963.

THE
SPINACH
KING

*The Rise and Fall of an
American Dynasty*

John Seabrook

W. W. NORTON & COMPANY

Independent Publishers Since 1923

For information about permission to reproduce selections from this book, write to
Permissions, W. W. Norton & Company, Inc., 500 Fifth Avenue, New York, NY 10110

For information about special discounts for bulk purchases, please contact
W. W. Norton Special Sales at specialsales@wwnorton.com or 800-233-4830

Manufacturing by Lakeside Book Company
Book design by Lovedog Studio
Production manager: Lauren Abbate

ISBN 978-1-324-00352-6

W. W. Norton & Company, Inc., 500 Fifth Avenue, New York, NY 10110
www.wwnorton.com

W. W. Norton & Company Ltd., 15 Carlisle Street, London W1D 3BS

10 9 8 7 6 5 4 3 2 1

For Lisa

Plant a carrot, get a carrot
Not a brussels sprout!

CONTENTS

ACT IV

Old Bulls and Young Bulls, 1939–1954

ACT V

The Prince and the Reporter, 1954–1959

EPILOGUE

Seabrook & Son

A NOTE ON SOURCES

My father, John M. Seabrook, kept meticulously detailed office diaries throughout his career at Seabrook Farms. He started in the family's frozen food business on graduating from Princeton in the class of '39. By 1955 he had succeeded his father, Charles F. Seabrook, as CEO. Dad's astringent, lemon-scented cologne still clings to the soft manila covers of the diaries, typed from handwritten notes and indexed by Betty Gaunt, his loyal secretary and secret keeper, to whom he was "JMS." For the 1950s there are close to a thousand 4" × 6" lined pages per year, loosely bound with metal rings. I know what JMS was doing, but rarely what he was thinking, nearly every hour of every working day and night. I know his weekend plans, and the parties he attended and hosted. I know his girlfriends' telephone numbers—Eva Gabor, Ann Miller, Lady Jeanne Campbell—with glamorous Manhattan exchanges like Butterfield 8 and Longacre 4.

I have also relied on pretrial documents relating to my father's and his brothers' challenge to the estate of C. F. Seabrook, after attempting to have him declared legally insane. These papers include more than fifty interviews with Seabrook Farms board members, employees, and personnel, along with my grandfather's household staff and extended support group—the butler, the chauffeur, the masseur; assorted doctors who kept the old man supplied with drugs; and Dolly, the greeter at the Engineers Club, on the south side of Bryant Park, where my grandfather lived when in New York City. The lawsuit was settled before trial, but my father kept the interviews, and after his death I found them among his papers, along with love letters he wrote to his first wife, Anne, in several cardboard filing boxes labeled "Save for JMS Jr." in black Sharpie. The interviews portray my grandfather, enfeebled by old age, as an addict, a predator, and a paterfamilias who seemed to hate his own flesh and blood. Having left this material for his writer son, my father must have wanted the true story told, even if he couldn't bear to tell it himself.

THE SPINACH KING

Aerial view of Seabrook, New Jersey, ca. 1950.

BOOTSTRAP VILLAGE

M Y LONDON-BORN GREAT-GRANDFATHER, ARTHUR P. Seabrook, emigrated to the United States at the age of five. He arrived with his family at the Battery, on the southern tip of Manhattan, in January 1859. Over the next three generations, Arthur's fifty-eight acres of vegetable and produce fields in southern New Jersey became the largest farm in state history. At its peak, in the mid-1950s, Seabrook Farms owned or controlled fifty thousand acres in the southwestern corner of the Garden State, employed up to eight thousand people or more at one time, and grew and packed about a third of the nation's frozen vegetables. As a model of agricultural engineering, there were few farms in the world that compared. Asparagus could be cut, trucked to the plant, trimmed, washed, blanched, packaged, and quick-frozen to -40 degrees Fahrenheit in less than two hours; one was the goal. A 4-page photo essay that *Life* magazine published in January 1955 called Seabrook Farms, with only some hyperbole, "the biggest vegetable factory on earth."

The Seabrook Farms brand stood for family, freshness, and domestic modernity. Its advertising promised an end to drudgery through food engineering. As a 1959 Seabrook print ad blared "Food Miracle Frees Wife . . . Delights Husband!" Seabrook Farms Frozen Creamed Spinach, sold in the boil-in-the-bag Mylar Miracle-Pack, became the brand's signature product, known and sought after up and down the East Coast. Seabrook's cutting-edge packaging materials lent a space-age feel to its wares. In Stanley Kubrick's 1968 film *2001: A Space*

Odyssey, Floyd, one of the astronauts, is briefly glimpsed sucking from a meal of Seabrook Farms Liquipacks—a liquified carrot, fish, and leafy vegetable—while transiting to the moon.

✺

CHARLES FRANKLIN SEABROOK, my grandfather, was the principal dreamer, main promoter, political fixer, master builder, and autocratic ruler of this industrial farming empire—and ultimately its destroyer. The original vegetable factory was built on land his father, Arthur, purchased in 1893 and called Poplar Brook Farm. Arthur and Charlie, who started the Seabrook & Son partnership in 1905, were the first farmers in the region to use overhead irrigation. The processing plant was modeled on Henry Ford's Highland Park automobile factory, which opened in 1910; Seabrook management even installed a time clock out in the fields, where farm hands punched in and out of work. Instead of Model T's, which Ford introduced in 1908, the Seabrooks' vegetable factory turned out fresh, canned, and eventually, frozen vegetables on a massive scale.

Henry Ford, nineteen years older than my grandfather, was Charlie's inspiration. Both grew up on farms and looked to industry to save them from the drudgery and monotony of farm work. Both industrialized what had previously been cottage industries—in Ford's case, the artisanal carriage trade; in Seabrook's, market gardening. Both men enjoyed paternalistic relationships with their workers but had difficult and ultimately tragic relationships with their sons.

Although his passport gave "Farmer" as his profession, C. F. Seabrook saw himself as a builder. He hoped to emulate figures like Henry Kaiser, who parlayed a paving business into a shipbuilding empire, and Warren Bechtel, a Kansas farm boy who founded the Bechtel Corporation, which became the world's largest home construction company. The great-grandson of the owner, Brendan Bechtel, now runs the company, which is still owned by the family. C. F. had something like that in mind for his own family. Things didn't quite work out that way.

IN 1912, Charlie misled his too-trusting father about the value of the farm and purchased Arthur's share for far less than it was worth. Then, backed by the Wall Street investment firm of W. A. & A. M. White, he created, in five years of furious construction, the surrounding infrastructure of roads and railways to support an industrial farm. At Farm Central, the Seabrook headquarters, a brick smokestack, built by Kelly Brickworks in Philadelphia, with the name SEABROOK painted vertically, rose 225 feet in the air. The five-thousand-gallon water tower, with the Seabrook Farms logo on it, could be seen from miles away, a reminder of the role irrigation had played in the Seabrooks' beginnings. Six magnificent greenhouses enclosing three acres of land stood beside the highway that C. F. himself had built as a New Jersey highway commissioner.

The labor necessary to realize C. F. Seabrook's vegetable factory was supplied by thousands of worker-tenants. From the turn of the century through the early 1950s, displaced Italians, Russians, Syrians, Jamaicans, Barbadians, Germans, Poles, Hungarians, Czechs, Japanese Americans, Estonians, and Latvians came to work for Seabrook Farms. In the 1920s, Blacks migrating from the Deep South arrived in large numbers. During and after World War II, more than two thousand Japanese American men, women, and children, and a small number of Japanese Peruvians, came from the incarceration camps where they had been confined by Executive Order 9066, signed by President Franklin Roosevelt on February 19, 1942, in the racist hysteria that followed the attack on Pearl Harbor. Some seven hundred Estonians came to Seabrook from postwar Europe, under the auspices of the Displaced Persons Act, all of them personally sponsored by C. F. Seabrook.

Workers and their families lived in houses and barracks for which they paid rent to the Seabrook Housing Corporation, which was wholly owned by C. F. Seabrook. Collectively, these largely segregated worker villages made up Seabrook, New Jersey, the company town. The community had a Seabrook fire department, a Seabrook police force, a

Seabrook glee club, a Seabrook Buddhist temple, and a Seabrook Estonian Evangelical Lutheran Church. My grandfather used his political connections to get the U.S. Postal Service to open a Seabrook Post Office, so that all correspondence was stamped "Seabrook N.J."

C. F. Seabrook was an exemplary American to many of his workers, a man who, with no more than an eighth-grade education, had hauled himself up by his bootstraps, Horatio Alger–style. Seabrook is remembered by some former inhabitants as a "bootstrap village": a sort of laboratory where workers could hope to emulate the great man's success by working hard for the company. The village was unusually diverse, which was a result of recruiting labor from distant regions; it was a workforce comprised of people who had no other options. Still, Seabrook formed a multicultural outlier in a part of New Jersey where de facto Jim Crow segregation remained long after the passage of the 1964 Civil Rights Act.

❧

EACH OF C. F. SEABROOK'S THREE SONS inherited a different one of their father's talents. His intuitive mechanical engineering genius passed to Belford, the oldest, who designed and engineered the infrastructure for the quick-freezing process in the 1930s, pioneering breakthroughs that became industry standards. Courtney, the middle brother, got his father's gift for marketing. Courtney created the family brand, that peculiarly American form of heraldry, and oversaw package design. John, called Jack, the youngest, was endowed with his father's capacity for finance, as well as his need for total control. Their sister, Thelma, would have liked to work in the family business too, but as a woman she was excluded from anything greater than secretarial or plant work. C. F. felt strongly that women didn't belong in business, and he never discussed business around Thelma or my grandmother, Norma Dale Ivins Seabrook, whom we knew as Nana.

As a famous American agriculturalist abroad in the 1920s, C. F. Seabrook garnered invitations to weekend parties at immense feudal estates in England that had been in the same family for five hundred years. He advised his titled hosts on how to manage their lands more efficiently and scientifically; in return, he got to observe the British aristocracy up close. He brought what he learned home and set about creating a South Jersey peerage of his own, made up of the land, housing, infrastructure, and workers of Seabrook Farms: a sort of feudal kingdom ruled by Seabrooks, to be passed down according to the law of primogeniture for the next five hundred years. "All his life," Uncle Courtney wrote in a timeline of the family, "he stated to me that he was working and slaving to build up an estate for his children and grandchildren. . . . He told me of his trips to England and Charleston, South Carolina, to look up members of his family, and of his life's ambition to create a lasting business in Seabrook Farms that could be perpetuated in his memory for generations. This was a continuous idea he told me about for twenty-five or more years."

Divide and conquer, C. F. Seabrook's go-to method of controlling his workers, was also his strategy for managing his sons. Tensions arose when Jack, the youngest, was chosen to be their father's successor instead of his older brothers. Even so, the three stuck together and mostly supported each other. Jack started out running the farming division and proved equally adept as his father at management and corporate finance. Still in his mid-twenties, he was effectively running the company during World War II, when Belford enlisted and their father was sidelined with a mysterious illness in Florida.

But although John M. Seabrook was in all ways C. F.'s ideal successor and a seemingly perfect son, his father could not surrender control. It required a devastating inland hurricane—Hurricane Hazel, in the fall of 1954—and the prospect of ruin and scandal to force him aside. Still, the old man did everything he could to undermine Jack. C. F. humiliated his son in board meetings. He refused to call him by his name. He spent the last years of his life destroying everything the family had worked so hard to create. Ultimately, C. F. sold the business to outsiders in April 1959, the year that I was born, and left a smoking crater just over the horizon of my paternal heritage.

By the end of the 1970s, the old Seabrook Farms was gone. The plant was demolished to save on insurance, and the land was given to the township to avoid having to pay taxes on it. What remains is a Rust Belt–like patch of postindustrial decline. The site of the former plant is now a large sunken rectangle of open space, with grass growing over earth, shattered concrete, and broken bricks. All that's left of the world that my bootstrapping grandfather built is a small museum at one end of the basement of the Upper Deerfield Township Municipal Building, which is open to the public four days a week and is run by the families of former workers. Here the memory of C. F. Seabrook, his multicultural workforce, and his vegetable factory is preserved, swaddled in gauzy nostalgia.

Thirty years ago, when I first began to imagine writing about the Seabrooks, my mother advised me against it. "Don't write about your family," she said. Coming from a former journalist, who met my father on the job, this carried some weight. Why not?

"Just don't," was all she said. Maybe she knew what I was going to find out.

C. F. Seabrook with workers, 1950s.

ACT I

SEABROOK FAMILY REUNION, 1994

> Though the mills of God grind slowly, yet they grind exceedingly fine.
>
> *—Henry Wadsworth Longfellow*

CHAPTER 1

A CEO OF HIS
OWN PAIN

JACK SEABROOK TOLD A GOOD STORY. LONG BEFORE
"getting the narrative right" became a management strategy, my
father used stories to get what he wanted in business as well as in life.
The moral was always the same: His way was the best way.

That's why it was odd that, in the spring of 1994, when Jack was
asked to give a speech about his father at a reunion of former "Seabrookers," he froze. Normally, drafting and delivering a talk came as easily
to him as breathing. My mother called me in New York, alarmed.

"He just keeps going over and over the details of the farming business," she worried. "Pat has been doing research for him," she went
on, mentioning JMS's executive secretary, Patricia Anderson, who had
replaced Betty Gaunt. "She told him that nobody cares how many tons
of spinach his family could process in a day!" My mother said that
the topic he'd been asked to address was "What were the qualities of
C. F. Seabrook that enabled him to create this unusual community in
South Jersey?"

"They should have added, 'but to wreck his own family,'" I said.
"I'd like to hear *that* speech."

My mother was a former journalist, who, as Elizabeth Toomey, had
written a column for United Press out of New York in the 1950s. She
had met my father while covering Grace Kelly's star-studded wedding
in Monaco in 1956—my father was a guest of the Kelly family—and
had joined the Seabrooks in South Jersey just in time to watch the family fall apart. She had offered to help Dad with his speech, but he had

rejected her suggestions. The event wasn't until October, so there was plenty of time.

"He's very down," my mother went on. "Maybe you could help him, honey."

"That would be a first," I replied. I was a professional writer, but Dad had never before asked for my help with his writing, or with anything else, for that matter. Showing less than total mastery was never his style.

"Please call him," she said. "Come down and look at what he's researched. He and Pat have turned up some interesting things. I'm sure he could use your professional help in organizing it."

"All he has to do is ask."

"Why don't you invite him to lunch, darling? Now that you've got your fancy office." My mother was proud of my success in her former field, although she was also my harshest critic. She added, "Or better yet, I'll suggest he ask you to lunch, and you can meet at your office."

⁂

THE INVITATION TO SPEAK ABOUT his father had come from the South Jersey chapter of the Japanese American Citizens League. Between 1944 and 1947, more than two thousand American citizens of Japanese ancestry came to work for Seabrook Farms from western incarceration camps, where they had been confined by the U.S. government after Pearl Harbor. People who had been college-educated professionals in prewar California—doctors, accountants, engineers—became agricultural tenant-laborers for fifty cents an hour on the Seabrooks' industrial farm. The JACL was organizing an event to commemorate the fiftieth anniversary of the arrival of those workers from "camp" and had asked my father to deliver the keynote address.

As a speaker, Jack seemed to talk off-the-cuff in his speeches, but behind that apparent ease lay careful preparation. During family time in the evening, he would sit in his chair near the fire, still in his suit but with Belgian slippers on his feet instead of wingtips, a writing board on his lap, filling sheet after sheet of yellow legal paper. The only visible flaw in my otherwise perfect father was his handwriting, which was awkward, almost childish—nothing like the beautifully dressed and groomed gentleman on the other end of the pen. His penmanship was the only vestige of the awkward boy he had once been. Since the age of twenty-one, he'd had Betty Gaunt to type his scrawl.

The scratching of the fine ballpoints he favored mingled with the spitting and hissing of the fire and the sounds made by the ormolu clock on the mantle, ticking and softly chiming the half hour, always in sync with the other clocks in the house, giving the impression that our lives were inching imperceptibly forward with precision and inevitability, just as Seabrook Farms used to hum along. Everything ran like clockwork with Jack Seabrook. Three of his four children, "out of" two wives (which was understood to be horse-breeding lingo), had the same birthday. I arrived twelve years to the day after my half sister Lizanne, and my brother, Bruce, followed me two years later. Our mutual birthday was nine months and one day after our father's birthday, which was April 16. One could surmise that either the thrill of his own existence was so stimulating that he was at the peak of his powers on that night—or that he got off on screwing the taxman, as his father had.

One of my earliest memories is of him writing a eulogy for his father, in the fall of 1964. Unlike in most families, the paper of record had written the first draft.

Charles F. Seabrook Dies at 83; Pioneer in Quick-Frozen Foods; Jersey Farmer Developed System with Birdseye—Irrigated Fields Overhead.

The *New York Times* obituary hadn't made the front page, which upset the family. But at least it was the lead item among the deaths the *Times* recorded on October 21, 1964, securing left-side placement and more column inches than Anthony de Francisci, the man who designed the World War II veterans' eagle-in-a-circle insignia that GIs call the "Ruptured Duck." Jack noted with pleasure the use of the present tense in the obit's headline, an honorific reserved for very important people. The Seabrooks sweated those details.

My father read aloud the whole obituary, which explained how Grandad had brought irrigation to South Jersey, led the transition from horsepower to manpower, and industrialized market gardening by introducing Henry Ford's assembly line to vegetable processing. Later, by pioneering quick-frozen foods, C. F. Seabrook changed "the eating habits of the nation," the paper said. In our family history, he was Thomas Edison and Henry Ford in the same Dagwood sandwich: a great American who had elevated us from dirt farmers to the ranks of industrialists in a single generation, hurtling the middle class without breaking stride.

Much later I would come to know the real story of how C. F. Seabrook became the farm boss of a baronial plantation in New Jersey. Ambition, energy, and ingenuity drove his rise, but violence and terror allowed him to maintain control. We often bury the details of how large fortunes are made, as the brutality underlying them is less inspiring to read about than eureka moments of accomplishment. Had the obituary writer checked the *Times*'s own morgue, they would have found front-page coverage of tear gas and billy clubs, mobsters and vigilantes, and the burning crosses of the KKK.

❧

IN THE SPRING OF 1994, my father and I arranged to have lunch at "21." He would meet me first at *The New Yorker*, at Twenty-Five West Forty-Third Street, where I had recently been given an office and a staff job. My father had initially dismissed my desire to write as an unserious pursuit. He imagined I would tire of it eventually and go to law school. But now that I was publishing pieces and working in the magazine's midtown office, I had risen in his estimation. *The New Yorker* was always on display in the library at home, although I don't remember him reading it.

My office was down the hall from Joseph Mitchell's, the North Carolina farm boy who became a giant in the field of narrative nonfiction. Joe hadn't published in the magazine since 1964, but he still came in every day, dressed in a suit and a fedora. There were pictures of fish stuck round the walls of his office, relating to an ongoing writing project. On another occasion, I would watch as these two formally dressed gentlemen, Jack and Joe, sized each other up while discussing the woes of the farmer, game recognizing game.

My byline was still something of a sore point. My father regarded the name I had chosen to write under, John Seabrook, as his name, even though he only used it legally, and always with the M. He thought I should use "Jr.," since that was the part that was mine; otherwise, I was squatting on his mark. But I had never liked being John M. Seabrook Jr., his namesake, and I was damned if I was going to pin that belittling suffix "Jr." on the end of my hard-earned byline. He could be John M. Seabrook Sr. if he liked.

Outwardly at least, Jack Seabrook was a man supremely satisfied with himself and his place in life. He had created his world and was the absolute master of it. His once blond hair had darkened in adulthood, going pewter-colored in his fifties, and then, by his sixties, a distinguished aluminum silver. He was tall, blue-eyed, and slim, and his skin was still smooth. He dressed in the finest British tailoring, served only the best French wines, and drove a coach and four vanilla-colored horses along the country roads that ran through his Jersey estate, like an English duke. Although the Seabrooks were new money compared to the Protestant elite of Philadelphia, whose Quaker ancestors came over with William Penn, Jack Seabrook had been accepted by the Lippincotts, Scotts, and Bissells as one of their own. He had even become a member of the Farmers' Club, an ultraexclusive fraternity of Philly grandees who met for elegant black-tie dinners in each other's homes and played at being farmers, as their forebears had been, solemnly reading the recent Pennsylvania crop reports into the minutes before tucking into the beef Wellington and Château Palmer. The fact that Jack Seabrook had actually been a farmer at one time added a whiff of authenticity to these Marie Antoinette-meets-Old MacDonald gatherings.

A great deal of work, care, attention, study, and money went into being Jack Seabrook. The farm required a staff of twelve, at least.

Indoors, there was a cook, a butler, a housekeeper, and a driver; outdoors, a barn manager, two stable boys, a gardener, a groundskeeper, two more all-around hands in the machine shop, and Pat, his executive assistant. JMS, as he was referred to by the staff when talking among themselves, called his place "the farm," as gentleman farmers do. Apart from hay, however, the only crop was him. His upkeep also required frequent trips to New York, where he maintained a pied-à-terre in a high-rise on East Sixtieth Street and Lexington Avenue, a perk during his CEO days that he eventually was forced to purchase himself. He saw his tailor, Anthony Zanghi at Bernard Weatherill Civil and Sporting Tailors, who kept up with Dad's changing physique. He had his hair trimmed by "Little Joe" Cione, the barber in the lower level of the Time-Life Building, who in his prime had coiffed heads from the Beatles to Brooke Shields, but now had plenty of time.

✺

WE WALKED UP FIFTH AVENUE TO THE 21 CLUB, on West Fifty-Second, where my father's old friend Walter Weiss, the maître d', greeted us warmly and discreetly pocketed the cash Dad peeled from the folded and rubber-banded wad he kept in his front trouser pocket, right side. Walter seated us at one of the power tables along the banquette, under the Jets helmet hanging from the ceiling, where we always used to sit during Jack Seabrook's heyday.

My father had been CEO and chairman of IU International, a Philadelphia-based transportation and utilities corporation, where he had spent twenty years after the end of the family business. He had been forced out in the early 1980s, in part because of an SEC investigation into his misuse of company funds. Since that rather sudden retirement, Jack had had time to reflect on his extraordinarily eventful years as a young executive under his father at Seabrook Farms, working alongside my uncles Belford and Courtney, beginning in 1939, at the outset of World War II. He toyed with the idea of writing a memoir about those tumultuous twenty years, which ended with the selling of the company and his break with his father. My mother was in favor of the project; it would keep him busy, instead of brooding, she said. When the opportunity to speak had arisen, he accepted it gladly as a way of launching himself into the writing. But something had blocked his normally facile flow of words.

We ordered martinis. I horrified him by asking for mine to be made with vodka. I had yet to prefer what John Cheever describes in his journals as the "galling" taste of gin. The sommelier stopped by; a few years earlier, I had written a piece about him for GQ, to Jack's delight. During the reporting I had won a case of Château Palmer for guessing the relative amounts of Cabernet and Merlot in one of the vineyard's blended wines. "An excellent foundation for a cellar!" my proud father declared. The wine was soon gone.

We both selected sauteed soft-shell crabs, which were in season, and he chose a bottle of 1983 Meursault, a white Burgundy, to go with it. After several large gulps of my martini, I said, "Maybe the trouble you're having with your speech is that your audience saw your father as their supreme leader, this benevolent dictator who helped them get back on their feet after the calamity of losing everything. But that wasn't your truth."

"Well, I guess it's not a lie if it isn't the whole truth," he replied. His voice, usually full of pep, was listless. He was always hyperaware of his audience, which in this case would be six hundred or so returning Seabrookers: former Seabrook Farms workers who had mostly held the Seabrooks in very high esteem.

"But your father tried to destroy you," I blurted out. "I mean, I never knew him, but he sounds like your worst enemy."

I had met my grandfather only once, a scary encounter in 1963, when I was four, the year before he died. My understanding of the character of C. F. Seabrook mostly came from my mother, who had known him only toward the end of his life. Elizabeth Toomey Seabrook was an outsider, born in Spearfish, South Dakota, where her grandfather had staked out a homestead in 1877. She had a complex view of her husband's family, one that alternated between a populist scorn for East Coast establishmentarians like the Seabrooks and a latent insecurity that they would find her provincial, or worse, uncouth.

She had missed the visionary farmer-entrepreneur who created Seabrook Farms, but she had experienced the destroyer he became, the man who evicted us from our home, disowned her husband, and refused to acknowledge my birth. In a letter to her mother in 1957, the year after my parents were married, and two years before everything fell apart, my mother wrote,

Jack's father is without doubt one of the most remarkable men of all time—cunning, domineering and spiteful beyond belief almost. I guess he will always work to undermine Jack because he resents so bitterly that Jack is running the business. He is a man whose life has been motivated by a single force—to control. He must control the people and the property around him—he knows no security except financial dominance, and he has no basis for having people as friends—only to have them kowtow to him as dependents or to oppose him and be enemies. He couldn't run the business without Jack, though I guess he would try. If I had been born a Seabrook, I wouldn't have stayed around here for all the vegetables in the world. Why all of his family has lived under his malicious spell all their lives I can't understand. By alternating kindness with unexpected vicious thrusts, he keeps people in his orbit constantly off-balance. He is fiendishly clever and I suppose is punished more than he punishes others by the suspicious, conniving resentful old age he is living.

"No he wasn't my enemy," Dad said now, cutting his crab with surgical precision. We'd moved on to the wine. He added, "Yes, you never knew him." Silence ensued. I'd gone too far. Regardless of whatever my grandfather had done to my father—alternating kindness with "vicious thrusts" to maintain control sounded right—he was still fiercely protective of him. As I was of my dad, despite our differences.

"To this day," he went on, swirling the wine in his glass, "I can't say that for me personally this was a tragedy." He spoke in the same judicious, boardroom voice that he once used in addressing shareholders.

Now, sitting there on the 21 banquette, he sounded like the CEO of his own pain.

Dad wasn't given to introspection. He used this aspect of WASP identity like razor wire to guard his true feelings. Once, when I pressed him on why we didn't talk more about emotional things, he came back with, "Well, you know we Anglo Saxons just don't do that." On another occasion, when I asked him why he wasn't more interested in me, he told me, "Well, my father was *too* involved in my life, so I decided not to be involved in yours." In other words, his lack of interest was for my own good. In fact, he was involved deeply in my life—or, rather, in the life of John M. Seabrook Jr. It was his decision to send me to St. Andrew's, a small prep school founded by the DuPont family in Middletown, Delaware. It was his great desire that I attend Princeton, which I happily did, and then at his suggestion I spent two years at Oxford University. After I had failed to obtain a Rhodes Scholarship, he paid for me to go on a Seabrook Scholarship.

He rarely spoke of the decade that preceded my birth, when he and his father were locked in their steely war of succession. When he did, it was in delphic barnyard aphorisms like "You can't keep old bulls and young bulls in the same pasture." Perhaps he had kept so busy in Philadelphia to avoid having to dwell on the circumstances that wrecked his relationships with his father and his sister, Thelma, altered the arc of his life, and cast a shadow over our family. I wanted—needed—to find the source of his reticence.

"You landed on your feet," I agreed cautiously, adding, "no thanks to him."

Dad ignored that. "Of course," he went on, returning to his crab dissection, "it's conceivable we could have done great things with the business. Seabrook Farms might today be one of the great companies in the food industry. But when you inherit something, you always have that doubt: Could I have done it on my own?" Was that directed at me? We were both aware that my writing career was subsidized in part by family money.

"But you lost your home," I said, "your job, and your future, and

the author of that was the man you are supposed to be celebrating."
Clearly, this wasn't helping. We finished our meal and "broke camp."
I suggested that, if he liked, Lisa and I could drive down for Easter
weekend and we could sit together with his notes and see if I had any
helpful suggestions.

Catching the waiter's eye, he touched his thumb and fingertip lightly,
almost tenderly. Not committing to any editorial help from me, he said
simply, "We'd love to see you."

CHAPTER 2

DEEP SOUTH JERSEY

I MET LISA AT *MANHATTAN, INC.* MAGAZINE, IN THE Graybar Building in 1988, when she was assigned to copyedit a piece I'd written about Dan Quayle's golf game. She looked like my mother at her age, that same dark Irish coloring; maybe that explains the suddenness of it. But what I came to love about Lisa was her integrity, her generosity, and her concern for the poor. Lisa's parents had raised her to be compassionate to those less fortunate; in my family, comparisons with people less fortunate than us were intended only to reinforce how much cleverer the Seabrooks were. In her family, love came first. In mine, accomplishments seemed to take precedence and love came further down the line.

We married in 1991. I wanted to start having kids right away. Part of my eagerness, I told myself, was so that Lisa and I could raise children differently from the cold, best-foot-forward, stiff-upper-lip way that I was raised. That is one of the great benefits of marriage, in my view—the chance to graft yourself onto a different family tree and learn and grow from that bond. Lisa came from a large, warm family of five siblings who enjoyed each other's company and even organized vacations so that they could spend time together. I love my siblings, but a weekend in each other's company every couple of years is fine. We are loners in our own ways—as was our father. But I could spend every day with Lisa.

On Good Friday 1994, Lisa and I joined the holiday traffic headed down the New Jersey Turnpike for the long weekend. The turnpike is a 120-mile stretch of tarmac and tolls that leads from the sulphureous refineries of Elizabeth and Edison to the expansive corporate campuses of Big Pharma in the central part of the state, and finally to the vegetable and grainfields of South Jersey. If you take the last exit before crossing the Delaware River and head southwest, you'll soon be in Deep South Jersey. Were the Mason–Dixon Line to be extended beyond the northern border of Maryland and drawn straight across the state, Deep South Jersey would lie below it. Geographically, the area is a cul-de-sac, with the Delaware Bay on two sides. Culturally, it's a redneck Shangri-la. On Saturday nights in summer, the Cowtown Rodeo is the place to be. The farms are prosperous, but there is poverty everywhere you look: poor white people in the rural areas, poor Black people in run-down parts of Salem and Bridgeton.

In between the farms are swamps, piney woods, and lonesome crossroads where the stop signs are cored by bullet holes, circles of sunlight glowing in the metal. The earth is flapjack flat. The power lines have orange ribbons dangling from them so that the crop dusters won't get tangled. The big gun irrigation systems blast 300-foot-long arcs of water across crops. Tractors leave muddy, crosshatched tire marks on the roads. Every now and then there's a colonial-era brick farmhouse in which rich Quaker farmers once siloed their wealth. The marshy border of Delaware Bay feels like the edge of the known world. Out in the narrow channels that run through stands of cattails, people fish for carp and catch muskrats. Crab traps are piled up in hay wagons by the riparian edges. On the distant horizon, steam rises from the twin reactors of the Salem nuclear power plant, built on an artificial island in the mile-wide river. At night you can see the twinkling lights of the dual-span Delaware Memorial Bridge, five miles across the meadows and marshes.

One thing that South Jersey and North Jersey do have in common is a deeply rooted culture of political corruption. Both are on the wrong side of two rivers across from two major cities, which makes New Jersey, in Ben Franklin's famous phrase, "a barrel tapped at both ends." From the beginning, political power and wealth could be derived from tolling the roads and river crossings that lie between New York and Philadelphia, and from government contracts and public works to build more roads. The state's 21 counties contain 560 municipalities, which in turn hold boroughs, townships, and villages, each with its piece of toll revenues and road construction contracts. It's a bouilla-baisse of baksheesh. The Seabrooks might have made their fortune in other states, but the culture of political corruption in New Jersey literally paved the way. As a New Jersey highway commissioner in the 1920s, C. F. Seabrook spent public funds to build a four-lane concrete highway from Camden to the farm.

My résumé had been blotted by one of the most famous cases of political corruption in New Jersey history, a high bar that includes such notorious scandals as Bridgegate in 2013, in which state officials under Governor Chris Christie caused traffic jams on the George Washington Bridge to Manhattan as political payback aimed at the mayor of Fort Lee, the town at the base of the bridge. In the summer of 1979, when I was a rising junior at Princeton, my father leaned on his political connections to get me an internship with New Jersey Senator Harrison Williams. I'd worked for the Labor Committee, which he chaired. That was the same year the senator and others accepted bribes from FBI informants posing as the representatives of an Arab sheik who had millions of dollars to invest in the United States. Among those ensnared was the mayor of Camden, Angelo Errichetti, who was recorded boasting, "I'll give you Atlantic City!" The following year, Williams was convicted of extortion, the first senator in eighty years to go to prison and the last until former New Jersey Senator Robert Menendez exhausts his appeals.

༄

MY PARENTS HAD MOVED into their colonial-era farmhouse in Salem in 1959, after being exiled from Seabrook. My father had added various wings and outbuildings over the years. The furniture was mostly composed of Regency pieces that lent a French country house feel, like a vineyard château. Nothing was terribly valuable, except the Aubusson carpet in the Pine Room, which as children we were not allowed to walk on. But when put together by the masterful eye of our father, the sum was greater than the parts.

I greeted the staff, including Delores Hiles, the cook, and her brother Norman, who would be serving dinner tonight, and had on his white jacket and black pants uniform. The Hileses were a white family who lived less than a mile down the road from us. Delores's parents, Virginia and Buck, had raised seven children in poverty, in a house without indoor plumbing. My father had attempted to recruit and train all of them, at different times, as members of his indoor and outdoor staff. The Hileses were as much my family as my actual relations, partly because the Hiles family had been there for me as a child on the many occasions when my parents had been elsewhere. I loved them in an uncomplicated way that I wished I could love my parents.

The Hileses were the un-Seabrooks. Whereas tragedy never seemed to touch us, always splashing just to the stern, bad luck struck the Hiles family amidships again and again. Alcoholism, divorce, untimely death from car wrecks and farm machinery were common among the extended Hiles clan. Buck, the patriarch, died of a massive heart attack on our property, sitting at the wheel of his Oldsmobile one Saturday morning, while my brother and I played nearby. Delores's husband, Bobby, had been pinned underwater when the tractor he was driving toppled into the swamp, and he drowned. (Bobby couldn't swim, so he kept hold of the steering wheel; when they found him, he was still clutching it.) Delores and Norman's brother Billy slid off the barn roof when he was patching it and broke his back. But instead of blaming poverty, and its effects—poor nutrition, lack of health care, minuscule education—my parents placidly put the responsibility on the Hileses themselves. While they were supposed to be a cautionary tale for us, I learned empathy and humanity from them. Without the Hiles family, life on the farm would have been a lot bleaker.

Before the Hileses, in the early to mid-sixties my parents had a Black couple living with us. Arthur and Catherine were kind, intelligent people whom my father had recruited from the Seabrook Farms workforce for his domestic staff, and whose surnames I never even knew. They lived in the apartment over the garage. One day, I was alongside the road playing army with some local boys. The game was to set up small green plastic soldiers in a field and then bomb them with dirt clods, reenacting the nightly violence on the evening news, which was a distant but growing concern of mine. I feared that the war would last long enough for us to be drafted. The oldest Hiles boy, Earl, was over in Vietnam.

I saw our station wagon, a Country Squire, approaching, driven by Arthur, who had been to the Acme supermarket in town. As the car was passing, one of my friends shouted out the N-word, loud enough for Arthur to hear. White kids in South Jersey used that word among themselves, but I had never heard it flung as an epithet at a Black person before. Arthur was crying when I got home.

My parents held somewhat progressive if parochial views on race, shaped by their own families and their small-town origins. My mother had grown up living with Native Americans in Spearfish, and in New York she had worked with Blacks, whom she called Negroes. On the farm, Black people were "coloreds," which was the word I was taught until I was thirteen and used it to Vincent Johnson, a St. Andrew's School scholarship student from Richmond, Virginia, who became my first roommate. "What color?" he asked.

My mother didn't hesitate to explain why the N-word was so hurtful, and why it must never, ever be spoken. She called the boy's parents. We both talked to Arthur. I thought my mother was wonderful that day, and maybe that was why I confided in her about James, a Black man who worked with Billy Hiles in the machine shop, behind the barn, my favorite place on the farm. It reeked of gasoline and cigarettes, and there was a calendar in the nasty workers' bathroom with naked ladies. James showed me how to tie someone's hands behind their back with a rope, and then how to get out of it, like WHO-dini, James said. I'd beg him to tie me up, and I'd spend hours trying to escape. James had cautioned me not to tell my parents about our WHO-dini game, but when my mother asked what I did out in the shop all day, I shared our secret with her. The next day James was fired. I cried and begged my parents to bring him back, but it made no difference. I still feel awful about it, almost sixty years later.

☙❧

"YOUR PARENTS ARE IN THE PINE ROOM," Delores said. The rooms
in the house all had names, a custom begun by my grandfather, who
had affected the style of the grand British country estates he had been
invited to in the 1920s, when he was at the height of his fame as an
industrial farmer. A guest bedroom was the Toile Room, for the French
fabric that covered the walls; next door was the Silk Room, and down
the hall was the Pink Room.

The Pine Room, which my father had built in the early 1970s,
was the grandest room in the house. It was part of a new wing that
included, upstairs, a master bedroom and bath, and in the basement,
a new, greatly enlarged wine cellar. The big Palladian window at the
west end of the Pine Room was designed by Guy Roop, a prominent
mid-century interior designer, who wrote a monograph on Andrea
Palladio himself, and who was my father's old friend from Jamaica,
where he and his first wife used to go in the winter. Roop was a clos-
eted gay man who may have been in love with Jack; he lived with us
for long periods of time. My father wasn't gay, but gay men were often
interested in Jack Seabrook.

The Pine Room was named for the wide-plank pine paneling on the
walls, which had come from some old English pile, built in an era when
any pine tree sixteen inches in girth or greater was called the "King's
Pine" and by law reserved for the Royal Navy's masts. Ergo, it was the
kind of paneling one would have needed connections to get. The Pine
Room had a marble floor, partly covered by the Aubusson carpet, an
upright Steinway piano that my mother no longer played, and a pair of
life-size male Nubian blackamoors with gold rings in their noses and
houseplants resting on their heads, posed by the east windows.

My father shook hands, offered a hearty "Welcome!" and quickly
ventriloquized the dog. "Mona is certainly happy to see you," he said,
gesturing toward the pit bull terrier's madly wagging, stumpy tail.
My mother beamed and offered her cheeks. I could see in the way
she looked at Lisa that she was searching for signs she might be preg-

nant; she was keen on becoming a grandmother. No one hugged. I can remember my father kissing me as a child, his thin papery lips on my big sloppy mouth, but I can't remember him hugging me. When I broke my shoulder using a zip line in Vermont in the summer of 1984, he sat behind me in the car on the way to the hospital, grabbed a fist full of my hair from the back, I suppose to keep the bones stable for the drive, and held it.

The cocktail hour was my favorite time of day with my parents, when the clawed feet on which the furniture rested, ready to pounce, seemed to relax their coiled tendons a little. Two cocktails generally got me loose enough, and with wine and after-dinner drinks, the evening would unfold along a familiar groove. Alcohol was almost always involved, one way or another, in my interactions with my father, usually in highly ritualized ways. Just as with clothes, there was always the right drink for an occasion, in the right glass, from the Calvados at the end of a long evening of rarefied eating and drinking ("Bring the Calvados!" I would cry, in a Spanish accent, by then well into my cups, as Jack went into the bar to get the bottle) to a bullshot—Worcestershire sauce, beef broth, and vodka—for the morning after.

With Seabrooks, it didn't matter how much you drank; it was your "capacity" that counted. I had learned this lesson the hard way in the spring of 1972, when I was thirteen. The Devon Horse Show, an annual ritual of the horsey set in an ultrapreppy region of the Main Line, was under way, and there was a large tailgate picnic, with horses and horse vans, in a big open field with an eighteenth-century house nearby. An older boy I knew, whose father was one of my father's horsey friends, brought me a Budweiser and said we should chug one together. The first one was pretty hard to get down, but then I drank two more in quick succession, easily. Not long after that, my parents said it was time to go.

The car was a maroon Jaguar XJ-6, license plate NIMROD2, that Jack had recently gifted Liz. It smelled new, almost like a ripe melon. It wasn't long after we set off along the twisty, hilly roads alongside Brandywine Creek that the melon scent began to curdle the beer in my stomach. I lay back, my eyes open, hoping to ride the wave of nausea. I got the spins. Suddenly, my stomach flipped, and I knew I was going to throw up. I fumbled for the window control, but I couldn't find it, discreetly hidden next to the ashtray, and I puked all that beer and whatever I'd had for dinner into the leather map holder on the side of the door.

My parents were shouting as I finally found the power-window switch and, too late, hung my head out the window, the night air cooling my blazing shame. The blurred lights became fixed as my father pulled over. After they had done what could be done, we got back in the car and went to a gas station for paper towels and water, then drove home with all the windows open, in roaring silence. I went immediately to bed. The next morning, I was on the floor of the upstairs bathroom, leaning my pounding head over the bowl, suffering the first of many hangovers. No one came to see how I was, but through the floor I could hear my parents' voices coming from the breakfast room, directly below, talking about the incident. My mother's voice was low. My father's judgment, however, was loud, clear, and devastating: "I guess Johnny is not as grown up as we thought he was."

LISA, NO DRINKER (another thing I was drawn to about her), asked if she could have a glass of white wine. My father pretended to be befuddled by this simple request. "A *glass* of wine," he repeated, as if the concept of drinking wine by the glass had never occurred to him; wine came in bottles, not glasses. Once you opened a bottle, you drank it.

"You can open a bottle for Lisa," I said, annoyed. I heard the moist pop of a cork, and soon he reappeared with a glass of something.

I was grateful to my father for my excellent education, as well as for supporting my early literary efforts and life in New York. But we weren't particularly close. I found it hard to be myself around him. We played father and son as though we were acting our parts in a Restoration comedy. There seemed to be a reluctance on both sides to engage honestly, perhaps even a mutual suspicion that genuine affection might be used against you. The prudent course of action was to remain wry and detached.

Delores was preparing a dinner of spring lamb, fingerling potatoes, and fresh local asparagus to welcome home the "prodigal son," as my father never failed to call me at some point on my weekend visits, even though I was hardly extravagant or reckless. Naturally, we would need the right wine to pair with the food and the occasion. Would I care to accompany him to the cellar to choose a bottle, so that it would have time to breathe? Lay on, Macduff.

✺

LEAVING MY MOTHER AND LISA in the Pine Room, I followed my father down the narrow, winding stairs to the basement, noting how carefully he took the steps, clinging hard to the railing. Many years earlier, he had been thrown from his horse while out riding early one Sunday morning. He had fallen astride an irrigation pipe and broken his back. After the horse showed up riderless back at the barn, they searched and found him lying in a field. This story, which alarmed me greatly as a child, was notable because it is the only one he told in which he didn't come out ahead.

At the bottom of the stairs was cabinetry for storing excess kitchenware and picnic baskets, and next to that, a floor-to-ceiling plywood bookcase, painted white with green trim, which held old volumes of children's books that once belonged to Carol and Lizanne. These included *Eloise*, signed by the author, Kay Thompson, a friend from Dad's bachelor days (her phone number was also noted in JMS's diaries), *Black Beauty*, and *The Happy Hollisters*. I remembered the first time he had revealed the cellar to me, how he had stopped in front of the bookcase and asked, with a slight smile, "See anything?" and I studied the books. Among them was *The Boy Who Drew Cats*, a Japanese folktale about a rebellious artist-boy who defeats a goblin-rat that lives in the temple and that has killed many mighty warriors, simply by drawing pictures of cats on the walls and going to sleep. In the morning, when he finds the goblin-rat dead in the temple and can't explain it, he notices that the cats' mouths in the drawings are dripping with blood.

Dad grasped the shelves and pulled to the right, and the whole bookcase slid noiselessly into a recessed pocket behind the cabinetry. Before us was a wide, arch-shaped wooden door, painted glossy gray. A key marked W.C. fitted the brass key plate and the heavy door swung open, drawing the cool air of the cellar behind it. The viney scent of wine, cut with the stringent reek of strong alcohol, enveloped us. Inside it was dark, and as a kid, in the second it took to turn on the light, I used to imagine a goblin-rat rushing past us and disappearing into some other part of the house.

The main part of the wine cellar was directly below the Pine Room; it had been excavated during construction. It was a square room, about twenty feet per side, filled from floor to ceiling with wine and liquor, resting in sturdy wooden bins stacked four high, stained dark brown, and built around three sides of the room, along with a two-sided row of bins in the middle, forming two bays. The first bay held champagne on the left and bottles of liquor and port on the right. There were exotic spirits such as Framboise, Calvados, and Poire Williams; liqueurs one comes across in Hemingway—Eau de Vie, Armagnac, Mar; and others in garish colors, like Chartreuse.

In the next bay were the red and white wines, all French—great châteaux such as Cheval Blanc, Latour, Margaux, and Palmer. Bottles lay on their sides to keep the corks moist. The bottles of Burgundy, whether white or red, had gently sloping shoulders and expansive, deeply dimpled bottoms. The red Bordeaux wines, with their boxy shoulders and skinny butts, were called clarets. If a bottle was upright in front of the bin, it meant that that wine was ready to drink. Some of the wines predated me. It pleased our father that the year of my birth, 1959, and that of my younger brother Bruce, 1961, were first-rate vintages, in both Burgundies and clarets. Later, after the wines had further matured and become famous—wines that Gordon Gekko might have sent Bud Fox as thanks for an insider tip in Oliver Stone's film *Wall Street*—they featured prominently in our early-adult milestones, homecomings, and celebrations. No birthday toast was complete without the flourish: "1959 was a *very* good year." But the drawback of always being measured against one's birth wine is that the wines keep getting better.

The bottom row of the reds contained the magnums—two bottles of wine in one. There were also a few double magnums, and one jeroboam: six bottles. As a boy I was thrilled to learn that there were still bigger bottles, including a Balthazar (sixteen bottles), and a Nebuchadnezzar—twenty bottles! When I heard in Sunday school about how the Babylonian king Nebuchadnezzar cast Shadrach, Meshach, and Abednego into his fiery furnace, I pictured a gigantic bottle of wine, tipped forward aggressively, towering over those godly men.

Two bins in the cellar were reserved for the "ETS" wines. These had been created after a notorious incident in which my mother had gone down to fetch some wine to make her signature dish, coq au vin, and chosen a bottle of Cheval Blanc, '55. "And she cooked with it!" my father would cry—the punch line of this oft-told horror story—as his dinner guests shook their heads and moaned, "Ohh noo!" and my mother smiled gamely and played along as the simpleton housewife, which she most certainly was not.

After that, Jack had labeled two Rolodex cards, in red marker, with "ETS Red" and "ETS White" and placed them before bins filled with his most ordinary plonk, generally stuff that clueless dinner guests had brought as a gift. When I started coming home from college with friends and we would help ourselves to a bottle or two, we knew to avoid the ETS selections. ETS Red and ETS White became our shorthand for inferior wines in general.

In the back corner of the first room was a narrow archway that appeared to have been walled up with gray bricks, which on closer inspection turned out to be a painted facade. On it hung a dustpan and a broom. Behind the dustpan was a keyhole with a key in it. Turn that key and push, and a section of the false wall opened, revealing another room, with wooden crates of wine stacked along the walls.

These wines were for laying down, still years away from drinking. The extra layer of subterfuge seemed a bit much, given that a Deep South Jersey cat burglar was unlikely to have consulted Robert Parker's *Wine Advocate* before breaking in.

At the very back of this secret room, partly hidden by wine crates, was an old iron safe. Dad said that this was the original safe that his grandfather, Arthur Seabrook, and his father had used to store cash in, when the family business, originally called Seabrook & Son, was beginning to take off, in the early years of the twentieth century. He had kept it for sentimental value, he said; the combination had been lost long ago. Bruce pledged to crack the safe for him, and we spent hours down there twisting the cold steel knob this way and that way. It was not until after he was gone—and my therapist pointed out that the very last thing this careful, meticulous man would ever do is lose the combination to a safe—that I understood why it was hidden behind a sliding bookcase and a false wall, and what was inside.

❧

WHEN WE HAD SELECTED a bottle of Château Petrus 1985 (that Petrus was fellow Jerseyman Frank Sinatra's favorite château went without saying), we came back upstairs to open and decant the wine. Uncorking and decanting, a procedure my father undertook with the care and precision of a neurosurgeon extracting a brain tumor, occurred in the bar, a small, booze-crammed antechamber off the dining room that took up a significant portion of my headspace as a child.

In third grade, our teacher, Mrs. Hall, had given the class a homework assignment to draw a floor plan of our parents' house or apartment. I had to restart a couple of times until I got a feel for the proportions. I liked the way the assignment made me think. I was momentarily outside the familiar rooms and the lives we lived there, looking in. Eventually, I managed to fit all the rooms into the square boundaries of my plan. I was proud of my work and showed it to my mother.

"Oh dear," she said and laughed.

"What's so funny?"

"It's just the size of the bar, darling." My bar (labeled "BAR" in big, blocky letters) was a large rectangle exactly in the middle of the plan, as big as the kitchen. She laughed again—light but with a hint of tension. "It's so big! Mrs. Hall will think we're alcoholics!"

The bar was like a magic hat from which a magician pulls impossibly long scarves of colored silk. It sounded big—the violent rattle of the cocktail shaker and the muted explosion of a champagne cork reverberated throughout the house. The liquor cabinet was a men's club of masculine archetypes: someone's ornery grandfather on the whiskey bottle; on the gin, a British Beefeater, dressed like the real ones we had seen at the Tower of London, wearing bright-red jackets and round black hats and holding long spears. There were chrome-plated grippers and squeezers and shakers that my father washed and laid out on a dish towel before the guests arrived. The exotic names of the cocktails delighted me: martini, Daiquiri, Manhattan, old-fashioned. My favorite was the bullshot, because it sounded like "bullshit."

I dutifully erased the rectangle marked "BAR" and made it smaller, but now it was smudged, and more of a focal point than ever. So I redid the whole plan, trying to draw the bar to scale, but it still came out larger than it was.

"That's better, thank you, darling," my mother said, but I could tell she was still worried about what Mrs. Hall was going to think.

Decanting was always done by candlelight, because only when the decanter was lit from below could the sediment be seen properly. I watched as my father poured the crimson liquid through the little glowing circle of candlelight and onto the broad glass lip of the decanter, alert to the first dark bits of wine waste—the hated sediment. Sometimes, with an old bottle, a whole glass of wine was left, so thick was the crud. White wine, of course, didn't require decanting; the bottle sat in a terra-cotta sleeve that kept it cold. If the wine was a chilled Beaujolais, which was served on that fall day when the new vintage arrived, a day as eagerly anticipated as Christmas around the

Seabrook house, the bottle sat on the table, shoulders steaming, in a pewter coaster inscribed with the words "A Dinner Without Wine Is Like a Day Without Sunshine." A smiling Provençal sun split the sentence in half. As a boy, I had spent mealtimes listening to the adults talking, staring at that vinous proverb. As an adult, it had become my watchword.

After the wine was decanted and we were seated at the oval-shaped polished walnut dinner table, I poured. Pouring wine properly, another aspect of my patrimony, requires a symphony of fine motor skills. The right hand cradles the bottom of decanter, while the left hand grasps its throat with a white linen napkin. Approaching the drinker over his right shoulder, the pourer's left forearm is near the seated diner's right ear, as the left hand holds the lip of the decanter over the glass (never touching the rim), while the right arm comes up to initiate the flow of wine. When the proper amount has been poured, which varies depending on the size of the glass, the wine, the number of people at the table (not counting my mother, who wouldn't have any), and those like Lisa likely not to want a second glass (a calculation the pourer must make afresh with every subsequent pour), the right wrist rotates laterally, decanter neck spinning in the curved fingers of the left hand, so that the wine drips are held by centrifugal force, while the napkin in the left hand slides up to blot the lip. The slightest breakdown in muscular coordination results in spreading scarlet stains of shame on the spotless tablecloth, for all to see.

I was allowed a full glass of champagne when I turned thirteen. I had a crystal flute set at my place at the table, and as a special honor, I got to try my vintage year, the 1959 Bollinger, which by 1972 was a good deal more mature than I was. Before this, I had been permitted to take small sips of champagne from my father's glass, but now I had my own. As he poured the wine, I heard the faint whistling of breath in his nostrils and caught a whiff of his citrusy aftershave. I kept perfectly still, hardly daring to breathe, lest a micro flutter disturb the delicate procedure. Then there was a toast I can't remember, except that it concluded with, "1959 was a VERY good year!" I took a sip.

The shocking dryness of the grape practically gagged me, but I pretended nothing was amiss and took another. I felt something. What? Did anyone else feel it? I looked around. The adults were talking about what they always talked about—how the wine tasted (notes of peach, white pepper, and chocolate), where the grapes were grown, and how it had rained at the right time on the 1959 crop. They talked about everything but the most basic fact about the wine: the feeling it gave you. It felt as though my good spirits had emerged from a cave in my lower jaw where they usually hid away. It was a revelation, but no one at the table spoke a word about it, and I quickly learned to conceal the feeling. That was my first lesson.

∽๛๛

THAT EVENING WE SAT in our usual places at the dinner table, with my father in front of an oil painting of himself, dressed in full Coaching Club regalia. Whenever you looked at him, you'd see the portrait behind, like an aura.

Jack Seabrook was a leading "whip," or driver, in the ultimate rich man's pastime: four-in-hand coaching. He was the first American since Alfred Vanderbilt to be admitted to the Coaching Club of Great Britain. He became one of the leading promoters of four-in-hand driving in the U.S. His carriage collection, which he kept in a large building behind the barn—the Carriage House—contained buggies, buckboards, gigs, surreys, male and lady's phaetons, park drags, road coaches, and the horse-drawn sleighs that Dad delighted Bruce and me by pulling our Flexible Flyers behind when it snowed.

The signature piece in the collection was the Nimrod, a 1906 reproduction of a road coach that had once carried travelers between London and Oxford, stopping at the towns painted in gold on its wooden sides. The Nimrod offered seating for twelve on top, including the driver and a coachman, and room for four more, six in a pinch, inside the cab. The cab had small windows above the doors on both sides, set in wooden frames, which were opened by yanking up on a thick leather eyeholed strap attached to the lower sash. That dislodged the frame from its slot, and then you could lower the whole window into a pocket inside the door.

In 1969, after he had been admitted to the Coaching Club and had the proper clothes made at the original Bernard Weatherill on Savile Row, our father commissioned the portrait of himself with the Nimrod. The artist, the New York society painter Aaron Shikler, had posed him standing in front of the vehicle, with his foot resting on the step, like a hunter posing with an impressive kill. Jack wore a cutaway jacket, with the Coaching Club insignia—CC—engraved on the brass buttons; a high, stiff shirt collar; dove-gray bow tie, perfectly knotted by himself; and a stiff shirtfront placard with a burnt-meringue waistcoat, gabardine trousers, spats, and patent-leather shoes. His left hand drooped languidly over his top hat, while his right hand grasped the whip and the calfskin driving gloves. Shikler had put some of Jack's shrewdness into his eyes and arched brows, but he had made his jaw too square. Jack Seabrook wasn't Tom Buchanan, who moves with a creak and crunch of boot leather through *The Great Gatsby*. He was sleeker and stealthier, and much cleverer. He entered via a side door, and you wouldn't hear him coming.

Over the years, Jack's association with Nimrod had expanded beyond the road coach to include the quasi-historical figure of Nimrod himself, who according to Genesis was a "mighty hunter before the lord" who became "mighty on the earth." Who was Jack Seabrook to Nimrod, or Nimrod to him? I had plenty of opportunities on coaching outings atop the Nimrod to think about that. He secured a NIMROD1 vanity plate for his Mercedes sedan and scored NIMROD2 for my mother's Jaguar XJ-6. When Mom bought him a Mercedes coupe to cheer him up after he was forced to step down from IU, that became NIMROD3. When he purchased a former dairy farm in Vermont in 1973, it was christened Nimrod North, and a wooden sign was made for the barn. When he bought a winter property in Aiken, South Carolina, in the mid-eighties, that was Nimrod South. During horse-drawn picnics atop the Nimrod, you sipped mint juleps and G&Ts in plastic glasses on which the word NIMROD was stenciled. He got the township to change the name of Griscom Road, our street, to Nimrod Road. But frat boys kept stealing the sign, so now it's Seabrook Road.

Unfortunately, as Jack Seabrook was aligning his personal brand with Nimrod, twentieth-century popular culture was transforming the name into an insult. The agent of this etymological cataclysm was Bugs Bunny, the wascally wabbit of Looney Tunes, Warner Bros.'s long-running animated franchise. Bugs taunted his nearsighted nemesis, the hapless hunter Elmer Fudd, by calling him "Nimrod." The show's fan base made "You nimrod!" into an all-purpose Gen X put-down free of racial or sexual overtones. By the 1980s, if you went for a drive with my parents in one of the Nimrod fleet, you could count on honking and flashing lights at the very least. More than once, they were mooned by real nimrods.

Bruce and I tried to impress on our father the seriousness of the problem. "Nimrod doesn't mean 'mighty warrior on the earth,' or whatever, anymore Dad," I said. "It means 'a mighty doofus.'"

"I'm sorry," he said, "is that the Looney Tunes translation of the Bible?"

He refused his tormenters even the slightest satisfaction, handling these mortifying highway encounters as Nimrod himself, son of Cush, would have, with the haughty disdain of the truly mighty of the earth.

☙

UNLIKE MOST WOMEN who sat at his dinner table, Lisa Reed was not in Jack Seabrook's thrall. She had kept her name, although both my mother and Lisa's mother addressed letters to Mrs. John M. Seabrook Jr. When the subject of Lisa signing a prenup was delicately broached, I knew she was going to have none it, and I supported her. Plus, the idea of not being with Lisa was unthinkable.

My father's money, finery, and expensive tastes held no sway over Lisa. He realized it, and it made him vaguely uneasy, an amazing thing to see. She knew that kindness and fairness are what overcome the barriers we create to our own happiness, and that was something my father didn't know. At dinner that night, he made several attempts to provoke her by saying something politically incorrect that he hoped would get under her skin. President Clinton was at the time caught up in a scandal involving Paula Jones, an Arkansas state employee who was suing the president for sexual harassment. Dad wasn't put off by the president's alleged cheating on Hillary; what bothered him, he claimed, was "her looks." Clinton's character, infidelity, misogyny: surely one of these would get Lisa's goat. But she only smiled, and my mother said, "Jack, that's enough," and I got up to pour myself another glass of wine.

After the pie and champagne, I had a large brandy (Remy Martin, blue) in exactly the right glass and sat in the Pine Room with my father and the Nubians. We made a plan to meet the following day at 10:00 a.m. out in his office, where he had assembled the materials for his project, he said. After another ten minutes, he went upstairs to bed.

"Your father pretends to be hard-hearted, but he's not really," Lisa said, when we were in my too-small bed in my former boyhood bedroom.

"He claims to have been what he calls a 'hot-eyed liberal' once," I said.

"That's hard to imagine."

"I know, right? But I actually think he was."

"What happened to him?"

"Whatever happened with his father."

CHAPTER 3

MY FATHER'S CLOSET

THE NEXT MORNING, A LOW RUMBLE CAME THROUGH the bedroom ceiling: the sound of my father getting dressed. His closet, located in his dressing room, appeared to be the well-appointed closet of a successful businessman. Only when you stuck your head inside did you see a much larger collection of suits, hanging on a dry cleaner's motorized apparatus, extending up through the ceiling of the second floor and looming into the attic, which was filled with his life story, as told by his clothes. You could stand in the doorway, press a button, and watch as outfits from different eras of Jack Seabrook moved slowly past. Drape suits, lounge suits, and sack suits, in worsted, serge, and gabardine; white linen suits for Jamaica before air-conditioning; glen plaids and knee-length loden coats for brisk Princeton-Harvard football games; a raccoon coat for Princeton-Dartmouth, which was later in the season. Suits for a variety of business occasions, from wowing bankers (flashy pinstripes) to mollifying angry shareholders whose stock was diluted by a new stock offering (humble sharkskin). Suits for increasingly rarefied social events, from weddings at eleven to open-casket viewings at seven, to christenings, confirmations, and commencements, culminating in the outfits needed for four-in-hand coaching. The "sport" demands the mastery of a daunting range of wardrobe challenges, determined by what time of day the coaching event is taking place, whether it's in the country or in town, whether one is a spectator or a participant, or a member or a guest of the club putting it on. Three-quarter-length cutaway coats, striped trousers, fancy waistcoats, top hats: his four-in-hand outfits were the part of his closet that verged on pure costume.

Next to the closet door were the carousel's controls. Jack could use the directional arrows to browse his wardrobe, or punch in a three-digit code for a specific garment. A numerical key below the control box divided his clothes into nine categories: Dressing Gowns, Overcoats, Country Clothes, City Clothes, Odd Jackets, Odd Trousers, Formal Evening Wear, Formal Day Wear, and Odd Waistcoats. Under each category were subcategories based on patterns, colors, and fabrics. Odd Trousers, for example, were subdivided and labeled Colorful, White, Linen, Gray Flannel, Tan, Checkered, Extra Heavy, and Corduroy.

The 1960s had burst against Jack Seabrook's solid shoulders of English wool and receded, leaving one very interesting trace behind. This was a blue velvet Nehru smoking jacket, decorated with light-blue and navy flower and ivy psychedelia and matched with midnight-blue velvet pants. It was made by Blades of London, and dated April 25, 1968, a period when the Nehru was enjoying a brief vogue among fashionable men in London and New York. I had never seen my father wear the outfit, but there it hung, among all the sober garments in his closet, a sign that somewhere inside the businessman was a poet.

Some pieces had stories stitched into them. The black cashmere cloak with purple silk lining and a velvet collar, for example, was a garment originally made for Bishop Fulton J. Sheen of New York, the soulfully handsome mainstay of mid-century Christian TV. Seabrook and Sheen both patronized the U.S. branch of Bernard Weatherill on Madison Avenue, as did many other celebrities, socialites, and movie stars. Jack happened to be visiting Anthony Zanghi on the very day that Father Sheen died: December 9, 1979.

"Six months it took me to make that thing!" Zanghi exclaimed.

"Seems a shame for it to go to waste," Jack replied, fingering the velvet collar. With Zanghi's help (the tailor was a foot shorter), he slipped the coat on and—praise the Lord—the "sainted father" and my father had the same measurements. "Twas a miracle!" he'd exclaim, dropping in a bit o' brogue. The kicker was that the Church paid the bill. Glancing heavenward, he'd say, "Hallelujah!"

This morning, the mighty sartorial machine was hard at work as Jack dialed up his wardrobe for the day. On weekends, the mechanism seemed to be at its most active—corduroy Odd Trousers for family time; Country Clothes for an afternoon horse show; Formal Evening Wear to follow, perhaps with an Odd Waistcoat.

Today, my father was dressing for a morning writing session with his son—an unprecedented wardrobe scenario. He'd met the challenge boldly, with a tweed jacket, bow tie—always a good choice, for a literary man—a yellow sleeveless wool sweater, a pale-blue Brooks Brothers shirt, and a club tie. On his feet were butterscotch-colored suede chukkas, made by Edward Green of London.

We ate in the Breakfast Room, which was off the kitchen. The morning was chilly, so he had a fire going. The making of fires was Dad's domain. He took the time to instruct me carefully in the proper method of doing it, when I was still very young for lighting fires—maybe six. He showed me how to make a foundation of small sections of logs, and into that place five sheets from *The New York Times*, each one individually wadded up into a grapefruit-size paper ball. Then a log cabin of kindling—never a teepee—and then a few more small logs, preferably birch. Finally, just before lighting the fire, he took a half dozen wooden matches and stuck them in crevices in the bark.

"Pretend they're people," he said, lighting the paper with the next match.

I thought we were going to save them, but we didn't. We watched as one by one their heads exploded into flame and their bodies shriveled and turned black.

۞

AFTER BREAKFAST, I followed my father through to the outbuilding where he had set up his home office after he retired. The azaleas and rhododendron bushes were blooming, adding smears of colors to the pale-green spring pastures and the recently plowed fields that surrounded the property. Seabirds followed the plows, sampling worm meat instead of their usual aquatic diet.

Most of the home office was filled with dozens of three-drawer metal files. Jack's vast filing system was an extension of his extremely well-organized mind. There was also his private office, which had a door, and a large open area where Pat worked. On the wall above Pat's desk hung pictures of four older men who had influenced JMS in business—a sort of WASP hall of fame. His father held first position, then came three more father figures—Charles Thornthwaite, Ben Sawin, and Howard Butcher. Each became a surrogate father for Jack, whose own father was so irrationally critical of his talents. For these men, Jack Seabrook was the perfect son, who eagerly absorbed their wisdom and experience.

On his desk sat a Rolodex 3500-T, the Brooklyn-based company's top-of-the-line model, capable of holding up to two thousand cards in side-by-side carousels. Professional, personal, and commercial connections were categorized by card color. He had four duplicate 3500-Ts for which Pat had typed identical cards, one for each of his addresses: New Jersey, New York City, Nimrod South, and Nimrod North.

"Can I see what you've written so far?" I asked. Dad prided himself on his writing talent. He sometimes mused that, had he been given the choice, he might have pursued a literary career. A swashbuckling novelist named George Agnew Chamberlain had made his home nearby in South Jersey, and as a young man my father had been much impressed with that now forgotten author's lifestyle and world travels. Chamberlain played golf at Cohanzick Country Club with Amelia Earhart. Jimmy Doolittle, the pilot, would fly in for a weekend.

He handed me some pages Pat had typed for him, and I read in silence. Jack Seabrook belonged to perhaps the last generation of businessmen who could go through life without learning how to type—and be proud of it. I could see he was agitated, waiting for my reaction;

I took my time, enjoying his discomfort. My mother was right: he was lost in facts and figures about the former Seabrook Farms. It was always a place where size mattered, in part perhaps because the company's driving force, my grandfather, stood five feet eight inches tall, in shoes. Dad seemed determined to include every financing, every financial lender, and every record harvest of spinach and lima beans in his manuscript.

One passage caught my eye. It was his account of the first big financing deal my father was involved with, in September 1941, when he was just twenty-four. This was a large sale of securities that raised almost $30 million in today's dollars. He and his father had traveled by train to New York for the closing, taking C. F.'s longtime corporate lawyer, state senator Albert R. McAllister of Bridgeton, along with them. The financing represented "a momentous turning point for the company," my father had written. The money had helped Seabrook Farms expand to meet wartime demand for frozen and dehydrated vegetables and to begin experimenting with its own branded product line that would debut at the war's end. Culturally, the deal marked the end of the start-up phase of the bootstrap enterprise that my grandfather and Belford Seabrook had created over the previous decade, and the beginning of a modern corporation run by managers and beholden to its lenders and shareholders, as well as government regulators—a job for which my father's blend of talents perfectly suited him.

Like many farmers who had lived through the collapse of food prices after World War I, and the wave of bankruptcies that followed in the 1920s and '30s, my grandfather saw bankers as his natural enemies. To C. F., bankers, and in particular investment bankers, represented something he didn't have, which was capital—financial capital but also cultural capital. My father, on the other hand, had attended Princeton with the sons of these bankers, even if they had never registered his presence on campus. At least some of the later conflicts between my father and his father can be attributed to their belonging to different social strata. Maybe the Seabrooks came up too quickly from the lower level of the social hierarchy, and their dizzying ascent triggered a psychic case of the bends, caused not by nitrogen bubbles in the blood but champagne bubbles at the dinner table.

"We got the money," my father had written, of the 1941 financing, "shook hands with the bankers, and went out onto Wall Street. The Senator and I automatically turned west to head for Hudson Terminal, the tube to Newark, and the train home, but C. F. turned east. I asked him if he wasn't coming home, and he simply said no and walked away."

I looked up from reading. "Your father just walked away? He didn't want to celebrate?" My father shrugged. "Weren't you disappointed?"

"Not particularly," he mused in that CEO-of-his-own-pain way. He added, "My father wasn't as concerned with his sons' feelings as your father is." Ha ha. I returned to reading.

"On October 3, 1941, C. F. was incapacitated by a serious illness, probably a stroke. Prior to the 1941 illness, C. F. had exuded the confidence that he could and would tackle anything. His heroes in life were the great builders, men like Steve Bechtel and Henry Kaiser. He had their outlook. 'Tackle any job no matter what or how big, get it done, and move on to the next.' But after his long illness, C. F. never regained that confidence. And although he learned to project a strong public image, he simply lacked the old confidence when he was with people who were his peers—directors and bankers."

I looked up. "He had a stroke?" I asked, surprised. "Is that true?" I had never heard anything about a stroke before.

"Of course it's true."

"So that's the explanation for why he turned on the family? The stroke affected his mind?"

"He was never the same after it."

The timeline didn't really line up. "All these workers who came from the camps—they met him a couple of years later. He seems to have projected the old confidence in his dealings with them, at least."

"Maybe he did," my father replied. "But to the family, he wasn't the same."

"So the stroke affected his relations with his family, but not with his workers?"

I was trying to understand Dad's intentions. He was planning to tell a crowd of adoring Seabrookers that the man they had venerated wasn't right in the head. Why did the story need to turn on a medical event no one had heard of until now? What was really going on here?

CHAPTER 4

IT COULDN'T
BE HELPED

T HAT FALL, I DROVE DOWN TO SOUTH JERSEY TO HEAR
my father's speech. Cornstalks were bleaching in the fields;
pumpkins were everywhere; and in the early mornings the crackle
of shotgun fire could be heard from the duck blinds in the marshes.
The mosquitos and strawberry flies were finally gone. In good fall
weather like this we'd go on family picnics. Dad would take four
horses and his Bar Harbor Buckboard, a more casual vehicle than
the Nimrod, which had four rows of two-person upholstered love
seats. The vehicle had originally been built by a wealthy Philadelphia
family called Ludington, who used it on the beach at their Maine
estate. My father had found it in a barn in Lancaster, Pennsylvania—
Amish country—and had made numerous improvements, including
welding an iron frame on back to hold a cooler. During the hour-
long drive to the spot where we picnicked, the people in the back row
took cocktail orders from the other seats, and passed them along. At
the picnic grounds we unhitched the horses and tied them to trees
and Dad grilled steaks. These family picnics were the best part of my
father's coaching.

Like the other attendees, I was an adult returning to a place where
I had memories of being a child. Something traumatic had also happened to my family here, but I had been too young to know what it
was. As I turned off the turnpike at Exit 2 and paid the toll, I felt the
powerful pull of nostalgia—which comes from the Greek words for
"return home" and "pain." The pain is especially acute when the place
you are nostalgic for was ground zero in your family explosion. When

I was little, driving over to Seabrook to have Sunday lunch at Nana's used to give me a stomachache.

By 1994, Seabrook, New Jersey, had long since taken on the forlorn look of a company town without the company. The local grocery store no longer carried a large selection of Japanese food. In the center of town was a large empty space: the former site of the power plant, torn down in 1979 to save on the cost of insurance. Seabrook Farms was hardly the only employer in the area to close. Ritter shut its tomato processing plant in Bridgeton. The glass-making company Ardagh Glass moved away in 2014.

〜

MY FATHER HAD WORN one of his Savile Row suits despite the warmth of the October day. His yellow bow tie was his only concession to the summery temperature. But whereas I was already a puddle of perspiration, Dad never seemed to spritz; now that I think of it, I can't recall ever seeing him sweat. Not once. If there was a job that might induce perspiration, he'd have one of the staff do it, or he'd call on me or my younger brother, Bruce. Not because Dad was lazy, just because that had been the way on the family farm: the workers did the physical labor, the Seabrooks did the brain work. As for me, I was always happy and grateful to be tasked by my father with menial jobs that required physical labor, because it seemed to me that Jack Seabrook was more relaxed, and more himself, with the people who worked for him than he was with me.

On entering the Seabrook School, we passed a bronze stele of my grandfather, with a paragraph describing his role as founder of Seabrook Farms and, in 1924, as the builder of this school, a gift to his workers' children's education in the seventies. Generations of local schoolchildren have been schooled on C. F. Seabrook's genius and positive impact on the community. The auditorium was crowded with Seabrookers registering for the weekend. Most of the crowd were Nisei and Sansei—second- and third-generation Japanese Americans, who were children at Seabrook in the 1940s. Many moved back to California with their families after the war; a smaller number had lived here all their lives. There were several Issei—first-generation Japanese—including a ninety-six-year-old man named Fuju Hironaki Sasaki, who had been "mayor" of the postwar Japanese American community in Seabrook. There were a few Yonsei—fourth generation—as well.

We picked up our Seabrook Fiftieth Year Celebration tote bags and were shown to our seats, in a row near the front that was set off by a yellow ribbon. I nodded down the row to my father's older brother Courtney, my gentle, soft-spoken uncle, the middle brother of the three, now with snow-white hair and a new wife. The aisles were filled with people embracing each other, some with tears running down their cheeks: tears of joy at seeing old friends, and perhaps tears of pain at recalling former hardships. The event began with a percussive blast from the Seabrook Hoh Daiko Drummers.

Then the master of ceremonies, Ed "Mas" Nakawatase, said, "I'm a former resident of Dormitory 8, Apartment 10, 819 Garden Street, and I'd like to say to all of you, Welcome home." I saw my father smile. He was home too. Children and grandchildren of Japanese Americans who were incarcerated during the war typically find it difficult to get their elders to talk about their wartime experience. The younger generation want to know what happened in the camps, so they can pass along this almost biblical event in the family history to their children; the older generation don't want to talk about it, because the pain of the terrible experience is still too alive. When members of the younger generation ask their parents about the camps, they often hear the word *shikataganai*, a Japanese bit of stoicism that means "It couldn't be helped." Richard Ikeda, who came to Seabrook as a boy, told me *shikataganai* was a way of saying, "OK, life is unfair. Now get back to work." Theodora Yoshikami, who was born in camp and spent most of the first twelve years of her life in Seabrook, told me, "You could never talk about the camps with my parents. I never knew what went on. Until I was nine, I thought when people said 'camp' they meant summer camp." Seabrooker Seiki Murano's father testified before Congress about life in the camps but was reluctant to talk to his own son about them. A powerful nostalgia seemed to hold many of the returning Seabrookers in its grip. Seabrook was a nightmare for the parents but something of a paradise for kids. As adults they clung to this childlike view of Seabrook as a happy place. The alternative was an agonizing replaying of prior generational trauma.

The local Boy Scout troop led the crowd in the Pledge of Allegiance to one nation under God indivisible with liberty and justice for all. The Reverend William Borror, pastor of the Deerfield Presbyterian Church, which was my grandfather's church (his employees called it "St. Charles's Cathedral"), stepped forward and said a blessing. "We thank you that you are a God of mercy and that you are a God of justice, and that your purposes are worked out in time and in the lives of those who seek to do your good."

One of the speakers was Michi Weglyn, the author of *Years of Infamy: The Untold Story of America's Concentration Camps*, who came to Seabrook as a child. Like many other returnees, she had been sheltered from the hardships her parents endured, although she did recall how cracks in her mother's hands from sorting beans all day wouldn't heal. She had planned to memorialize "Mr. Seabrook" as a benevolent figure, but in preparing her remarks, she told me, she had asked an elderly Seabrooker about working conditions in the plant. "It was awful," he said. "I hope you're going to give them hell." Weglyn thought to herself, "Oh my God, what have I got myself into?" She also reread Seiichi Higashide's book, *Adios to Tears: The Memoirs of a Japanese-Peruvian Internee in U.S. Concentration Camps*, which contains a section about the three hundred Japanese Peruvians who had been taken from Peru to a camp in Texas, and then, eventually, to Seabrook Farms. "We were required to work 12 hours a day. Initially, men were paid 50 cents an hour and women 35 cents an hour, with no overtime pay or differential for night work. If one arrived at work late, or if one went home sick, that portion would be subtracted from his hours in five-minute units. We had only one free day every two weeks, when we moved from one shift to the other. There were no paid holidays, no sick leave. Even for that time, these working conditions were considered to be severe."

Nevertheless, Weglyn gave a mostly nostalgic speech, her voice vibrating with the emotion of what she could not say.

※

JACK SEABROOK ROSE to long applause. He had always been popular with the workers, and he had perfected the art of noblesse oblige. He had been a twenty-seven-year-old boy wonder in 1944, who was already running the company, as his father continued to recover from his mysterious illness. The former workers remembered Jack with great fondness, and you could hear that in their applause. When it finally died down, my father said he was going to speak about "a man of incredible accomplishments and incredible contradictions," his father C. F. Seabrook. He first recalled his grandfather, Arthur, was "a genial man with great flowing white mustaches," and then the terrible fights that C. F. used to have with his father. He described how, after agricultural prices dropped sharply after the end of World War I, my grandfather lost the business. "He was out, and he didn't look back," my father said. "This was another of C. F.'s great contradictions. He never cared about money." That was where he differed from his father: he cared.

Then Dad dropped his bombshell about the stroke, explaining that physical weakness had cost C. F. his confidence, and that the effort to make up for lost confidence had caused all the trouble that followed. This was his version of *shikataganai*: It couldn't be helped. I looked around to see if the audience was surprised, but no one seemed taken aback.

The closest my father came to speaking of his own truth was to observe how ironic it was that this man, who had treated his workers like they were his own children—here he glanced up at the rapt faces in the audience—"was never close or intimate in any way with any of his family. None of us thought this was odd, it was just the way Seabrook life was. In fact, it was not until 1953, when we three boys were grown men and a psychiatrist . . . pointed it out, we realized how odd this was. Seen up close, as we saw him, C. F. was cold and distant, but, in public, he was highly successful at projecting a warm, caring, friendly image to a large group." Otherwise, Dad gave the attendees of the reunion the C. F. Seabrook they wanted to hear about, dressed in all the oratorical trimmings. "Leave 'em smiling" was one of my father's public-speaking maxims, and that's what he tried to do with his closing line. "I sometimes wonder if the outcome would have been different if C. F. had educated at least one of his sons as a psychiatrist instead of an engineer." That was his kicker. Yes to mental health, but only if the Seabrooks got a piece of it.

❧

THE NEW SEABROOK MUSEUM, which we toured after lunch, was located in the basement of the Upper Deerfield Township Municipal Building, right below the courtroom. It was run by a nonprofit, the Seabrook Educational and Cultural Center. Ellen Nakamura, who had been one of grandfather's biggest supporters in the community, was a driving force in creating the museum. It was paid for in part by the $20,000 reparations checks the federal government sent to the victims of Executive Order 9066 in the 1980s.

In the corridor leading to the museum, we passed the ragged wooden piece of siding on which eleven-year-old "Mr. Chas Seabrook" had carved his signature in 1892, a relic saved from the shed before the structure was demolished. The time clock that the company installed in the fields was also here. Inside the main exhibition space, a 10" × 10" 3-D scale model of Seabrook depicted the plant, with its brick smoke-stack, the water tower, and the workers' villages. Around the walls of the room were black-and-white photographs of life in those villages and of work in the factory and fields, most from the 1940s and '50s. I saw one elderly Seabrooker pause at a picture of the plant and ask another man, "Were you there when they dynamited her?" referring to the demolition in 1979. "It was unbelievable. The dynamite took the first story clear out from under her, so that you could see clear through to the other side. But she just hung there in the air for about five seconds. It was like she didn't want to come down."

In the Seabrook museum, history had been quick-frozen in an imaginary past. The two-room diorama depicted a "global village" in South Jersey, represented by flags of twenty different nations hung around the room. My grandfather was portrayed as the farsighted and compassionate creator of this community. There was no mention of the 1934 farmworkers strike, and no pictures of Black workers, although there was a photo of Black children gathered around my father sometime in the 1940s.

At the center of the room was a black-and-white photographic portrait showing C. F. Seabrook surrounded by adoring employees. It was bizarre, to say the least, to see the man who had cast such a shadow over our family represented as a savior.

~

FOR LOTS OF FAMILIES, including mine, the reunion was a chance to visit with rarely seen relatives. My family's reunion took place in the backyard of my parents' house on Saturday afternoon.

Everyone was talking about my father's speech. To Carol, I said that the story of the stroke was a good compromise—a way of respecting C. F. while at the same time acknowledging that something had gone wrong—because it meant our father could blame a physical infirmity for the trouble that came later in the family. She said, "Of course, it's also nice to believe we didn't inherit the genes that caused this kind of behavior." That was a chilling thought.

At lunch, I sat next to my cousin Jim, one of Belford's three sons. We spoke about our grandfather in a reserved way, treading cautiously. With the Seabrooks it was often hard to tell what people were thinking. Jim and his brothers Charlie and Larry had founded a new company, Seabrook Brothers & Sons, that packed frozen food three miles from the old plant. Unlike the original company, Seabrook Brothers didn't own the land or grow the crops. By the mid-1990s, it was often cheaper to buy a container of frozen brussels sprouts grown in Poland, ship it to Seabrook Brothers, and repackage the sprouts to sell at Walmart, rather than to source the vegetables locally.

Jim's three sons worked there, and so did his nephews. Until that year, Jim said, he packed vegetables only for other labels, because he was not permitted to sell his vegetables under the Seabrook name. But that spring, thirty-five years after C. F. sold the brand, Jim bought it back.

"It's a good feeling," he said.

My mother had hoped that the younger generation would play a softball game, but nobody really wanted to. She turned to cousin Wessie and remarked, "Hasn't the weather this fall been incredible?"

"Good for the spinach," Wessie said.

I heard my father telling Cousin Jim that he was planning to expand his talk into a book. "Where do you think John gets his talent from?" he said, laughing, but I knew he wasn't really joking.

That night we had several especially good wines with dinner. Carol's husband, Jacques, proposed a toast "to Jack," and we raised our glasses to him, his portrait with the Nimrod looming behind.

C. F. Seabrook, 1942.

ACT II

THE HENRY FORD OF AGRICULTURE, 1859–1924

"This is the age of the engineer. . . . We telegraph without wires, and neither under nor upon the ocean, but through the air, annihilating space. We fly with the speed of birds of the air by a spark of gasoline as wings. We speak to each other through the telephone . . . and listen to the finest music in our homes from the imprisoned voices of the greatest singers. All this would have seemed miraculous to our grandfathers."

—*Andrew Carnegie, Address at the Engineers Club inaugural banquet, December 9, 1907, New York City*

CHAPTER 5

STRANGERS' GRAVES

"SEABROOK" FIRST APPEARS IN HISTORY AS THE NAME of a medieval hamlet in Buckinghamshire, England, not far from the present-day village of Ivinghoe. Today it's a cow pasture, but from the air RAF pilots once identified the remains of the settlement of Little Seabrook. The place evidently got its name from a brook next to the pasture, which tends to overflow. When I visited, Mr. Keable, the owner, told me, "When it rains, you see, that brook floods, and this field becomes a shallow lake."

"A sea, like," his wife added.

People who lived near this sea brook probably took it as their family name in the fourteenth century, when the Crown began to require surnames for the purpose of recordkeeping and taxation. Perhaps the Seabrooks had hoped to be the Woods, the Fields, or the Meadows, but those more attractive natural features were all taken by the time they reached the front of the surname queue.

In the seventeenth century, certain of those home county Seabrooks crossed the ocean to the coastal islands of South Carolina, where they created a long-grain rice plantation and owned many slaves. Other Seabrooks migrated east, to Cambridgeshire and Suffolk, and became tenant farmers. In the 1920s my grandfather commissioned a genealogy that claimed to find a line of descent from the South Carolina plantation owners to us. For a story in *The New Yorker*, I collected DNA from as many Seabrooks as I could persuade to swab themselves and sent the swabs to the lab of author and geneticist Brian Sykes in Oxford, to try to establish a connection between the two branches. I found that despite my grandfather's efforts to prove a paper connection, these two sets of Seabrooks don't appear to be genetically related. Our line descends from the eastern branch—not from the slaveowners but from the serfs.

Toward the end of the eighteenth century, the first of our Seabrooks learned to read and write. Thomas Seabrook, who was C. F.'s great-grandfather, entered Caius ("Keys") College, Cambridge University, in 1792 as one of the college's "sizars," or scholarship students. He obtained his MA in Divinity from Cambridge in 1798 and was ordained as a deacon in the Church of England in 1802. He married his childhood love, Frances Brewster, but she died giving birth to their first child, a son he named Brewster, in 1804. In 1806, Thomas married Mary Jay and had nine more children.

Thomas Seabrook's Church of England career was unspectacular. After eighteen years as a curate, he finally obtained a vicarage in the parish of Wickhambrook, Suffolk, in 1828, only to die suddenly eight months later, at the age of fifty-six, leaving his family penniless. The older children were apprenticed in London; the younger ones went with their mother to an almshouse for vicars' widows in Cambridge. Brewster, the eldest, became a doctor in Brighton, and continued his father's charitable work with the poor. The youngest boy, William Macro Seabrook, who was thirteen when his mother died, "wandered from place to place, making his living by gathering rags and bones," according to his death notice in *The Bury and Norwich Post*.

✍

AT THE TIME OF THE 1841 UK CENSUS, Samuel, my grandfather's grandfather, the sixth of Thomas's children, was a police constable living in the city of Essex with his wife, Clara. The 1851 census has him working in a beer hall in Surrey. Clara died in 1854, leaving two children, and within the year Samuel had remarried Clara's much younger sister, Fanny. In 1855 he was a warehouseman in London, living in Southwark, then a working-class area on the south side of the Thames. A son, Arthur Peters Seabrook, was born there in 1856. In January 1859, Samuel decided to try his luck in America. In Liverpool, he and his family boarded a transport ship called the *Underwriter*, traveling second class. They arrived at Castle Clinton in Manhattan nine days later. Samuel was listed as a "merchant," his fourth profession. One hundred and forty years would pass before the American Seabrooks and the British Seabrooks met again, when in the course of researching my family, I rediscovered its UK branch and was able to contact my fifth cousin, Colin Seabrook. We arranged to have tea in Essex. I recognized him immediately in the car park. We share a nose.

In the 1860 U.S. Census, Samuel Seabrook, now forty-four, had taken on a fifth profession—"herdsman." The Seabrooks had three children and were living at the Meadows, a produce and dairy farm near Rhinebeck, New York, that belonged to Charles S. Wainwright and his brother, William. The farm had a Gothic manor house on the property, which burned in the 1970s, and numerous outbuildings, including a stone barn and the still-standing cottages where the Seabrooks lived. It's a lovely spot, not far from the Hudson River. But the Seabrooks weren't there long.

Charles Landis, a Philadelphia lawyer turned property developer, had a vision for a utopian-sounding metropolis in South Jersey that would combine the best aspects of city and country living. Having determined that the soil was good for grape growing, Landis named the place Vineland and placed ads in New York papers offering cheap land in a "healthful" climate. The Seabrooks bought thirteen acres of scrubby wilderness from Landis in 1867, with a two-hundred-dollar loan from Landis himself. They arrived about the same time as Thomas Bramwell Welch, a teetotaling Methodist doctor who had invented a way to stop grapes from fermenting by pasteurizing them, and created Welch's Grape Juice.

Samuel proved to be as unsuccessful at farming, his sixth and final profession, as he had been at the previous five. After two years in Vineland, he wrote a letter to Landis asking for more time and financial assistance to carry out the improvements he had agreed to in the purchase contract. This letter, dated September 18, 1867, which I found in a box of unsorted odds and ends kept in the back of the Vineland Historical Society, is the only physical evidence that Samuel existed at all.

Dear Sir,
I am quite without means to carry on my improvements
to which I am so desirous of doing. Can I receive some
small assistance from the benevolent association to make
a beginning? In the meantime, will you kindly urge on
the sale of the land, your answer will oblige. Respectfully
Yours, S Seabrook

In 1869, Sheriff Samuel Peacock of Cumberland County repossessed the Seabrooks' thirteen acres. The family became tenants on a farm just outside the colonial town of Greenwich, pronounced GREEN-wich. According to the 1870 U.S. Census, only the two youngest sons were living with the family. Arthur, fourteen, was apprenticed to a local farmer, Alfred Davis, who would teach him truck farming.

Samuel died on the sixth day of January 1871, at the age of fifty-four, leaving his children as impoverished as Reverend Thomas had left Samuel and his siblings. According to a story Uncle Courtney told me, Samuel was buried in the "Strangers' Graves" section of the Deerfield Presbyterian Church cemetery, and a long-ago flood had washed away his stone. But though it was not uncommon for cemeteries to have sections for strangers, especially in agricultural areas like South Jersey where a lot of itinerant farmworkers passed through, Deerfield Presbyterian has never maintained one, according to church records. There is no notation in the sexton's book of a Samuel Seabrook being interred anywhere in the churchyard. It seems more likely that his family lacked the funds to bury Samuel, and some generous neighbor—perhaps the wealthy farmer Alfred Davis, who is interred there—took pity on the widow Seabrook and made part of his plot in the churchyard available as Samuel's resting place.

If so, Elizabeth "Fanny" Seabrook, who lived for another fifty-one years after her husband's death, never got around to marking his grave, nor did any of his children. Fanny and Arthur are in the churchyard, but there's no trace of Samuel. The man who brought the Seabrooks across the ocean and deposited us in Deep South Jersey, where we would flourish, is missing.

I asked my father about what Samuel had done, or not done, to merit such disregard. He had no idea.

"Doesn't that seem odd to you? That he's just gone? It's like he's been disappeared."

Dad shrugged. "People lose things, sometimes on purpose," he said cryptically.

I suspected the hidden hand of his father. With his long résumé of failure, Samuel simply wasn't qualified to be the crossing ancestor of an American as distinguished as C. F. The South Carolina Seabrooks were far more suitable. So Samuel needed to disappear.

Before C. F. himself died, he made sure that no one would ever misplace his grave. He commissioned a thirteen-foot-high slab of granite worthy of a pharaoh, with the name SEABROOK carved at the top, high above all the other names in the churchyard, and far removed from the word's origins as muddy cow pasture. At the base are the words "Look up to the realm of light and song, where no one says farewell."

CHAPTER 6

TRUCKERS

I N DOWNTOWN MANHATTAN, JUST BELOW COOPER
Square, Third Avenue turns into the Bowery, a word derived
from the Dutch *bouwerie*, for "farm." Now the site of expensive lofts,
restaurant supply stores, and a mix of unhoused people and the elabo-
rately clothed contemporary art fans at the New Museum, the Bowery
was where Dutch settlers grew fruit and vegetables and raised livestock to feed the citizens of New Amsterdam. Bowery farmers were
well situated for two reasons: proximity to the people who consumed
their products and to the manure produced by those people and their
horses, which could be spread on the fields to keep them fertile.

Around the turn of the century, millions of European immigrants
came to America through Ellis Island and the Port of Philadelphia,
bringing with them recipes that relied on culinary vegetables, grown
in backyards that did not exist behind the tenements of the Lower
East Side. The huddled masses were yearning to breathe free; more
prosaically, they were also yearning for celery, cabbage, carrots, parsley, peas, and spinach to make traditional dishes from the old country. At the same time, prosperous city folk, eager to show off newly
acquired manners, began to favor salads instead of potatoes, the
workingman's veg.

As population in the mid-Atlantic states increased, farmland near
the cities became expensive, and that pushed these "truck farmers," as
vegetable and berry growers were then called (from the archaic meaning of "truck" as produce or goods), out to Queens and Brooklyn, and
then farther away, to Long Island and New Jersey, which had been

colonial America's bread basket. By the mid-nineteenth century, Jersey grain farmers had gone west, and truck farmers took their place. Also known as "market gardens," the farms were so plentiful that New Jersey became known as the (Market) "Garden State," a reputation that survives on its dun-colored license plates, which hordes of metro commuters stare at daily in bumper-to-bumper traffic.

Arthur was by all accounts a first-rate truck farmer. Fourteen at the time of his father's death, he served a five-year apprenticeship with local farmer Alfred Davis. In 1875, Arthur became a tenant farmer on Davis's land. He lived in a small stone house near Beebe Run, regional dialect for a tidal creek. He married a local girl named Elizabeth Riley in 1878, and Fanny Seabrook was born two years later. Charles Franklin Seabrook (called Charlie) followed during the short-lived administration of President James Garfield, who was inaugurated in March 1881 and assassinated that September. Then came another daughter, Ida, and finally Sidney, Charlie's younger brother.

In 1893, after eighteen years of tenant farming, Arthur was able to buy a fifty-eight-acre spread of his own in Deerfield Township from a farmer named David Findlay, for $3,000, a bit more than $100,000 today. He named it Poplar Brook Farm. The family built a large house with generous porches on Parsonage Road, in the place that would become known as Farm Central. The land had gone unworked for years and was thickly grown over with brambles, scrub oak, and vines, which Arthur and Charlie, together with a hired man or two, laboriously cleared.

Poplar Brook Farm was in a sweet spot: far enough away from urban centers for the land to remain inexpensive, but close enough to Philadelphia and New York to ship goods in a day by rail, and to economically transport city manure, both animal and human (known as nightsoil) to fertilize crops. New York City produced a million pounds of horse manure a day by 1900. Farmers also relied on crushed oyster shells, which were produced locally in the nearby oystering towns of Shellpile and Bivalve, and bat guano that came by ship from South America.

Poplar Brook sat atop a particularly productive patch of earth. The reason was a mineral called glauconite, the nutrient that made Jersey's market gardens so fertile. One hundred million years ago, in the Cretaceous Period, a shallow sea known as the Interior Coastal Plain arced from the Raritan Bay in Perth Amboy to the Delaware River around Salem. The bodies of sea creatures as tiny as protoplankton and as large as hundred-foot-long mosasaurs settled on the shallow ocean floor and were transformed over eons into glauconite, or "marl," as farmers call the stuff. As far back as late colonial times, South Jersey farmers were "marling" their fields with the greenish-blue mud that they could see in the eroded sides of creeks. The present-day town of Marlton took its name from the nearby marlstone deposits. Many a Jersey farm boy began a winter's day with a wagon run to the marl pit.

Clues to Earth's past also lay buried in the marl pits, which were packed with fossils. Othniel Charles Marsh and Edward Drinker Cope, the founders of American paleontology, were both inspired to their life's work by the strange bones dug up and cast aside in the marl pits of South Jersey. In 1858, from a pit in a field that had once belonged to a farmer named John Haddon (now Haddonfield) came the bones of the first complete skeleton of a dinosaur ever assembled—the three-story-high "Hadrosaurus" that was put on public display in Philadelphia's Academy of Natural Science in 1868 and declared the state dinosaur.

≈

FROM HIS EARLIEST YEARS, according to family tradition, Charlie Seabrook could not be controlled. He was headstrong, impulsive, and lacking in respect for his parents' authority or the conventions and pieties of farm life in South Jersey. He had a singular focus on getting what he wanted and not letting anyone stand in his way. Both his parents were afraid of him and his terrible outbursts. His mother later regretted not taking a firmer hand in raising him, according to stories my grandmother Nana told my mother, imploring her not to make the same mistake with her children. She would not.

Bridgeton was the banking and commercial center of the surrounding towns, as well as the county seat. Every evening, Arthur and Elizabeth loaded their produce into a wagon. Before dawn the next morning, Arthur, sometimes with Charlie's help, hitched a two-horse team and drove along the rutted dirt road into Bridgeton, to the greengrocer, Kotak's, on Commerce Street. It was a five-mile trip—two hours each way—and Arthur and Charlie were back by nine and ready to begin work.

Farming gets into a family's blood. Despite the consolidation that has occurred in American agriculture—there are only two and a half million farms remaining in the U.S., a third the number there were in 1910—the family is still the dominant ownership model in farming; 90 percent of the farms in the U.S. today are family owned. Even large corporate farms tend to be controlled by families, many in their fourth or fifth generation of ownership. Agriculture is the original family business, going back to the days when the business was survival and producing children was a form of DIY labor recruitment. Sons were potential lifetime farmworkers; farmers who were blessed with half a dozen boys had a ready-made crew to put on any job. The continuity of the family farm depended on sons, and this is still largely true: more than 90 percent of the owner-operators of farms in the U.S. are men, and 97 percent of those are white men. Sonless farmers needed hired hands, apprentices, and migrant and immigrant laborers to do the work.

But the dual role that a farmer's sons played, as both workers and potential successors to the boss farmer, made father-son relationships fraught on the farm. The sons had to prove themselves capable of doing the same hard work that the hired men did. Perhaps there was an unspoken understanding that the oldest son would inherit the farm, but this was subject to revision. The situation was ripe for conflict. The father could try to keep control by playing the sons off against each other. Brother might undermine brother. Cain and Abel, sons of Adam, the first farmer, found themselves in a similar situation. It ended badly.

❧

WORK ON POPLAR BROOK FARM was year-round. In addition to planting, cultivating, and harvesting during the growing season, there was manuring and marling during the winter months to prepare the soil for next year. Charlie began working at the age of seven. Children, being closer to the ground, were anatomically better suited to cultivating and picking row crops than adults were. Charlie never forgot plucking maggots off lettuce leaves in the heat and mosquito clouds. His later refusal to abide by child labor laws when a field needed picking was grounded in these childhood hardships. He had endured it, and so could they.

Charlie eventually became the boss of his brother, who was seven years younger. Sidney disliked working under his older brother's direction so much that at eighteen he supposedly hit Charlie in the head with a shovel, or maybe an axe, and ran away from home. The event was covered in several of the local papers as well as *The Philadelphia Inquirer*, which reported that Sidney planned to get to Europe on a cattle ship and see the world. He didn't make it further than Philadelphia, however. *The Bridgeton Pioneer* reported, "He soon wearied of the outside world and longed for his home as the dearest spot on earth."

Sidney spent most of his life working for the Salvation Army. He played Santa Claus in the Salvation Army Hall in Bridgeton every Christmas. The Reverend Thomas Seabrook tradition of poverty, temperance, and benevolence ran through Sidney, much to his older brother's disgust. The two brothers only ever spoke to each other once again, at their father's funeral in 1937.

❧

CHARLIE OFTEN TALKED about how much he disliked working on the farm and told anyone who would listen that he'd be getting out of South Jersey as soon as he possibly could. Builders, not farmers, were his paragons. Who can blame him? As anyone who has tried to grow vegetables in the backyard knows, the labor involved is hard, dirty, and smelly—the sort of work that gets deep under your fingernails and that you feel in your back. You're in nature, but you're also at war with it. Bugs and animals want to eat your crops, slugs and maggots slither over it, the sun bakes it, the rain floods it. There are thirty thousand different types of weeds and three thousand species of nematodes ready to attack the plants. That's the reason the painted sign on the farm stand near our farm in Vermont says HOME GROAN. In a newspaper interview in 1912, Charlie said, accurately, "Those who sing hosannas to country living never worked on a farm."

Truck farming was an early form of production agriculture. By investing heavily in agricultural inputs, which include fertilizer, seed, water, machinery, and labor, the truck farmer sought to maximize outputs. Instead of one crop a year, truck farmers might grow three or four on the same land in a single season. Many truckers "intercropped"— planting strawberries between the rows of onions, say, so they got two crops where other farmers got one. Spinach, lettuce, and celery were the big moneymakers because their growth cycles were short—the farmer could be in and out of a crop in forty days. Timing was critical, especially in the New York market, where South Jersey farmers had the advantage over farmers further north, because their truck ripened sooner. Prices per bushel could shift dramatically from one day to the next depending on demand.

Truck farming was labor intensive. One worker per acre was the rule, with extra help needed around harvest time. Then the farmer had to lay off most of his crew, until he needed them again in the spring. Cities offered workers year-round employment at higher wages, with indoor work. Fortunately for Eastern Seaboard farmers, immigrant labor (mainly Southern Italians) was plentiful around the turn of the century. The Port of Philadelphia, in Gloucester, was the second busiest point of entry for European immigrants after Ellis Island.

Despite South Jersey truck farmers' natural and demographic advantages, a crucial element of agricultural technology was missing from their fields in the early years of the twentieth century. Without it, farmers would never reap the productivity gains that modern fertilizers and soil science promised, and farming would always be a game of chance against the weather that, sooner or later, every farmer lost. That element was irrigation. Incredibly, before 1907 no farmer in South Jersey had any better means of irrigating his fields than a watering can and a bucket. The lack of irrigation in the East is a major reason why the average farm east of the Mississippi was no more productive in 1914 than it had been in 1865.

CHAPTER 7

THE SKINNER SYSTEM

O N THE DAY CHARLIE SEABROOK CELEBRATED HIS
twenty-second birthday, May 28, 1903, Cumberland County
was in the middle of a six-month-long drought that the Vineland *Evening Journal* called "the long and most disastrous drought that has
visited this State during the past forty-one years . . . All vegetation previously at a standstill is now deteriorating. Plowing has become impossible, and there is much corn yet to plant. Early sown wheat is in head
but the late sown is short and thin; late sown oats is a very poor stand;
grass and hay crops are past recovery, timothy and clover, sown with
wheat, is nearly all killed."

In a 1917 newspaper interview that sounds as if the reporter wrote
the answers to his own questions, Charlie said, "In the main, the controlling element of chance was rainfall. Just when the crops needed
water most, the skies withheld their bounty and the sun shone and
withered or stunted the maturing products." He added, "We had nothing at our disposal that made it practicable [*sic*] to hand-irrigate on any
extensive scale, nor could labor be supplied in sufficient quantity to do
this profitably."

Irrigation was first employed on the alluvial flood plain of the
Euphrates River, in the Fertile Crescent of Mesopotamia, where the
annual rains sent irrigating waters throughout the newly sown fields.
By 4500 B.C.E., farmers had worked out how to control floods by
digging networks of canals, trenches, rills, and terraces through their
fields to redirect and capture the water—a practice today known as
surface irrigation. The biblical figure of Nimrod may have been among

the inventors of this technology. The ex-biblical sources say that the name "Nimrod" could be derived from the Assyrian god Ninurta, a god who was specifically tied to irrigation. Some suggest Ninurta was the first king—a farmer king.

Irrigation, more than any other single innovation, allowed agriculture to become civilization's standard-bearer. Irrigation made green crops a reliable food source to supplement dry grains, improving nutrition. Instead of merely surviving, farmers figured out how to achieve surpluses of storable grains to ward off future famines. By greatly increasing and regulating the supply of food, agriculture allowed humanity to thrive. Surface irrigation was first practiced in North America more than a thousand years ago, by the Hohokam Indians in the Salt River Valley, now part of Phoenix. In the eighteenth century, Franciscan padres who had come north from Mexico improved on the dams and ditches the Native Americans had built, lining them with stone and transforming the parched land around their missions into gardens and orange groves. In California's Central Valley, once an arid desert, farmers had been growing fruit and vegetables for more than a century before irrigation arrived in South Jersey.

In the East, surface irrigation was impractical. Ideally the irrigated land should gently slope, so that water moves from one place to another without pooling. The right amount of water retention and the right amount of drainage are essential. Flatland farmers might as well have been living in the Stone Age. There was simply no force that could move the water across the land. If a farmer could pump enough water high enough into a tank, gravity supplied the pressure. But before electric motors and internal combustion engines, there was no practical source of power to drive a pump.

※

IN 1898, Patent No. 614,507 was awarded to Charles W. Skinner of Troy, Ohio, for his invention, "A System of Irrigation." The late nineteenth century saw a flurry of patents for lawn sprinklers—residential irrigation for golf courses and rich people's lawns. Skinner, a truck farmer himself, was the first garage inventor to create an irrigation system for farmers like the Seabrooks, growing intensively on heavily fertilized soil. Skinner kits were available by mail order. The system was simple. An engine drove water through inch-and-a-quarter galvanized pipes that were joined together in long parallel rows, sixty feet apart, with tee junctions at the ends. The pipes were mounted on fixed wooden posts, about six feet high, so that a horse with a plow could get under them. Two small holes were punched into the pipes at two-foot intervals with nozzles that could oscillate to throw "artificial raindrops" over a sixty-foot span—thirty feet in each direction. The system could be adapted to different uses, including the spraying of pesticides. Skinner advertised in the ag mags such as *The Rural New-Yorker* and *Farm and Fireside* that forward-thinking farmers like the Seabrooks kept up with.

In 1907, Arthur and Charlie set up a Skinner system that covered two acres behind the barn. It cost $400 ($13,000 in today's money), including the 8-horsepower engine. Celery, a very thirsty vegetable, was the first crop they planted under the pipes. That year Seabrook celery was so succulent that the crop earned $1,500 ($50,000 today). In 1908, they put $400 back into irrigation, doubling their coverage to four acres, and intercropped celery, onions, and potatoes under the pipes. That year they sold $17,000 of truck—half a million in today's money. They reinvested another $400 and bought two more acres of Skinner pipes. They also built a wooden water tank that held five thousand gallons and was fifty feet high—the first of the company's iconic water towers. Later, under Courtney's direction, an image of the water tower would become part of Seabrook Farms' brand—a reminder of the transformative change that irrigation brought not only to Poplar Brook but to their neighbors' land as well.

CHARLIE HAD MARRIED NORMA DALE IVINS, a well-educated farmer's daughter from Newfield, in Gloucester County, in 1905. She moved into her in-laws' gray-and-white farmhouse with its wraparound porch on Parsonage Road in Deerfield, down the road from the church, where the sound of steam compressors competed with the ringing of church bells. Norma Dale, known to me as Nana, was taller than her husband, and also better educated. She assisted Charlie with the correspondence courses he pursued to buttress his seat-of-the-pants engineering talent with math and science. Norma and her mother-in-law were also responsible for preparing meals for the hired men. That same year, Arthur made his son a full partner in the farm. The iron safe with the name of their partnership, Seabrook & Son, welded onto the front of it—the same safe that would eventually wind up in the furthest reaches of the Salem wine cellar—sat in the kitchen of their mutual home. The younger Seabrooks soon got busy populating the house with future farm hands. Belford was born in 1907, Courtney in 1909, and my father, John, in 1917. Thelma Dale, the only girl, came in 1910.

Charlie's ambition, like Napoleon's, was inversely proportionate to his stature. He stood less than five feet eight inches tall, and never weighed more than 150 pounds. His eyesight was poor from birth, and he wore gold-rimmed spectacles. He had the type of skin that never tans, only burns—Seabrook skin—and his blond hair was so fair that it was almost white, an odd look in a young man. He was a bantam rooster: brisk, careful, humorous, and unflappably confident, leading with his chin when talking. He considered himself a man of the people. He could talk to anyone, but he was only truly comfortable among working people—provided they worked for *him*. He was an excellent motivator of men, in part because he seemed to be an example of what hard work could achieve. When Charlie Seabrook did something, he did it in as big a way as possible. His longtime driver, Jonas McGailliard, once told me that my grandfather even wrote big. "He made numbers like they made 'em in Bible times," Jonas said, still seemingly awestruck fifty years later by such monumental digits. "When he wrote something down, you knew it was *down*."

Charlie played no sports and pursued no pastimes. He didn't make friends, exactly, but he developed close associations with certain individuals who were useful in getting him what he wanted. He and Sidney were estranged. He had no relationship with his sisters, Fanny and Ida, or with his parents, except as concerned work. He never took vacations until his health broke down in the early 1940s. Later, he was notorious in Philadelphia social circles for not even trying to discuss anything other than business at social events; hostesses had to be careful about where they seated him. Workers began referring to him as "the old man" long before he was old. He was in too much of a hurry to stay young for long.

※

CHARLIE SAW HOW OVERHEAD IRRIGATION, electricity, and internal combustion had transformed Poplar Brook Farm, and he had heard about the new gas-powered tractors and combines that were going to mechanize the growing of grains. He had read about what Henry Ford was doing in Detroit, using assembly-line manufacturing and time-and-motion studies to industrialize the carriage trade. Although Charlie had been determined to leave agriculture for work in engineering or industry, as Ford himself had done, he now began to see a way to bring industry and big business to the farm, through mechanization. He would become the Henry Ford of truck farming.

Arthur, who began styling himself "A. P." as he prospered, was friendly and well liked. He traveled to Philadelphia and New York to meet the commission merchants who bought Seabrooks' produce wholesale. Charlie remained on the farm. He took charge of labor recruitment, and as the workforce grew, he oversaw the construction of more workers' housing. He had a knack for building things, and far preferred contracting and construction to agriculture.

The 1910 U.S. Census, conducted during the slowest season at Poplar Brook, in February, shows ten hired men in A. P.'s household who were born in Italy, along with one Russian, in addition to his and Charlie's families. In 1910, a reporter from the *Bridgeton Evening News* came and walked the "famous truck farm" with A. P. The article says there were twenty-five Italian men living on the farm for nine months of the year as laborers, and ten to twelve of those men stayed all year. Most lived in two recently constructed boardinghouses in the back of the farm—the beginnings of what would be known as the Italian Village. The reporter was impressed with the neatness of the gardens the Italians kept. "The Italians live in their own way and make good money, for the whole family works," the piece says, noting that a woman and her nine-year-old son made $19.78 in a week bunching celery. The only mention of "Charles" in the story is that he is the farm manager; he isn't quoted, an omission that can't have pleased the ambitious young man.

Another reporter, from *The Rural New-Yorker*, visited A. P. at the farm around the same time. The journal covered the entire northeast, so the correspondent was familiar with the state of irrigation technology beyond South Jersey: "One of the prettiest productive sights of Cumberland Co., N.J., th[is] past Summer was the farm of Arthur Seabrook . . . [who] has 14 acres under the Skinner irrigation system, and in this way can raise two and three crops from the same ground in one season." The writer emphasizes how the Skinner system "enables Mr. Seabrook to secure the maximum returns with a minimum of expense." Again, there is no mention of Charlie. The farm's 1911 income was $40,000 ($1.3 million in today's money), half from truck and half from dairy, meat, and poultry. The Seabrooks' truck included strawberries, onions, celery, cabbage, beets, radishes, lettuce, spinach, parsley, potatoes, carrots, string beans, peppers, eggplants, tomatoes, asparagus, watermelons, cantaloupes, leeks, parsnips, and lima beans.

SEABROOK AND SON had very different ideas about how to handle their newfound prosperity. A. P. wanted to bank the money, buy a house in town, and retire. Charlie advocated putting everything back into the farm, to get bigger—more irrigation, machinery, infrastructure, and workers. They quarreled fiercely. Arthur was reportedly afraid of his son's rages and threats of physical violence. According to my father, Charlie did physically assault Arthur. Charlie's mother recounted fierce fights over business policy that she witnessed while they all lived under the same roof. My grandmother later cautioned both my parents they should never, under any circumstances, live with their in-laws.

The solution was for Charlie to buy his father out, but he lacked the funds. If his vegetable factory was ever to be more than a dream, he needed not just thousands but millions of investment capital. The only place to find that kind of money was on Wall Street.

CHAPTER 8

THE VEGETABLE FACTORY

A LEXANDER MOSS WHITE (HARVARD '92), WAS THE sort of man Charlie Seabrook pretended to admire but secretly despised. In education, class, politics, and social conscience, White was everything the unlettered and parochial farm boy was not. White was the cofounder of White, Weld & Co., the Wall Street investment house, with Francis M. Weld (Harvard '97). Called "Alec," he and his family had a country place at Cove Neck in Oyster Bay, Long Island, near Theodore Roosevelt's place on Sagamore Hill. An exemplary citizen, White gave generously to the Brooklyn Academy of Music and the Brooklyn Library and enjoyed pastimes Charlie Seabrook disdained as a waste of time, such as fly-fishing and hiking in the Adirondacks around the Whites' camp on Upper Ausable Lake, which was close to the Welds' camp.

The family made their first fortune in the fur trade in Danbury, Connecticut, in the eighteenth century. Alec's great uncle, William Augustus White (Harvard '63), a Shakespearean and Elizabethan scholar, lived at 158 Columbia Heights, the largest private house in Brooklyn, where he kept a twelve-thousand-volume library. William's brother Alfred was a pioneer in housing reform and a supporter of historically Black universities and colleges in the South, in particular the Hampton Institute in Virginia, and the Tuskegee Institute in Alabama. William and Alfred had founded a Wall Street investment firm, W. A. & A. M. White, which their grandnephew Alec now managed, in addition to his role at White, Weld.

C. F. may have had an introduction through Alec White's wife, who was an Ogden from South Jersey, a common name in the Deerfield cemetery. According to a story my father told me, Charlie went to see Mr. White one day, without telling his father about the meeting. He carried his one pair of good shoes in his satchel, along with his business plan and whatever else he had to help promote his vision of a vegetable factory. Only when he was outside the Whites' office at 40 Wall Street did he put on his good shoes. Or so the story goes.

Why would Alec White, who supported progressive institutions and cared deeply about social justice, have entertained Charlie Seabrook's vegetable factory pitch? Maybe the Whites saw my grandfather as acting in the public interest, by providing fresh, nutritious green vegetables to the meat-and-potato-eating masses. Maybe he saw the farm as a gateway for Black migrants fleeing violence and terror in the Jim Crow South. Or maybe he was dazzled by the potential profits promised by mechanization. In any case, it is a measure of twenty-nine-year-old Charlie Seabrook's promotional skills that he sold Alec White on his idea of a vegetable factory. White became the majority owner of the new Seabrook Company, the corporation that served as a holding company and investment vehicle for the farm. Seabrook's title was general manager.

✒

IN 1911, Arthur agreed to sell his land and his half of Seabrook & Son to his son Charles. In fact, his son's behind-the-scenes financial backers, the Whites, were the new owners. The price for A. P.'s share was $24,000, the equivalent of $796,500 today, figuring 3 percent inflation. Given the amount that the buyers would end up investing— about ninety million, valued in today's dollars—this transaction seems like theft. It is the original sin in the Seabrook story. "Arthur had no real idea of the true worth of his half of the partnership," my father wrote, which was possibly what attracted the White group to the investment in the first place: it was a steal. Once the Whites were in, Charlie "was able to finance the new business on a very favorable basis to himself," according to my father. Perhaps Arthur should have

known the true value of his holdings, but he trusted his son and partner to tell him what the business and land were worth. Business may
be business, but family is family. What kind of man would cheat his
own father to get ahead?

An article in the January 24, 1913, edition of the *Dollar Weekly
News* of Bridgeton describes Arthur P. Seabrook upon his retirement,
after thirty-eight years of farming, as the "famous truck farmer" who
was the first to introduce overhead irrigation to the area. The story
says A. P. made his "last delivery to Bridgeton on Saturday, January 4,
1913. Hereafter he will reside in his handsome new home on Fayette
Street, acting as agent for the West Jersey Marl and Transportation
Company." The article ends by saying that "few indeed have succeeded
so well" in truck farming. The story also notes A. P.'s farm "has been
taken over by a corporation capitalized at $150,000, and that the new
owners have already purchased additional acreage."

A. P. and Elizabeth moved out of the house at Farm Central, which
now belonged to Charlie and his family. In 1914, the Seabrook & Son
safe was moved from the kitchen into the new administration building where "C. F.," as Charlie now styled himself, kept his office. Belford remembered visiting his father in his office that year, when he was
seven. He wrote, "My first recollection of my father was during the
blizzard of 1914 when the snow was deeper than I was tall. My father
had an office in the corner of a building adjacent to the house in which
we lived on Parsonage Road. In that office there was a safe which was
taller than I was that contained the name Seabrook & Son. My father
told me that it was the name of our future partnership."

A. P.'s retirement didn't work out as he'd envisioned it. His wife Elizabeth died after a short illness in 1919. Their unwed daughter, Fanny,
died three years later, leaving her son, Earl, who had been raised as
her sibling to avoid the shame of her unwanted pregnancy, and A. P.
alone in the big Fayette Street house. When Arthur ran out of money,
he asked Charlie for financial assistance, but his son refused. According to my grandfather's driver Jonas, A. P. would come by the office
when his son was away and ask his secretary, Pauline Ober, for money,

a practice my grandfather knew about and tolerated. Jonas called this arrangement "pity-full." Out of necessity, Arthur continued working as a salesman for the West Jersey Marl Company; his sales book is preserved in the Cumberland County Historical Society. When he died in 1937, A. P. was at least allowed a stone in the Deerfield cemetery, which is more than his father Samuel got.

Once he had control of the farm, Charlie set about erasing his father from its history. Instead of a second-generation farmer building on the hard work and skill of his father, C. F. Seabrook would reinvent himself as a first-generation founder, the family patriarch who began with nothing and raised himself up by his bootstraps. He became that most American of success stories: the self-made man. A.P. had nothing to do with it. In a 1917 interview, C. F. takes sole credit for bringing irrigation to the farm. "My attention was called to an overhead system of irrigation—nothing more complicated than perforated piping that made it possible to spray considerable areas with a very close simulation of nature's showers."

≈

C. F. COULD NOT HAVE CHOSEN a better time to build his vegetable factory. Food prices, already rising in 1913, were further boosted by the outbreak of war in Europe, causing agricultural production abroad to contract severely. The price of a bushel of corn in Minnesota rose from 59 cents in 1914 to $1.30 in 1919. Wheat went from $1.05 a bushel to $2.34. Mechanization was bringing tractors, threshers, seed drillers, and combine harvesters to the cultivation of wheat, rye, oats, and barley, greatly increasing production. Land prices rose accordingly. Farmland was 70 percent more valuable in 1920 than it had been in 1913. The Federal Farm Loan Act, passed in 1916, was part of a package of farmer-friendly legislation included in the Wilson administration's New Freedom program that allowed farmers to buy more land and machines and to produce even more food.

No farmer embodied the promise of mechanization in agriculture better than Thomas D. Campbell, the "world's wheat king." Born in a log cabin in North Dakota in 1882, less than a year after my grand-father, Campbell married the daughter of George Bull, the founder of Cream of Wheat, and moved to California for the climate; his wife had tuberculosis. In Pasadena, he worked for Jared Sidney Torrance, a California real estate developer who commissioned Frederick Law Olmsted Jr. to design the planned community the developer named after himself.

When the United States entered the war in 1917, Campbell sent a telegram to Woodrow Wilson, asking for the federal government's assistance in subsidizing mechanized wheat production in the Great Plains, which, Campbell insisted, would help the allies to win. ("To Farm Is to Arm" went one wartime slogan.) Wilson took him up on the idea and helped arrange for Campbell and his associates to lease two hundred thousand acres of Native American land in southeastern Montana, about ninety thousand acres of which was put under the plow and planted with wheat. Campbell, seeking capital for his enter-prise, traveled to New York City and pitched J. P. Morgan himself. After hearing him out, Morgan said, "Young man, your project is the most romantic, the most patriotic, the most interesting and, I believe, one of the most profitable ideas that has ever been presented," although his thoughts may not have occurred to the banker in that order. He loaned Campbell $2 million, and Tom Campbell used the money to introduce mechanized corporate farming to the world, which would eventually lead to the consolidation of small family acreages into the family-owned megafarms that dominate U.S. agriculture today.

Like Campbell, C. F. went looking for capital for his farm at a time when mechanization was drawing investors to agriculture. Perhaps he even quoted Campbell: "Modern farming is 90 percent engineer-ing and 10 percent agriculture." In addition to securing the Whites' backing, C. F. sold shares to local farmers and businessmen as well as to commission merchants who handled Seabrook produce in urban markets. On Sundays he would roll up in his big 12-cylinder Pack-ard and pitch his neighbors on the company. Of all the hats Charlie Seabrook wore—farmer, contractor, engineer, entrepreneur, corporate executive—promoter is the one that fit him best. *The Dearborn Independent* reported, "The presidents and cashiers of the four local banks each took moderate blocks of stock. So, too, did a couple of commission men in New York and Philadelphia." The paper also noted, "the elder Mr. Seabrook, who was so doubtful back in 1911, has since purchased $20,000 worth of stock in the company and is one of its firmest adherents."

If a potential investor didn't think about the matter too deeply, he might assume that the wondrous efficiencies Tom Campbell had achieved with wheat would apply to all forms of agriculture. But mechanization had a much greater impact on the production of dry goods like wheat, corn, soybeans, rice, and cotton—the five crops that make up much of the planted acreage in the U.S.—than on melons, berries, most leafy greens, green beans, peas, cauliflower, and cucumbers: the crops the Seabrooks grew. Those still needed to be cultivated with a hoe, selectively harvested, and delicately handled; machines were too clumsy and dumb for that type of work. Of all types of agriculture, truck farming was the least receptive to mechanization. To mechanize a truck farm, especially one that grew as many different varieties of vegetables and fruits as the Seabrooks grew, the farmer would need a different machine for practically every single crop.

Even when machines were developed for harvesting some types of vegetables, they weren't always a clear advantage over human labor. Wheat could be bred to ripen all at once, but green beans and peas, like strawberries and melons, ripen unevenly. Human laborers could pick a bean field every few days, selectively harvesting the ripe ones and leaving the rest for the next pass. But a mechanical "viner," a huge, combine-like machine for harvesting shell peas, limas, and green beans that the farm began using in the 1930s, hoovered up everything, including the vines, all at once. The farmer had to calculate whether the money saved by mechanical labor offset the money lost by destroying the vines before much of the product was ripe. The answer often depended in part on how little the pickers could be paid.

CHAPTER 9

"NEW YORK TALKING, MR. SEABROOK!"

A FTER BUYING HIS FATHER'S HALF OF THE BUSINESS, C. F. wanted nothing further to do with A. P. But his father's younger, college-educated brother, Albert Seabrook—called Uncle Bert—became an important adviser, as well as a corporate officer, serving as secretary and treasurer of the Seabrook Company. Charlie couldn't abide the softhearted liberalism of his own father, a Democrat, but Uncle Bert's conservative Republican politics spoke to him. After working as a schoolteacher for years, Albert had become the owner and publisher of a conservative weekly newspaper called the *Glassboro Enterprise*, for which he wrote fiery editorials in support of mid-1890s Republican policies such as maintaining the gold standard and high tariffs, in addition to espousing nativist views. Uncle Bert marched at the head of the 1896 Republican victory parade in Glassboro, dressed as Uncle Sam. He was also an avid bicyclist, who held the speed record from Glassboro to Pitman.

Albert Seabrook was a disciple of Ohio Senator Mark Hanna, a wealthy industrialist-businessman politician who was a Republican champion of expansive capitalism. Hanna, who went to high school with John D. Rockefeller, epitomized the close relationship between titans of industry and politicians during the Gilded Age. The robber barons who built the railroads had been brutal, corrupt, and wasteful, but they demanded total autonomy, claiming their efforts benefited the public. Hanna wanted the next generation of American builders—C. F.'s cohort—to enjoy the same permissive political climate. Businessmen should be able to act unheeded, Uncle Bert and

C. F. thought, because growth drives everything. Today the same American spirit animates venture capitalist Marc Andreessen's "The Techno-Optimist Manifesto." "We believe growth is progress—leading to vitality, expansion of life, increasing knowledge, higher well-being. . . . We believe everything good is downstream of growth."

In 1913, Alexander White became the president of the Seabrook Company. C. F. was the farm's general manager. He had a seat on the board of directors and was a major stockholder, but White maintained control of the voting stock, which allowed him to make major policy decisions without consent of the board.

With the Whites' money, C. F. went on a building spree. He acquired another two hundred acres in 1913 and doubled his irrigated land from twenty-five acres in 1912 to fifty, which required installing fifty thousand linear feet of pipe overhead, plus underground mains and pumps. Having achieved control of precipitation, Seabrook took on climate next. He commissioned Lord & Burnham of Irvington, New York, to build six magnificent greenhouses, enclosing three acres under glass at Farm Central. It's telling that C. F. employed the architecture firm favored by the Vanderbilts, Astors, and Morgans—those stalwarts of the New York Four Hundred, who formed C. F.'s idea of how rich people live. Lord & Burnham adorned the Gilded Age Hudson River estates with glass-roofed greenhouses, conservatories, and solariums designed in a baroque Italianate style.

The Seabrook L & B greenhouses were outfitted with electricity, steam heat, and irrigation, and could accommodate a two-horse team inside with a plow. In the spring, lettuce, cabbage, and tomatoes that had been started in the greenhouses during the winter were transplanted as seedlings into the fields, just after the last frost, a labor-intensive operation that gained the farm a crucial two-week head start on its competitors in the New York market. Now the farm had greens, berries, and roses all through the winter months, when prices were at their highest.

At first, the farm was without railroad facilities: everything had to be hauled by horse and wagon to the Woodruff station for shipping.

But when officers of the Jersey Central line saw how much freight the farm was moving, the railroad built a spur right to the plant. C. F.'s contracting crews did much of the work on grading the rail bed. He discovered that he liked building railroads almost as much as he liked building roads. In addition to farming, his commercial interests were multiplying rapidly to include contracting, housing, car and truck dealerships, and soon, trucking—in the modern sense of the word. There were opportunities at every turn for the driven, grasping, and ruthless thirty-five-year-old entrepreneur to exploit.

C. F. and his family lived at Farm Central, in the house he had taken over from his father. The gray-and-white exterior color scheme of the Seabrook house matched the colors of the other farmhouses where the so-called "Americans," the native-born white people, lived. The Southern Italians resided nearby in the Italian Village. Eastern European and Russian workers were assigned in a large rooming house along the highway that locals called "the Pollack Hotel." There were also Dutch, German, and Swedish workers, and sixteen Syrian-speaking Chaldean Christian refugees who had fled from the Assyrian genocide of the 1910s. Within a mile of Farm Central, Jack could hear at least seven different languages spoken. In spite of the close living conditions, the Spanish flu pandemic of 1918 had almost no effect on the workforce. Thanks to a competent company nurse named Helen Burt, who maintained high standards of sanitation at the workers' housing, only one death, that of an infant, was attributed to the Spanish flu at the farm—a remarkable fact considering that the pandemic killed tens of thousands in nearby Philadelphia.

ᔐᖼᓬ

"THE HENRY FORD OF AGRICULTURE" was supposedly the coinage of Scottish-born journalist B. C. (Bertie) Forbes, the founder of *Forbes* magazine. The writer's intimate, celebratory biographical sketches of the tycoons of his time—men like Rockefeller, Morgan, Carnegie, and Frick, collected in Forbes's 1917 book, *Men Who Are Making America*—provided a template for business magazine profiles that endures to this day. Forbes's method derived from the 1859 book *Self-Help* by his fellow Scot, the Victorian reformer Samuel Smiles, a founding work in the self-help genre that became a publishing mainstay. In his multivolume *Lives of the Engineers*, Smiles told inspirational tales of personal improvement and advancement achieved by "the deserving poor." He emphasized humble origins and good habits, which included "diligent self-culture, self-discipline and self-control—and above all . . . that honest and upright performance of individual duty which is the glory of manly character." In B. C. Forbes's reworking of *Self-Help*, the rich are good because it's good to be rich.

A fawning press made C. F. Seabrook one of the best-known farmers in the country. *Collier's* put him on its cover in 1917. Bruce Barton, an influential business writer, who later cofounded BBDO, the ad firm that created Betty Crocker, profiled the farmer-industrialist in *The American Magazine* in 1919. C. F. was also featured in *The Rural New-Yorker, Country Life*, and *The Dearborn Independent*, among other publications. The back-to-the-land movement, which brought a wave of nostalgia for the rural life that many families had left behind on the farm, added a new twist to the bootstrapping narrative. C. F. Seabrook was living proof that a man could do very well without ever leaving the dear old family farm.

The Dearborn Independent story depicts the farmer-engineer-industrialist in action:

Charley [*sic*] Seabrook, a briskly-talking, briskly-moving young man, rolled up to the front of his office in one of his motor cars—the 12-cyclinder, it happened to be—and was told as he stepped out that he was wanted on the long-distance telephone.

"New York talking, Mr. Seabrook!" came the message. "Can you let us have a dozen carloads of lettuce tonight for tomorrow morning's market?"

"Sure, we'll have them right out!" was the reply.

A long train soon afterward slid away from Charley Seabrook's own siding. It carried not only the twelve carloads of lettuce, but a couple of carloads of celery, a couple of carloads of spinach, maybe a couple carloads of potatoes. Within forty-eight hours there arrived back at Bridgeton a check calling for several thousands of dollars.

A second article on Seabrook Farms in the *Independent* notes, "the people of New York wanted their salads and wanted them freshly green and crisp and the commission men knew that 'C. F.' had exactly the article required." Green salads had become aspirational items at upscale New York restaurants by the early twentieth century, catering to the public's growing awareness of the new science of vitamins and flattering the palates of diners refined enough to appreciate leafy greens. Restaurants seeking to attract women at lunchtime offered featured salads. The Waldorf Astoria's 1917 luncheon menu features salads made with escarole, chicory, romaine, endive, celery, and watercress. During the war, Americans at home were encouraged to eat more fruit and vegetables, to save the meat, wheat, fat, and sugar for the troops. Patriots planted their own "Victory gardens" for that purpose.

Distribution was another marvel. Goods shipped from the farm in the late afternoon by rail to Jersey City were floated across the Hudson on barges, kept in commission merchants' warehouses on Reade Street overnight, and available for sale in Washington Market early the next morning. Seabrook's famous "Honey Heart" strawberries ("Four inches around," declared advertisements) went for as high as sixty cents a pint in 1916—seventeen dollars today.

Across the street from the Seabrook home was the cold storage plant, powered by a row of Corliss steam engines built by the Frick Industrial Refrigeration Company of Waynesboro, Pennsylvania, with shiny valves and gleaming pistons that throbbed twenty-four hours a day. It was a one-story structure with a basement, measuring 320 feet long and 60 feet wide, with a washing room, a sorting room, and cold storage space for five hundred carloads of vegetables. The ammonia fumes from the compressors mingled with the smell of the horse manure spread around on the fields.

Steam was generated in the power plant, where three huge boilers ran night and day on sawdust and shavings from the sawmill that made the wood-and-wire pickers' baskets and hampers, as well as the shipping crates, from local lumber. Later, steam was replaced by six gas-powered compressors, also built by Frick. Across the main road was the cannery, which could turn out twenty-five thousand cans of vegetables a day at peak capacity. There was also a blacksmith shop with three glowing forges that gave off the smell of soft coal smoke and burning hooves, and the sounds—*tang-tang-ping-tang*—of farriers hammering horseshoes. The preindustrial soundscape of human-powered work coexisted unpeacefully with a twentieth-century racket made by belching engines and coughing motors. The machine shop was run by a German American worker named Schmidt, who told seven-year-old Jack exciting stories of chasing Pancho Villa in Mexico as a soldier with General "Black Jack" Pershing. Another engineer was a sailor who had stopped in ports all around the world and regaled the boy with tales of his adventures on the high seas.

With the passage of the first Immigration Act of 1918, the flow of Italian workers began to dwindle. In their place were about one hundred African American workers and their families, some of whom were seasonal migrants recruited in Georgia and Florida; others were part of the Great Migration out of the Jim Crow South. Black workers were forced to live farther away from Farm Central, in the camps and shanties. Black teamsters who drove the farm's seventy-two horses and mules lived with their families in dilapidated housing in Orchard Village, about a mile away.

In 1920, C. F. himself traveled down to Quincy, a town in northern Florida, to recruit Black workers. Among those he brought back were Mack Bradwell, aged fifteen, and his wife, aged twelve. According to their granddaughter Jeanna, Mack's family had taken possession of the girl to settle a debt and married her to young Mack. The Bradwells arrived in Seabrook in the spring of 1920 with a group of other Black laborers from northern Florida. At the end of the season, many went back to Florida, but Mack Bradwell and his bride stayed on.

By then, a fleet of motorized vehicles were zipping around the farm. The same year, C. F. sold off the farm's livestock and its animal-powered farm machinery in a large auction. The Ford dealer in Bridgeton, a man named Gus Westcott, calculated that by 1922 he had personally sold the Seabrook Company no fewer than fifty-three Fords—Model T's, Fordson tractors, and protopickup trucks. In 1919, Wescott had written Henry Ford himself a letter to tell him about Charlie Seabrook's wonderful irrigated farm. Ernest Liebold, Ford's personal secretary and closest aide, answered Wescott. A few months later, the two articles on C. F. Seabrook and his vegetable factory appeared in *The Dearborn Independent*, Ford's recently purchased weekly, where Liebold, a notorious anti-Semite, was general manager. Several months after the profile of Seabrook ran, the *Independent* began publishing the apocryphal "Protocols of the Elders of Zion," a forgery that claimed to be the minutes of a late nineteenth-century meeting where Jewish leaders discussed their control of the world's financial infrastructure as well as the international press. Later that year Ford himself began publishing his ninety-one-article series, "The International Jew: The World's Problem," in the paper.

C. F. Seabrook was a supremacist, but he was also a practical man who knew that providing education and health care to all workers, Black and white, would give otherwise migratory families a good reason to stay put, easing the constant pressure to recruit new workers. I believe he also sincerely wanted his workers' children to prosper with education. When Deerfield Township vetoed C. F.'s first request to build a new school for his workers' children, he lobbied for a new township. A referendum on splitting Deerfield into two entities passed the New Jersey State Legislature in 1922, creating Upper Deerfield Township. Seabrook Farms was by far the new township's largest taxpayer, affording C. F. the political power to get things done. The new

Charles F. Seabrook School, built by Seabrook crews, opened in 1924. My father was among its first students.

✧

INSPIRED PERHAPS BY BERTIE FORBES, C. F. also started a magazine: *The Seabrooker*. It was printed on glossy paper and published sporadically, beginning in 1919. Black workers were starting to arrive in large numbers for the first time on the farm. The Italian and Eastern European workers weren't welcoming. Management hoped that *The Seabrooker*, which featured both Black and white Seabrookers, would help to foster community. The publication also served as a platform for my grandfather's views on work and self-reliance, and on life in general. "The strongman's trick is to seem exceptional and yet to embody the national everyman, with all his endearing flaws," writes Ruth Ben-Ghiat in her 2021 book *Strongmen: Mussolini to the Present*. *The Seabrooker* was C. F.'s main outlet for doing just that. He presented himself as a Samuel Smilesian figure, a clever farmer-engineer who had made his fortune through brains, hard work, and good character. The dear leader's brief, tough-love exhortations, published in a box on the lower half of the front page, were probably written by Frederick Frye Rockwell, *The Seabrooker*'s editor, who also headed public relations.

ARE YOU PAYING SOMEONE TO THINK FOR YOU?

Every employee pays for superintendence and inspection. Some pay more and some less. That is to say, a three-dollars-a-day man would receive four dollars a day, were it not for the fact that someone has to think for him, look after him, and supply the will that holds him to his task. The result is that he contributes to the support of those who superintend him. Make no mistake about this: Incompetence and disinclination require supervision, and they pay for it and no one else does. The less you require looking after, the more able you are to stand alone and complete your tasks, the greater your reward.

Do your work so well that it will require no supervision and by doing your own thinking you will save the expense of hiring someone to think for you.

—C. F. Seabrook

But did any three-dollar worker succeed in becoming a four-dollar man?

Rockwell was a noted author of gardening books, including the popular 1917 *Around the Year in the Garden*. Later he was the garden editor of *The New York Times*. He also wrote for socialist publications, which may have been what drew him to *The Seabrooker*, where workers were the focus. But Rockwell would have been careful to conceal his political views from C. F. and Uncle Bert.

In the December 1921 issue, Rockwell describes climbing the new Seabrook Farms water tower to get a bird's-eye view of the whole farm.

The greenhouses loom up, one behind the other, until you realize that they cover nearly five acres! And behind them, the great cold storage plant, and the rail road tracks, and the cannery, and the foundations for a new building. And, so, with every step you mount up the big tower comes a new horizon, bringing into view something not visible before—steam shovels at work unloading manure, and coal, and excavating in fields far away. The new railroad siding, one of the biggest and best in South Jersey; acre upon acre covered with the thin grey parallel lines that indicate overhead irrigation, a carpet of several hundred acres, with strips and squares of different colored vegetation; and beyond that again fields and orchards with rows seeming to the horizon line. Some sight!

The work of manuring, sowing, transplanting, watering, and weeding was done by gangs of Seabrook field workers, overseen by gang bosses—a structure that came from the Padrone system installed at the farm by the Italian immigrants. Padrones, or bosses, were generally senior workers who acted as informal labor brokers in recruiting recent immigrants. *The Seabrooker* offers glimpses into day-to-day life on the farm and the relationships between bosses and workers. "Here is foreman George Tomlinson, who keeps things running—and from running amuck." Among the list of languages George needs to communicate with the multilingual workforce are "American, Italian, African, Assyrian, Polish, Dutch, and—last but not least—Baby-talk." The foreman speaks these languages "mostly with his hands, to be sure, but well enough to make himself understood."

THE SEABROOK FARMS Planting and Harvest Schedule for 1920–1921 reads as follows:

April 1920
4/13 first box of cucumbers shipped
4/22 completion of strawberry planting
4/23 strawberries planted for national farming corporation
4/24 first day of rhubarb bunching

May 1920
5/10 Hymie's gang started thinning lettuce
5/17 Hymie's gang started thinning carrots
5/18 Les Hewes gang started thinning beets
5/19 last shipment of radishes
5/21 first day of pepper planting
5/26 first shipment of lettuce
5/28 first strawberries picked

June 1920
6/9 first Chesapeake strawberries picked
6/16 strawberry festival brings many visitors and a good orchestra

6/17 cabbage is usually cut on CF's birthday, but this year they are one day early. 350 boxes cut

6/21 started again to pull rhubarb

6/24 first carrots shipped

6/25 first beets shipped

July 1920

7/7 Geo. Tomlinson was out in the beet fields at 4AM and has only been married a week

7/10 first second-crop of potatoes planted

7/12 new Italian gangs arrived

7/13 first onions topped

7/31 first romaine lettuce drilled in

August 1920

8/2 first leeks set out

8/4 first beans canned in can house

8/11 stopped digging potatoes on account of rain

8/13 Hymie's gang started to thin fall lettuce

8/26 first spinach drilled in

September

9/1 lettuce hoeing campaign started

9/20 no 1. Greenhouse set out with lettuce

October 1920

10/1 first romaine cut

10/2 first lettuce cut

10/5 first spinach cut

10/15 first pumpkin harvest

10/18 first celery cabbage cut

10/25 Grover Harris known as "runt" digs for potatoes

November 1920

11/8 first celery packed

11/15 first greenhouse lettuce cut from no. 1 greenhouse

11/24 lettuce seed for next spring planting sowed

11/26 first leeks pulled

11/27 completion of turnip topping

11/29 first radishes thinned in no. 1 greenhouse

December 1920

12/2 leek harvest complete

March 1921

3/10 first cukes planted in Huber's glass gardens

3/11 first onions set out

3/12 first cabbage set out—Geo. in charge of the operation

3/14 first lettuce set out

3/17 first leeks sowed. Smell 'Em??

On a single day that year, November 1, the farm shipped 82 barrels of peppers, 618 hampers of spinach, 400 hampers of romaine, and 1,425 hampers of green lettuce. (A hamper of lettuce contained 24 heads.) The year's end total revenues, in 1919 dollars (multiply by eighteen, roughly, for today's values) included $112,040 for lettuce; $39,244 for cabbage; $36,802 for radishes; $31,973 for spinach; $19,771 for onions; $19,794 for potatoes; $18,906 for strawberries; and $17,545 for cucumbers. Total revenue was about $300,000, with 20 percent of that profit.

On top of all that, the farm produced a world-record potato crop that year, according to the boss farmer. Six hundred and four bushels of potatoes were grown on a single acre, about four times more than the average yield. Some were skeptical of the photographic evidence, which was published in local papers, with a note of mockery that can't have pleased C. F. The Vineland newspaper editorialized:

"Many who have seen the photograph of this world's record-breaking acre have inquired: 'How much did you pay to have that picture faked up, Charlie?' "

At the end of each year, the family would throw a big party at their home at Farm Central. At the beginning, these affairs were for the forty workers, and Norma Dale would kill a hog and procure oysters from the nearby oystering towns, crab from Maryland, as well as prime rib and kegs of beer and liquor, even during Prohibition years. As C. F. rose in the world of business and politics, the end-of-year parties gradually became displays of Seabrook splendor as well as the family's powerful connections. Bankers, politicians, and businessmen from Camden, Trenton, and Atlantic City would converge on Seabrook for a night of feasting and revelry, and to pay tribute to the boss farmer himself.

CHAPTER 10

THE HIGHWAY
COMMISSIONER

In Jersey, anything's legal
As long as you don't get caught.
— "Tweeter and the Monkey Man,"
The Traveling Wilburys

B Y THE 1920S, C. F. WAS MAKING TWO TRIPS TO EUROPE
a year. As he built up his international contracting business,
he opened offices in London, Paris, and Berlin. Seabrook Engineering supposedly had an asphalt-making factory in Turkey that Ataturk
seized when he took over in 1924. Since he made two Atlantic crossings a year, and since each one took about eight days, C. F. was shipboard for a month out of each year, which is a lot of time for a man of
constant action and movement to be confined. Yet embarking for the
continent conferred its own kind of status during the heyday of luxury
ocean liners. C. F. preferred the *Berengaria*, and later, the *Île de France*
and the *Normandie*.

The first-class salons of the great liners became laboratories for
the farm boy's immersion in the manners and mores of the Anglo-
American upper class in the 1920s. He carefully studied the passenger
lists before each voyage, to make the most of the possible connections,
a mix of business travelers, socialites, celebrities, and well-off vaca-
tioners. He learned about table service, waiters, crystal, and cutlery
in the many hours he spent under the glass-domed Palm Court on
the *Berengaria*. At the bar he learned to savor a dry martini, recently
invented by Henry Craddock, the bartender at the American Bar in

the Savoy Hotel, London; Craddock's Savoy Cocktail Book would become a founding document in Seabrook culture. C. F.'s own celebrity and uniquely American combination of talents made his opinion sought after on matters of land reform and scientific agriculture in the gentlemen-only smoking room. He also learned about French wines and began to build his own wine cellar. In London, he visited the original Bernard Weatherill and ordered the first pieces in what would one day be an extensive wardrobe. His son Belford had no interest in clothes, but Courtney emulated his father's British style. My father would take C. F.'s passion for British tailoring to the next level.

Over time, C. F. Seabrook came to conceive of himself and his family as an American version of the titled British aristocrats on whose estates he had been a guest. He often told people that the purpose of his life's work was to recover the status the Seabrooks had once enjoyed in the old country—a complete fiction. He decorated his home to resemble the rooms and grounds he had seen in England and began planning a country estate of his own right in Deep South Jersey, complete with elaborate gardens. He ordered monogrammed sterling silver cutlery and ten-piece gold-rimmed Lenox china place settings capable of serving 256 people, much like the settings on the *Berengaria*. The famous year-end parties also evoked his time at sea, with an opera singer performing upstairs for the first-class people, and a house band of local musicians for the steerage-class workers in the basement.

Above all, C. F. formed the idea of an American dynasty that his three sons would carry on, keeping the land together through male inheritance, if not strict primogeniture, leaving himself wiggle room to pit his sons against each other. But the British nobles whom C. F. emulated had been wealthy for centuries, whereas C. F. had begun life as a dirt farmer on A. P. Seabrook's tenant farm on Beebe Run. A chasm in education, manners, taste, and worldview—class, in a word—yawned between my grandfather and real British aristocrats. My father, who was thirty-six years younger than his father, would mix with this crowd as though he were one of them, but my grandfather was always acutely aware that he was an outsider. As the years passed and his tall, debonair playboy son's nightlife was chronicled in the society columns, that resentment would fester.

❧

PEOPLE NOT FROM a farm background might think it is unusual to be both a farmer and a road contractor. As career choices, they seem to sit at opposite ends of the spectrum of possible avocations. The farmer husbands the soil so that it remains fertile year after year; the contractor pours concrete and molten tar over it, ensuring the earth will not grow anything again for a long time.

In fact, farmers were among the nation's first roadbuilding contractors, when roads outside cities first began to be paved in the early twentieth century. The Bureau of Public Roads, the precursor to the Federal Highway Administration, was a division of the Department of Agriculture until the early 1930s. Farmers needed good roads to get their goods to market, and they often had deposits of stone, gravel, and sand on their land, which could be used to make both concrete and asphalt, the two main paving surfaces. They had big machines to do the roadwork. And for farmers like the Seabrooks, who relied on seasonal labor, roadbuilding offered off-season work to keep workers employed.

As a farmer, C. F. built hundreds of miles of roads across his own property. He also built another railroad spur that connected to the Pennsylvania line, in addition to the Central Jersey spur, allowing him the leverage to bargain for cheaper prices for his freight. By the early 1920s, with Seabrook Farms infrastructure mostly in place, he began looking outside the farm for roadbuilding projects. On the farm, he had been absolute boss on any such job—both the client and the contractor. But the road to success in public works was paved with politics. Accordingly, in 1920, C. F. parlayed his roadbuilding know-how into an appointment as a New Jersey highway commissioner. Shortly after taking office he awarded his company, Tri-State, a contract to pave part of the forty-mile-long Route 6—now Route 77—that ran from the farm straight to Camden and the Port of Philadelphia. During his two-year term as state highway commissioner, C. F.'s contracting companies won contracts worth more than a million dollars ($17 million today), many of them local. He seems to have made some, but not that much, effort to hide these acts of self-dealing.

Route 6 was a concrete road, but C. F. soon moved onto asphalt concrete, a newer, more flexible material. Asphalt was tricky to work with, and it could crumble if the process wasn't followed correctly and moisture got into the mix, or if the roadbed wasn't properly prepared. But new, portable asphalt-making machines made the hot rolling process of applying asphalt faster and easier to automate than the cold process of pouring a concrete road, and asphalt was easier to work with in cold weather, when C. F.'s farmworkers were idle.

When C. F. built roads around Deerfield, he sometimes bordered them with sycamore trees. The trees gave his roads a stately appearance and earned him an additional commission, since they came from a nursery he owned. He preferred sycamores, with their distinctive scaly bark, because he had seen and admired the trees growing along the Seine in Paris. As my grandfather's contracting businesses grew and he needed more roadbuilding equipment to take on bigger jobs, he became the regional distributor for Caterpillar, the equipment manufacturer. He also held local dealerships for Packard motor cars and General Motors trucks. He sold the machines to his own contracting companies, which Seabrook Farms paid to build more roads and farm structures, which kept workers busy in the off months while constantly expanding the business. It was a win-win-win-win.

≈⁊⸫

C. F. SEABROOK ENGINEERING was headquartered at 50 Church Street in the Hudson Terminal in lower Manhattan. During the week, C. F. lived at the Engineers Club, a magnificent eleven-story building on the south side of Bryant Park near the Public Library. The main hall had a colored glass dome sixty feet above the entrance, which was surrounded by sculptures, in the style of the Roman Pantheon. On the third floor was an eighteen-thousand-volume library, as well as a billiards room, then six floors of bedrooms, bath-attached, sixty-six in all, one of them C. F.'s. On eleven was the 4,000-square-foot banquet hall, and there was a covered garden on the roof. Additional amenities included a wine cellar, a barber shop, and boot cleaning stands for the members and their guests. No wonder Jack's father spent all week in New York and came home only on weekends, if at all.

C. F. was proud of the fact that he had never been certified by any professional engineering society (which didn't stop him from enjoying the comforts of the Engineers Club). He was like a builder from an earlier era, before engineering was a science, when making things stand up was a matter of seat-of-the-pants reckoning. His real expertise, apart from motivating people to work for him, was in knowing how to bid low on a project and still make money on the job. But C. F.'s lack of formal training, a source of pride to himself, was also a liability, one that became more serious as the jobs got bigger. At a minimum, he needed credentialed engineers on his payroll who could sign off on the work. This gave rise to one of the old man's favorite maxims: "It doesn't matter how many degrees you have, it's how many degrees you have working for you that counts."

After the end of the war in Europe, food prices continued to climb throughout 1919 and into the first half of 1920, as U.S. producers supplied food overseas for relief efforts. In June 1920, crop prices averaged 31 percent above 1919 prices, and 121 percent above prewar prices. But the following month, prices began to fall, and by May 1921 they were a third of what they had been the previous June. Corn dropped from $1.30 per bushel to 47 cents. Wheat was down from $2.65 to $1.65 per bushel. As food prices cratered, the cost of gasoline, fertilizer, and seed rose. Then in August, at peak harvest time, the nation's railroads raised freight prices 25 to 40 percent. On top of everything else, cheap farm labor was no longer easy to find. Men returning from digging trenches to survive the war were unwilling to go back to digging ditches for 20 cents an hour. They hadn't survived the slaughter for that.

If there was a single factor, more than any other, that brought about the farm crisis, it was overproduction. Mechanization, which farmers like C. F. had gone all in on, was now producing too much food, especially after European agriculture came back online, driving down prices. It cost indebted farmers more to produce food than they could make from selling it. In a 1921 letter to Charles Lyman of the National Board of Farm Organizations, a New Jersey truck farmer wrote:

> I just threw 32 bushels of onions out on the ground to rot, as I would not ship them to the market for the price offered. . . . Container would cost 20 cents, freight 30 cents, and the commission 10 per cent—five cents. Total of 55 cents for 100 pounds. The price was 50 cents per hundred pounds. Therefore, I made a profit of 5 cents per hundred pounds by throwing away the onions.

Actually, the farmer avoided an additional loss of five cents.

Eventually the federal government would be forced to protect the American farmer by fixing prices, and by purchasing and sometimes dumping food that couldn't be sold profitably. And although C. F. railed against the federal government, he also used his political contacts to avail himself of federal assistance, as well as government contracts and low-interest loans whenever he could.

Like many farms, Seabrook had high fixed costs. It was massively overbuilt. Still, the business held out until 1924, and had it been left to C. F., he might have found a way to make it work. But Alec White, the majority owner, had apparently had enough of Charlie Seabrook. Although my grandfather had never been more than the farm's general manager, he acted as if he owned everything. The Whites also could have disapproved of C. F.'s obvious corruption as a state highway commissioner, not to mention his segregation of the workforce's growing Black community in Orchard Village.

In the summer of 1924, C. F. was abroad for an extended period, recuperating from dysentery he got on a contracting project in the Crimea. An Australian nurse, Leila Small, oversaw his recovery. White took this opportunity to declare their business bankrupt and to fire my grandfather as general manager. A bankruptcy receiver, a New York associate of the Whites named Meyer Handelman, was appointed to dispose of the assets that could be liquidated. When he returned to the United States, C. F. challenged the bankruptcy in New Jersey Chancery Court, but he wasn't successful. (Unfortunately, the case files burned in a fire at the state archive in Trenton in the 1970s.) Of the $5 million the Whites had sunk into Seabrook Farms, the receiver recovered less than a million. The big banks got most of it, typically. C. F. lost his stake, as did the local businesses, small-town banks, and ordinary investors he had sold shares to, including his father.

The farm became Del-Bay Farms, and Alec's son, A. M. White III, called Alex, a recent Harvard graduate, became the head of Del-Bay. The Whites took possession of the plant, cannery, vehicles, and real estate at Farm Central, including the house that A. P. built, where Charlie and his family had lived since he was married. Now it belonged to a rich Harvard boy. My father, who was seven, and his sister, Thelma, were forced to relocate quickly with their mother to the Cumberland Hotel in Bridgeton, while C. F.'s workmen readied a new house he had acquired, not far from the old one, on Polk Lane. C. F. retained ownership of several thousand acres of farmland, which he rented to Del-Bay along with farmhouses and worker housing. He owned that independently of the assets of Seabrook Farms.

The *Bridgeton Evening News*, always friendly to Seabrook interests and an eager promoter of "Bridgeton's Midas" and the "Wizard of Deerfield," reported that C. F. had merely "retired" from farming. But the farm's investors, who had lost their money, knew the truth. Bankruptcy was more of a stigma a hundred years ago than it is today, especially in the eyes of the conservative burghers of Bridgeton. For all his success and his accolades, C. F. had crashed and burned just like Samuel, his ne'er-do-well grandfather, whose series of failures had cost him a gravestone.

A vigilante leader with a choke hold on a striking worker.

ACT III

BLOODY HARVEST, 1929-1934

The day of the great promoter or the financial Titan,
to whom we granted anything if only he would build
or develop, is over.
—*Franklin D. Roosevelt, September 23, 1932,*
speech to the Commonwealth Club of San Francisco

CHAPTER 11

SHIRTSLEEVES

I WAS LITERALLY MEASURED AGAINST MY FATHER. AT the age of seven, the traditional age of reason, I received my first Brooks Brothers No. 1 Sack Suit. My father exclaimed approvingly as I emerged from the fitting room, "John, you look exactly like an investment banker!" Five years later, he brought me to have my first suit of evening clothes made; still later when A-Man Hing Cheong, his Hong Kong–based tailor, visited New York, my father took me to be "measured up" for a few "country" suits (a glen plaid and a windowpane check), presumably the first of many. "Big men can wear bolder plaids and more details without appearing to be fairies," Dad advised me.

My visit to A-Man turned out to be a rite of passage.

"Which side?" the tailor asked. He was kneeling in front of me, pointing at my crotch and waggling his forefinger back and forth.

"He wants to know which side you wear your pecker on," my father explained.

Andrew Carnegie's dictum about the rise and fall of American fortunes—"shirtsleeves to shirtsleeves in three generations"—was never far from my father's mind. He was at home in the clothing metaphor, of course, but he was keen to prove it wrong. He closely instructed me in clothes, beginning with my first short-pants formal outfits. Never leave the pocket flaps of the jacket tucked inside. Always make sure your suit collar is firm against your neck, with at most a half inch of shirt collar showing above; same with cuffs. (More than once, he came up behind me, pinched my suit collar from behind, and

yanked hard to close the uncouth gap between shirt and suit, half gar-
roting me.) He also taught me the "Savile Row Fold": how to drape
trouser legs in opposing directions on a hanger so that they can't slip
off. He stood behind me facing the mirror, his forearms resting on my
shoulders, guiding my fingers as I practiced a Windsor necktie knot.
These were intimate moments.

But despite all my father's efforts (or perhaps because of them), I was
not particularly interested in clothes as a boy. Shirtsleeves suited me
just fine. I wanted to be a worker. The people I spent my day with—the
staff—were the workers, with clearly defined roles in the larger family. Though I desperately desired to please him, I could never hope to
meet the expectations my father had for JMS Jr., his namesake and
mini-he. But I could work hard at haying, or at cleaning tack, mucking
out stalls, and moving irrigation pipes for the local farmer in the spring
after school—all jobs best performed in shirtsleeves. My hard work
did garner me some of the fatherly praise that I so craved, but it was
clear more was expected of JMS Jr. Much more.

The closet in my bedroom where the suits hung (the same closet from
which the monsters emerged at night) was a riot of passive-aggressive
behavior exhibited toward innocent garments. "You're so *hard* on your
clothes," my mother would say. Trousers (never referred to as "pants,"
which signified underwear) were bunched up on hangers instead of being
hung along the pleat line. I always forgot to pull out the pocket flaps of my
jackets, so that the next time I wore them the flaps would be full of creases,
paining my father terribly. Shirts had fallen off their hangers and were
puddled on the floor, with shoes chucked into a pile on top of them. The
shoes themselves were a mess—the leather, once soaked, was now flaking
off, and the backs had all been crushed by my habit of cramming my feet
into the shoes while they were still tied. My brother, on the other hand,
seemed effortlessly to acquire my father's ability with clothes. His closet
was like an Eagle Scout's version of my father's. Mine was the Anticloset.

My arrival in New York in the fall of 1983 as a twenty-four-year-
old would-be writer coincided with the heyday of magazine publishing. New York talking, Mr. Seabrook! I loved it. Starting out as a

staff writer at *Manhattan, inc.* in the mid-eighties, at the height of red-suspendered Wall Street greed, I wrote mostly celebratory articles about successful and powerful men like my father, and inventor-entrepreneurs like my grandfather, never straying too far from the B. C. Forbes template of biography as self-help. My mother seemed to be proud of my success, but she was also fiercely critical of my work. She hated it when I used the first person, which I was drawn to. She made her admonitions against writing about the family.

Not long after I moved to my first apartment in New York, my father took me to Weatherill to have a couple of his old suits refitted on me. By then the shop had moved from the Madison Avenue storefront, shown from the inside looking out in a wonderful Slim Aarons photograph from the sixties, to a place upstairs on a midtown side street. Charles Weatherill himself, now elderly and white-haired, measured me up. His slightly stooped posture seemed like a synthesis of class-based deference and the physical toll of years of bending down to measure the bodies of young gentlemen like me. His tremendous discretion sucked the oxygen out of the air.

The jackets fit almost perfectly. A little big in the body, but the length in the sleeves was beautiful. My father and the tailor beamed with pleasure. The pants, however, needed taking in; the tailor asked me to "stand naturally" as he marked them up. But for some strange reason I had suddenly forgotten how to stand. It was as if I'd lost the concept of posture.

"Why are you standing like that?" my father said. "Knock it off."

During most of the eighties, these suits hung among other pieces of my so-called wardrobe, like a landing party that had set up a base camp in my closet from which to launch an assault on the rest of my life. Among them was an inky-blue-black drape suit, double breasted, with three closely bunched parallel rows of silvery dot stripes. The peaked lapels extended to the bottom buttons of the jacket, while the cuffed pants had a deep pleat near the fly buttons and a shallower pleat two inches farther out, which was immediately echoed by the almost hidden slash of the pocket. The date inside the jacket pocket said "9/21/61," although in style it harkened back to the fifties—a suit that Burt Lancaster could have worn in *Sweet Smell of Success*. My father was forty-four when he had the suit made, in 1961. Seabrook Farms had been taken from him by his father, and he was meeting the financiers who would help fund his four-in-hand style of living. He needed something flashy.

I wore this suit to certain pre-crash 1980s evenings. I was aware of an authority in these clothes that I didn't feel in my body. Men followed the suit with their eyes as I walked through a restaurant. Women wanted to put their hands on the fabric. Worn properly, a suit like this was clearly capable of enormous leverage. Perhaps it could attract some of the money, beauty, and power that were in the air in the mid-eighties in New York—guys I had been in college with a few years earlier were making $2 million a year selling mortgage-backed securities—and redirect that energy into me.

My chosen career did not require much in the way of clothes. But on receiving payment for a writing project, I could think of nothing I wanted more to do with it than spend it on clothes. With my check in my pocket, I'd set out for the bank, and then for Barneys, at Seventh Avenue and Seventeenth Street. I was drawn to the most expensive brands. Only a famous label had the talismanic power to ward off the Savile Row succubus that lived in my father's clothes. To my father, the whole concept of designer labels in men's fashion was ridiculous, another triumph of the marketers. What did these swishy women's dressmakers know about making clothes for a man? Ralph Lauren has made a fortune imbuing his brand with images of people like my father, but my father would never, ever wear Ralph Lauren.

The first time I wore an expensive Italian suit I had bought with my own money, an Ermenegildo Zegna, was to meet my father at 21 for lunch. He arrived at the restaurant first, and as I walked in, I saw that his attention was instantly riveted on the boxy, ventless, close-to-the-hips silhouette of my jacket. P. G. Wodehouse, describing the reaction of Jeeves upon spotting his master wearing a scarlet cummerbund with his evening clothes, wrote that "Jeeves shied like a startled mustang." My father, watching this Italian garment moving toward him around the checked tablecloths, reacted similarly. He recovered in time to greet me cordially; then, plucking the lapel of the Zegna between his thumb and forefinger, he looked at the label.

"Hmp," he said softly. That was all: "Hmp." It was the sound of a world ending.

༄

AFTER THE PRAISE he received for his address at the Seabrook reunion, Jack was keen to develop the speech into a longer memoir. I offered to help him with research at the New York Public Library, where I knew my way around from my own work. One day, while browsing a database microfilm reel of periodicals, I had come across a long, two-part article in *The Nation*, the New York–based magazine of the Left, published in August 1934. The article was an account of a farmworkers' strike that summer at Seabrook Farms, written by Leo Huberman and Colston E. Warne, two professors at the Bryn Mawr Summer School for Girls, outside Philadelphia, who were present on the bloody final day of the conflict. The article cited eyewitnesses who claimed the Seabrooks and their henchmen crushed the strike using fire hoses, tear gas, mass arrests, an imported gangster named Red Sanders, armed vigilantes, and the local chapter of the Ku Klux Klan, who spread terror by burning crosses in front of Black workers' homes. One ACLU observer reported seeing my uncle Belford, of whom I had only fond memories, leading a tear-gas attack on a striking workers' house and setting it on fire with a woman and small children inside.

That was the first time I had heard of the strike. Dad had never mentioned it, and it occurred long before my mother arrived on the scene. Still, this was arguably the single most significant event in Seabrook Farms history. It also seemed to have been a defining event within the family that had bonded father and sons as never before. So it was odd, to say the least, that my father had never brought it up. How could I have remained clueless of an event that convulsed the family, the company, the county, and the state? My ignorance motivated me to find out as much as I could about the strike, and write something myself.

Should I bring the matter up the next time I was down in Salem? I was eager to know what part, if any, young Jack Seabrook had played in the strike. He was seventeen in 1934, a senior at Bridgeton High School. He was a careful and calculating young man, who would be attending Princeton University, after a postgraduate year at Mercersburg Academy in Pennsylvania. He was not the sort to lead a tear-gas attack on workers' families, if *The Nation*'s account accusing Belford was to be believed.

✴

LISA AND I DROVE DOWN to South Jersey for Thanksgiving that year, as we always did. Thanksgiving was the Seabrook holiday par excellence, because it coincided with the former end-of-the-year harvest parties and retained elements of excess. Also, everyone dressed to the nines. (I wore a black Prada suit that year; a provocation that Dad bore stoically.) The evening would begin with oysters, caviar, and cold vodka in cut-glass tumblers, all set into a large mound of shaved ice. The vodka always reminded me of a story in which Jack had outsleuthed the help. A Finnish cook, who was part of the staff for a time, was in the habit of sneaking nips from the Stoli bottle in the freezer and topping it back up with water. When JMS found the vodka had frozen, he knew why.

I didn't bring up the strike at Thanksgiving dinner. I thought I might raise the subject the following morning, after breakfast, when I'd agreed to go coaching with Dad. Coaching was my father's sole form of recreation. He could play no sport. He had no pastimes. He wouldn't take part in cards, Clue, Monopoly, chess, checkers, or after dinner parlor games. I am haunted by a round of Celebrity that Lisa had once cajoled him into playing. Players write the name of ten celebrities on slips of paper and put them into a hat and then answer yes-or-no questions from opposing teams. My father wrote his own name, ten times. The other team, which included Lisa, kept drawing "John M. Seabrook." "Is he a very important person around here?" Yes. "Is he a very snappy dresser?" Yes. "Does he drive a coach and four horses?" Yes. "Is it . . . ?"

"You could have at least written John M. Seabrook Jr. on one of them," I said, after we'd found all ten.

We were accompanied in the carriage that morning by Chris Higgins, JMS's English coachman. Chris had trained at the Royal Mews, the Queen's stables at Buckingham Palace. He rode on the backseat, ready to jump off and hold the leaders if need be. I was next to my top-hatted father in front, who sat on the elevated box seat, towering over me, so that he could see the leaders. Supposedly it relaxed him to take the team out for a drive. It was certainly relaxing for passengers, but being the "whip" seemed like a very stressful activity indeed. The four powerful horses could bolt at anything—a telephone repair truck, say, or a kid on a bicycle, or the drivers who pulled over to stare and sometimes take pictures, perhaps expecting that Charles and Diana were inside.

My father wore a suit from the "Country Clothes" region of his closet. He maintained contact with the horses' mouths through the reins, or "ribbons," that were threaded through different fingers of his gloved left hand. When his index finger moved to the left, the long rein that stretched all the way to the mouth of the left leader would pull on the bit and begin to turn the team. In his right hand was the whip, a varnished shaft of knobby holly wood. A whalebone "drop" at the end of the shaft was attached to a braided strand of whipcord made of white horse hide, with a tufted leather lash at the tip, also known as the "popper." The driver almost never needed to use it—the team only needed to know the whip was there.

As he drove, he concentrated on the horses' ears, because the ears were sure to telegraph trouble within the team. One flattened ear was mere annoyance; two flattened ears merited a tense "Eeeaaassseeee" from the whip. On learning this as a boy, I believed Daddy could also see trouble in our ears. Like the four horses he held in his hand, Jack Seabrook's team of four children could be turned this way or that with the tug of a finger. Our burden was to pull the Seabrook legacy into an even more glorious future. There was little danger that we would bolt: we knew the whip was there.

We chatted about Pete du Pont, then the governor of Delaware. The du Ponts of Delaware had achieved what my grandfather only dreamed about. The French family was already wealthy when they emigrated to the United States to escape the French Revolution. At

President Thomas Jefferson's urging, Éleuthère Irénée du Pont established a gunpowder factory on the Brandywine River near Wilmington in 1802. Pierre Samuel du Pont, born in 1870, and his brothers Irénée, born in 1876, and Lammot, 1880, guided the company beyond explosives into chemicals and finance, in the process creating the modern corporation, E. A. DuPont de Nemours. As was the du Pont practice, Pierre married his first cousin, Alice Belin, so that their immense land holdings would remain in the family. They built Longwood, their estate, now open to the public.

By my time there were three thousand DuPonts around Delaware. My father carried the complicated genealogies of the different branches of the family—DuPonts, Copelands, Carpenters, Sharps, Bissells, and Lairds—in his head for any chance encounter with a DuPont at the Wilmington Club, the historic townhouse in downtown Wilmington where the social elite could meet, and that catered my parents' parties. St. Andrew's School in Middletown, where I spent four years, was founded by Pierre to educate future generations, but there weren't any DuPonts there in my time. My father liked to say that inbreeding had kept the land together but diminished the bloodline.

Perhaps it was the whip, or the enormous power in the animals' rear haunches, but our coaching outing didn't seem like the right time to bring up the strike. I needed a cocktail first.

CHAPTER 12

SUSPENDED
ANIMATION

A FTER THE 1924 BANKRUPTCY, ALL THREE BROTHERS
had to grow up fast. Each had to reckon in their own way with
the fact that their infallible father had failed. Belford, the oldest, was
tired of butting heads with his old man. Courtney, who unlike Belford
avoided any direct confrontation with his father and had a studious
side, seemed content to manage the Koster Nursery. Jack and his sister, Thelma, moved with their mother into the Cumberland Hotel in
Bridgeton while Seabrook work crews readied their new home on Polk
Lane. They seldom saw their father. He spent most of his time in New
York, where Seabrook Engineering was headquartered. The company
also had offices in London, Paris, and Berlin. "Until I was 13 years old
in 1930," my father wrote, "I hardly knew my father at all. Even if he
was at home, he was not the sort of father who paid any attention to
small children, and after I was seven in 1924, I saw him only on his
occasional visits to South Jersey and had little contact with him."

Unlike his brothers, my father had been educated with the workers'
children in the Charles F. Seabrook School. His two best friends had
been Presto, the son of Sicilian immigrants, who lived in the Italian
Village, and Paul, the son of Black migrants from South Carolina, who
lived in Orchard Village. As a boy, he had accompanied his mother as
the family representatives at workers' celebrations—saints' days, weddings, funerals, and christenings. While they were in the Cumberland
Hotel, Norma Dale bought Jack a chemistry set, which he set up in
the suite's bathroom, the start of a boyhood passion. A few years later,
Courtney helped Jack create a semiprofessional laboratory in the base-

ment of the Seabrook house on Polk Lane, using discounted glassware from the nearby Corning Glass plant.

Jack became the "boy chemist." Soon he would be analyzing soil samples for Mark Loper, one of the farm's managers. Loper was impressed with his work and praised it to the boss. "C. F. was probably pleased with my laboratory work," Jack wrote, "but I never remember his visiting it or saying he was pleased. The nearest he ever came was to tell people, often in my presence, 'Jack is an example of the fact that, as time goes on, generations get weaker but wiser.' This was a reference to the fact that I was tall and very thin in my teens and certainly not the physical specimen that Belford, a high school athlete, was. Anyway, I took it as the nearest thing to a compliment I was ever going to get." From his father, that is. His mother was unstinting in her praise of her son's academic record, which was always outstanding.

ॐ

IN JULY 1929, the *International Herald Tribune* reported that the C. F. Seabrook Engineering Company, described as "one of the largest road-building firms in this country," had signed construction contracts with the Soviet Union's trade organization, Amtorg, totaling $150 million—$2.7 billion today—to build roads, canals, docks, irrigation projects, and other infrastructure improvements as part of Joseph Stalin's Five-Year Plan to modernize Russia. Seabrook Engineering was one of the dozens of firms Stalin had hired, representing the biggest industrial contractors and equipment manufactures in the world: GE, Ford, and Bechtel, among many others. Lenin believed that by training engineers and workers in Fordist methods of production—flow, assembly lines, time-and-motion studies—the USSR would be able to leapfrog the bourgeois phase of development that had corrupted the West and skip right to the higher proletarian phase, as outlined by Karl Marx in *The Communist Manifesto*.

Given this faith in the transformative possibilities of *Fordizm* and *Taylorizm*, it is no surprise that the American who was celebrated as "The Henry Ford of Agriculture" would be on the Bolsheviks' radar.

After all, C. F. Seabrook had already transformed a nineteenth-century agrarian society into a twentieth-century industrial one in southern New Jersey, through his own Five-Year Plan, when he built the infrastructure of what would become Seabrook Farms in a frenzy of construction between 1913 and 1918. C. F. and the Soviets also shared a passion for what Western commentators called "gigantomania": Stalin's insistence that size mattered in industrial policy. Still, for Charlie Seabrook to get himself included in this elite company of builders was an act of extraordinary chutzpah, and, as it turned out, overreach.

C. F. made his headquarters in Moscow, at the five-star Savoy Hotel. A marvel of czarist opulence when it opened in 1913, the hotel was somewhat run-down by 1929, but still grand. Seabrook's contract was to build ten thousand miles (roughly sixteen thousand kilometers) of roads in the province of Moscow, over a six-year period. By the spring of 1930, C. F. had assembled a crew of ten engineers and twenty technicians in Moscow and acquired and shipped a lot of roadbuilding machinery, all on credit. The plan for the first year, overseen by an experienced New York State–certified engineer, H. Eltinge Breed, was to pave seven hundred miles of roads in two hundred days, before winter set in.

In a talk that August at the Bridgeton Rotary Club in South Jersey, C. F. painted a rosy picture of the Soviet situation in general and his roadbuilding work in particular. But soon after that, the Moscow streets Seabrook paved began to disintegrate. The November 1930 issue of *Za Rulem* (*Let's Roll!*), a Russian automotive journal, carried an article titled "Road Works Failures in Moscow," which showed shocking photographs of crumbling roads paved by Seabrook. One photo, in which Muscovites can be seen climbing down steep embankments and walking in trenches where road surfaces had been only a few months before, is captioned "Circus exercises of Moscow residents when crossing from one sidewalk to another." The article blames a lack of proper research into materials suited for Moscow conditions.

There was talk of a lawsuit against Seabrook Engineering. Naturally the Soviets had withheld payment, and that meant C. F. could not pay the equipment manufacturers whose machines he had purchased on credit and had shipped to Russia. As Seabrook's asphalt concrete roads crumbled, so did Charlie Seabrook's dream of belonging to the ranks of industrial construction titans like Bechtel and Kaiser. C. F. Seabrook might be a big man in New Jersey, but in Moscow he was badly exposed. For the second time in six years, a C. F. Seabrook business venture went belly-up. He would channel his anger into a newfound hatred for Communists, his former business partners—a Red-hating blaze that would burn bright in the family's coming strug-gle with organized labor. He also suspected a Jewish banking conspir-acy was at the heart of his troubles, along the lines laid out in "The Protocols of the Elders of Zion."

✺

IN AUGUST 1931, C. F. convened an important family meeting over breakfast. He announced that he was broke, that his contracting busi-ness was at a dead end, and that the family was going back to farm-ing. He had put together a group of investors and had reacquired the remaining assets of Del-Bay Farms, which were sold after Alec White's death at the age of fifty-eight in 1929, the year of the crash. In addition to the cannery, there were the greenhouses, the processing plant, and the cold storage warehouse, as well as the fleets of trucks, tractors, plows, cultivators, seed drills, harrows, and other farm machinery.

Present at breakfast were Belford, twenty-six, Courtney, twenty-three, Thelma, nineteen, and Jack, thirteen. My grandmother was there too, and as usual kept quiet. C. F. was long estranged from his brother Sidney, but his sons were a team, and looked out for each other, despite their father's attempts to pit them against each other. Jack's circumstances were very different from those of his brothers, however. Belford and Courtney were both married with houses of their own, while Thelma and Jack were still living with their parents in the house on Polk Lane. Both older brothers had lived through the 1924 bankruptcy and knew what working for their father was like. They had seen him humbled. But to Jack, C. F. was a distant, rarely seen, all-powerful figure who could do no wrong and whose word was absolute.

C. F. told his family that he was returning to Moscow to try to collect his money from the Soviets, but that henceforth they should all consider themselves part of this new venture. As my father later wrote of this memorable morning,

> He told Belford and Courtney there would be no more engineering jobs anywhere. Thelma, now 19, was sent to work in the office over the truck and car agency at 41 Atlantic Street in Bridgeton, New Jersey, to which C. F. transferred his office after he closed the offices in Berlin, London, and New York. Belford and Courtney, halfway through college, were told they were to finish the next two years, but pay their own expenses. There was no cash at all, and we would use barter for many things. Mother suggested certain other economies, which C. F. promptly vetoed, saying, to maintain credit, he had to keep up appearances. He still had a man shave him every morning and bought a new Panama hat each summer.

Jack was made the grader in the cannery, a key position in the production line, at the age of fourteen. The boy was thrilled to be given such an important job. Everything depended on the grade. The grade of the produce brought to the plant by Seabrook's contract growers determined the price the company paid them for it. To determine what grades to award peas, or string beans, Jack used special measuring calipers. Spinach was graded on color and crispness, and how clean the crop was. Farmers sometimes objected to the grade the young master awarded their crop, but Jack would patiently explain his reasoning and stand his ground.

❧

JUST AS HE HAD DONE with overhead irrigation, C. F. hoped to build his latest venture by applying another new technology—quick-freezing—to the vegetables produced at Farm Central. Always an avid reader, C. F. knew about Clarence Birdseye's efforts to preserve fish by quick-freezing, which had been inspired by the inventor's visit to the Labrador region of Canada in 1917. Birdseye had observed the local Inuit catching fish that froze instantly in the Arctic air. The fish not only tasted fresh when thawed, in some cases they swam away. Quick-freezing seemed to put the fish in a state of "suspended animation," Birdseye later wrote.

The inventor set out to reproduce suspended animation in his home laboratory in Gloucester, Massachusetts. After a decade of experimenting, and some 180 patents, Birdseye had devised a viable process. The food was packed in waxed paper cartons, then quick-frozen between metal plates that chilled the packets to -25 degrees Fahrenheit with pressurized ammonia. The product debuted in 1928. The following year, Birdseye came to the attention of Marjorie Merriweather Post when her yacht, the *Hussar*, was docked in Gloucester, and she happened to sample a quick-frozen goose. Post, the wealthiest woman in America (she built Donald Trump's residence, Mar-a-Lago in Palm Beach), was the only child and heir of the breakfast cereal tycoon C. W. Post. She had inherited his company, Postum, in 1914, following her father's suicide. She insisted the company purchase Birdseye's business and patents, which it did, for $23 million ($424 million today), just before the crash. Postum, which soon changed its name to General Foods, created the Birds Eye Frosted Foods brand to sell its frozen line. The inventor remained with the company as the head of research.

Birdseye had had some success in his experiments with freezing fresh fruit, but quick-frozen vegetables had eluded him. Unlike fruits, green vegetables needed to be blanched before quick-freezing to preserve their color and to slow the loss of vitamins. In 1930, C. F. met Birdseye (who went by "Bob") in the Postum Building at 250 Park Avenue. The Seabrooks had been keeping vegetables cold since the 1910s, using the Frick compressors. But freezing veggies, at least by conventional methods, ruptured the cells and rendered them tasteless. Courtney had worked with the company's chief agronomist, Dr. Frank App, who came from Del-Bay Farms, on packing the vegetables in wooden boxes with dry ice. Although this method had not proven successful, the men learned which vegetables froze best. Lettuce leaves, being heavy in water content, would not freeze; spinach leaves, which are denser in cellulose, froze nicely. Corn, peas, beans, and kale froze well, but not cabbage or celery. The most freeze friendly of all was the lima bean, a vegetable not yet well known in the East, but thanks largely to the Seabrooks, soon would be.

C. F. made Belford chief engineer and put him in charge of converting the plant and cold storage warehouse into a frozen vegetable factory. Belford visited the Birdseye laboratory and studied the inventor's process and then adapted it to the existing plant and the Frick refrigeration system. C. F. recognized how instrumental Belford had been to the success of his second incarnation as an industrial farmer, and gave him stock in the company, but they frequently butted heads. They looked alike, whereas Jack and Courtney were much taller and resembled Norma Dale. Social and holiday gatherings were made tense when Belford's wife, Harriet, a free-spirited, independent woman, objected to C. F.'s treatment of her husband. Family dynamics did not improve when grandchildren began to arrive, beginning with Belford's oldest child, Margaret Dale Seabrook, born in 1929.

Vincent Salmon, seventeen, was working in a summer job at Del-Bay Farm in 1929, when C. F. bought back the business and its assets. Salmon worked at the farm in the summers until 1938, while attending college and graduate school at Rutgers. In a letter he wrote to me in 1995, Salmon recalled that in the early thirties, "Working with Birdseye, C. F. had a walk-in freezer installed for the very first experimental freezing operation at the Farm. I was put on a team that worked from 7am to midnight for two weeks on the experimental freezing of baby lima beans. We picked, sorted, packed, and froze them according to a planned experiment series. . . . At the end of the two weeks, a taster came from Boston for an evening session to select optimum conditions for picking, packing, and freezing. He used only a few mouthfuls from each lot to make up his mind."

For Salmon, as for many workers, Seabrook offered formative life experiences he remembered vividly almost seventy years later. In his letter, Salmon recalled that "jobs included looking at the south end of a mule going north; picking, grading, and packing fruit and vegetables; tending greenhouse roses with liquid cow manure; handling cold storage transactions; and in the garage helping mechanics, serving vehicles and driving truckloads of produce to market." To kill insects and aphids, the greenhouses were fumigated with cyanide gas. Salmon explained, "The greenhouses were sealed closed except for one exit to be used by the worker carrying cyanide pills. Jars of sulfuric acid had been placed at calculated locations, and the pills were dropped in as you quickly moved on to the exit to avoid the HCN fumes. The greenhouses were then opened and the fans started by a worker with a special gas mask."

Around 1930, C. F. brought from Holland Peter Koster, a well-regarded horticulturalist who was a member of a prominent Dutch family of nineteenth-century plant breeders. The firm, M. Koster & Sons, had created several popular species of rhododendrons and azaleas in Europe, as well as *Picea pungens "Kosteriana"*—the Koster Blue Spruce, a compact, luridly colored evergreen that would become a backyard American favorite. C. F. gave the nurseryman some land along Parsonage Road, down from his own place. Koster also established a rose- and tulip-growing business on the farm, both outdoors and under glass. In 1924, members of the New York Horticultural Society made a day-trip to Seabrook and reported forty acres of blooming tulips. Koster also bred a rhododendron he named the Grace Seabrook. The nursery supplied the sycamores that lined the roads that C. F. built as commissioner. When his contracting jobs dwindled, C. F.'s own estate became Koster's main client. Under the supervision of a landscape architect, who lived with the family at times, Koster became the supplier of trees, shrubs, and flowers for the magnificent gardens C. F. created at the Seabrook mansion on Polk Lane.

꩜

HAVING AGREED ON A CONTRACT WITH BIRDSEYE, C. F. had secured a large loan from the federal Reconstruction Finance Corporation in February 1933, during the waning hours of the Hoover Administration. (Presidents were inaugurated in March until 1937, when the Twentieth Amendment moved the date to January 20.) This money helped fund the retooling of the plant's cooling system as well as the cost of the research and development needed to produce frozen vegetables on an industrial scale. Still, cash was tight, and food prices remained depressed, as they had been since the end of World War I. The company offered snow-plowing services during the winter to generate income. The Seabrooks relied on the cannery business to pay the interest on the government loan and meet the company's payroll and operating expenses. But all they had to sell was canned cabbage, which no one wanted.

C. F. leaned on his political connections to convince the state of New Jersey to distribute sauerkraut, which is made of cabbage, to hungry people. At first, New Jersey claimed to lack revenues to pay the Seabrooks for the sauerkraut. However, the state came into a windfall when John T. Dorrance, the principal owner of Campbell Soup Company, died in 1930 and left an estate worth billions in today's money, of which New Jersey extracted a third. C. F. got the cash for his sauerkraut.

Like many wealthy men of the day, C. F. considered Franklin Roosevelt a class enemy. He saw the New Deal as a threat to the free hand he had enjoyed in his first iteration as an entrepreneur and builder. The federal government, for its part, seemed eager to get out of business with the Seabrooks. The farm's RFC loan was transferred to the Farm Security Administration, which faced pressure to wind up the Seabrook loan entirely.

The year 1934 was make-or-break for C. F.'s new enterprise. In spite of costly infrastructure improvements, mostly financed by the government, the company still had few revenues to show from quick-freezing.

As with electricity, gas-powered cars, the internet, and other epoch-making inventions, it took time to create the necessary infrastructure to realize the potential of frozen food. Without the kind of viable "cold chain" that Nicola Twilley describes in her book *Frostbite*—freezer trucks and railcars to transport the product to chilled warehouses, and from there to freezer cabinets in supermarkets, and then to the latest freezer-equipped Frigidaires at home—there was no way to reliably supply a potential customer. On top of that, marketers had to convince the public that quick-frozen vegetables tasted good, when most people associated frozen food with spoilage.

By the spring of 1934, it became necessary to cut wages and lay off workers. That was when the trouble started.

CHAPTER 13

"THE NEGRO JOINS THE PICKET LINE"

W HEN C. F. RETURNED TO THE FARMING BUSINESS IN
1930 and needed to recruit labor, the company looked to
Southern Blacks traveling north as part of the Great Migration. The
first wave of migrants from the Upper South brought many people
to Philadelphia, where the Pennsylvania Railroad offered work. As
the Great Depression began take hold, in 1933–1934, some of those
workers lost their railroad jobs and ended up working in the fields at
Seabrook.

Black and white workers lived in separate "villages," an arrangement that was both ideological and political, because it allowed C. F.
to play the different ethnic groups off against each other to keep control. Housing workers in separate villages with different levels of amenities helped stoke resentment. On the farm, Blacks were confined to
the fields and weren't allowed to work in the plant at all, to say nothing of management, which was entirely white, Protestant, and male.

The ethnic villages are described in *The Nation* article I came across
in the library. "The workers are divided into three sections, whites,"
who were Italian and Eastern European immigrants, "Negroes, and
Americans, with the rents for their houses ranging from two dollars a month to ten dollars. The Negroes are given broken-down
sheds . . . most often without water, light, or sanitary facilities."
Their account continues, quoting one of the Black workers, "The Italians . . . pay higher rent for better houses. The . . . sub-foremen are the
Americans who live in the best houses. In the winter months, when
we are laid off, rent continues just the same, only it is added up and

deducted from our spring pay checks. When we are working the rent is deducted in advance from our weekly pay checks."

Some of the poorest workers could not afford to pay the rent in Seabrook housing and lived in shacks in Bridgeton, where Lester B. Granger, a Black civil rights activist who later became the executive secretary of the National Urban League, described their living conditions in "The Negro Joins the Picket Line," an article that appeared in *Opportunity: A Journal of Negro Life* in the fall of 1934: "Half-clothed, half-starved, completely dirty children, poor white and Negro, run about in hopelessly squalid surroundings. Frowsy heads look out from half-open doors, through which may be seen badly ventilated rooms crowded with broken furniture and with broken humanity."

❧

IN THE SPRING OF 1934, with national unemployment over 20 percent and dust storms driving farmers and workers from the land in the Great Plains, the pay for men on the Seabrook farm was 17 1/2 cents an hour, or $1.75 cents for ten hours of work, which is about $40 today. (Federal wage laws weren't enacted until 1938, when minimum wage was set at 25 cents an hour.) Women made 15 cents an hour, and children 5 cents. It was common to see whole families working together in the fields; child labor laws did not apply to agricultural work in New Jersey, and even when those laws were later enacted, C. F. mostly ignored them. He himself had begun working full days at age seven, as had his children, and the old man expected no less from his children and his workers.

Because farm work is seasonal, there are busy times when the farm needs many hands, and slack times only a skeleton crew is required. At Seabrook, the hectic planting season in the spring was followed by a lull in May before the need for workers picked up again in June, when the pea harvest started. The custom was to stop paying the Black workers during slack seasons, and to keep the white, mainly Italian American workers. Black workers had long complained about this discriminatory practice, but nothing changed. What could they do? As the Great Depression deepened, the number of people willing to do farm work for low pay increased. If the strapped Seabrook workers didn't like their wages, someone truly desperate might.

Opportunities for collective action were limited. The American Federation of Labor showed little interest in supporting striking farmworkers, with so many industrial strikes going on at the same time. Factory labor was more attractive to union organizers than farm labor because most farmworkers were too poor to pay dues and too migratory for any one local to represent them effectively. As the State Federation of Labor secretary told *The New York Times* in 1935, "Only fanatics are willing to live in shacks or tents and get their heads broken in the interests of migratory laborers."

Thanks in part to the progressive policies of the Roosevelt administration, the mid-1930s saw legislative victories for unionism. But agricultural workers were exempt from most of the new labor laws, including the National Labor Relations Act of 1935, which guaranteed industrial workers collective-bargaining rights and made it illegal for employers to dismiss workers who joined a union. Farm workers were also left out of the Fair Labor Standards Act of 1938, which established minimum wage for the first time. Why were farmworkers denied the rights that other American workers enjoyed? Mostly because segregationist Southern Democrats opposed any tampering with the sharecroppers and farmworkers. The workers themselves were mainly people of color who lacked the political power to represent their interests in Washington.

Agricultural workers did have one great advantage over industrial workers when it came to collective action. A manufacturer might be able to wait out a strike by rejiggering the supply chain and working around shortages, but a farmer's product was perishable. A few days could make the difference between a valuable crop and silage, and that gave farmworkers leverage that trade unionists didn't have. A strike timed for a peak planting or harvest season could cause severe economic damage.

At Seabrook, the spring cabbage planting season offered just such an opportunity. Removing the cabbage seedlings from the greenhouses and cold frames and transplanting them in the fields was one of the many farm jobs that could not be mechanized.

≈

ON THE MORNING OF APRIL 6, 1934, a delegation of Seabrook workers approached the farm office with a list of ten demands. They included pay raises to thirty cents an hour for men and twenty-five cents for women, and time-and-a-half for overtime. Workers also demanded that during the slack season men be laid off according to seniority and not according to race.

The delegation was led by Jerry Brown, a senior Black worker who had been elected president of the workers' homegrown union— Farmers and Workers Association, Local No. 2.

The others included a mix of white and Black workers. As a striking Italian worker, Primo Busnardo, later put it, "Hunger pulls people together—prosperity separates."

The farm's administration building was one of the gray-and-white wood-frame houses that the farm's top managers lived in. The Seabrook & Son safe, where cash, stock certificates, and deeds were stored, was also kept here. C. F. was not there that day, but Uncle Bert was. He refused to see the delegation. Later that day, about 250 workers walked out. Many of the white cannery workers joined the Black field workers in solidarity.

The next morning, Saturday, April 7, a picket line formed on the highway outside Farm Central. Women of color, dressed in white uniforms, joined the men in the line. Striking workers stopped drivers and good-naturedly explained why they were striking.

C. F. had returned to Farm Central by then to take charge of the situation. Now fifty-six years old, he controlled Upper Deerfield Township absolutely. The railroads and the highways had been built by him. Much of the land belonged to him. The villages in which the workers lived were built and owned by Seabrook Housing, a separate entity that C. F. also controlled.

Leaving the administration building and heading for the picket line,

C. F. approached Jerry Brown. Lester Granger included their exchange in his *Opportunity* piece.

"Jerry," said Seabrook, "you know we've always been for the colored people. You know we've always hired them on our farms right along with the white folks."

"Yes," says Jerry, "hired 'em last and fired 'em first when slack season comes along."

"Break up the union," urged Seabrook, "and I'll take care of you. I'll fire all the Dagoes and just keep coloreds on. I'd rather have coloreds anyhow."

But Jerry Brown refused to dissolve the union. So the boss fired him.

The state appointed a mediator, a local man named Garfield A. McKeen, who was a newspaper editor, chaplain, and former Socialist candidate for local office. C. F. maintained to McKeen that the company could not possibly pay the workers thirty and twenty-five cents an hour because of the terms of the government loan he had received. "Mr. Seabrook explained to me that in order to negotiate a government loan last year," McKeen said to a reporter, "it was necessary to give the government officials a complete report of the budget, including wages, and the budget cannot be changed without governmental consent." McKeen also stated that "the increase in wages would have to come from the pockets of individuals of the Seabrook organization"—meaning executives.

The farm would have no cabbage crop unless management settled with the strikers, and C. F. would lose many thousands of dollars at a time when the company was struggling to survive. So Seabrook told McKeen they would agree to "temporarily" raise wages and to pay workers a bonus for working overtime, as well as to investigate improving the miserable housing conditions. It was, all things considered, a victory for the union.

But when McKeen urged the workers to accept management's offer the next day—Sunday, April 8—the union "repudiated his recommendations," so McKeen quit, according to a report in Camden's *Morning Post*. McKeen explained: "A group of four or five men with Communistic leanings have taken over authority among the strikers, and their attitude was such that there was nothing for me to do but discontinue my efforts at mediation." Given C. F.'s hatred of Communism, this was a serious outrage.

CHAPTER 14

REDS

O NE OF THOSE MEN WITH "COMMUNISTIC LEANINGS"
was thirty-two-year-old Donald Henderson. As an undergraduate at Columbia University, Henderson was active in the Social Problems Club, the leading radical students' organization. After graduating, he'd been a tenure-track economics instructor at Columbia from 1926 to 1933, while also heading the Student Union. He was a protégé of the university's president, Rex Tugwell, a key member of FDR's New Deal brain trust. Henderson's wife, the former Eleanor Curtis, was a member of the American Communist Party and was involved in civil rights activism in Harlem. Like many on the left, she was radicalized by the 1931 show trial and capital conviction of the Scottsboro Boys of Alabama, who were falsely accused of raping a white woman. Curtis took part in the League of Struggle for Negro Rights, the organization headed by Langston Hughes, also a Party member, and worked in Harlem to recruit African Americans to the Communist Party, with limited success. Many viewed the Soviet Union's interest in the plight of the American Negro as more of an anti-American propaganda tool than a genuine commitment to civil rights.

By the early 1930s, the Hendersons were living with their son, Curtis, at 174 West 109th Street. Eleanor ran unsuccessfully as the Communist Party candidate for City Council member in the 21st District of New York in 1932. The next year her husband was fired from Columbia for his membership in the Party. Because of his role in the Student Union, Henderson's firing became a cause célèbre for left-leaning students at the university and elsewhere in the city.

Since leaving academia, Donald had become a full-time labor organizer for the Cannery and Agricultural Workers Industrial Union
(CAWIU) and had gained field experience in helping to organize strikes
in California's Imperial Valley in the early 1930s. The Seabrook conflict was an ideal opportunity to garner publicity for workers' rights
and for the Party. Unlike most large farms, which tend to be in remote
areas, Seabrook was near enough to Philadelphia and New York to
attract reporters from major newspapers, as well as the interest of local
papers from Camden, Bridgeton, Millville, Vineland, and other towns.

Henderson had been involved, through the CAWIU, in trying to
organize Black sharecroppers in the South. The union had also played
a minor role in the walkout at the Campbell Soup processing plant in
Camden earlier in 1934, the first large agricultural strike in the Northeast, although it involved only cannery workers and not field laborers.
Shortly after the start of the Seabrook strike, CAWIU formed a local
in South Jersey and began organizing the Seabrook workers. Jerry
Brown remained president of the former union, but not for long.

In the spring of 1934, the Hendersons rented a house in Vineland
with the labor organizer Leif Dahl and his wife, Vivian, who were in
their mid-twenties and had worked together in North Dakota organizing wheat farmers. All were members of the American Communist
Party. The house, on West Landis Avenue in Vineland, became the
headquarters of CAWIU's organizing efforts across the region.

The Hendersons and the Dahls could not have been further removed
from the Seabrooks in politics and worldview. The former were committed to racial and social justice; the latter believed in the superiority
of their clan and in their own heroic narrative. They felt they had the
right to run their South Jersey empire as they saw fit. I grew up with
Seabrooks, but I have lived and worked mostly among Hendersons and
Dahls—idealists. The two camps don't mix well.

The organizers arranged for the Seabrookers to receive issues
of *The Daily Worker*, the American Communist Party newspaper.
But as was the case with Eleanor's earlier efforts in Harlem, they
met with widespread Black skepticism about the USSR and about

Communism. Fair pay and equal treatment were what the workers wanted, not the overthrow of capitalism. As Mack Bradwell, who had arrived in Seabrook as a fifteen-year-old in 1920, said years later: "We wanted more money—there was no Communism or nothing, we just wanted more wages to live on."

When Donald Henderson turned up in Seabrook, someone had alerted the Upper Deerfield Township sheriff, William Brown, to the presence of an "outside agitator." The *Bridgeton Evening News* reported, "Sheriff Brown took the party into custody this morning and after due process of law, will escort him to the limits of Cumberland County." With Henderson temporarily sidelined, the April strike was settled. The union and management signed a new contract that reestablished wages at twenty-five cents an hour and stated that the contract would remain in effect for one year from the signing date, April 10, 1934.

Just a few days later, members of the "White Legion" burned a cross outside Jerry Brown's house in Seabrook and fired fifteen shots through his window. Brown resigned from his position in the union soon afterward and left the area.

❧

THE REBIRTH OF THE KLAN as the "White Legion" in the 1920s was driven in part by the nativist mood of the country, not unlike the ideology fueling far-right hate groups today—claims that immigrants were polluting the Nordic gene pool. Catholics, Jews, and people of color were beginning to encroach on the previously all-white Protestant universities and corporations. The Great Migration had brought large number of Black people to Northern cities for the first time.

In July 1924, a Konclave in Long Branch, New Jersey, had attracted twenty-five thousand people, the largest KKK gathering ever in the Eastern U.S. Later that month, thousands of Cumberland County Klansmen held a clambake at Tumbling Dam Park, on Sunset Lake, where they had a camp. The women's auxiliary and the Junior Klan were also represented. Bridgeton Mayor Samuel C. Johnson led the group in prayer. Then, led by a white-robed man on a horse and a Klan band, the hooded Klansmen, who included prominent local businessmen, bankers, and clergy, marched through downtown Bridgeton. Five hundred people were "naturalized" as new Klan members. The *Bridgeton Evening News* reported, "A little girl of one of the members recited 'The Little Red Schoolhouse' and 'The Duty to the Flag.' "

Konclaves were family-friendly events that had parades with floats depicting church, home, and school, guarded by Klansmen with flaming swords. Klan christenings used "Klan water," which could be purchased from the national headquarters. Cross burnings were like fireworks displays. "Packaging its noxious ideology as traditional small-town values and wholesome fun," wrote Joshua Rothman in *The Atlantic* in 2016, "the Klan of the 1920s encouraged native-born white Americans to believe that bigotry, intimidation, harassment, and extralegal violence were all perfectly compatible with, if not central to, patriotic respectability."

In 1925, the Cumberland Country Club purchased Tumbling Dam Park and announced the building of a new amusement park. In May, the *Bridgeton Evening News* reported, "Rumor has it that the new club is sponsored by the Ku Klux Klan, but Bridgeton business men interested in the ownership of the property emphatically deny it." The paper also notes "there will be no gambling devices nor games of chance at any time. The plays and musical comedies put on are absolutely clean with not even lines suggestive of double meanings. The dress of the women will be beyond reproach." Two months later, the KKK held a "Klan Day" at the park, with canoe races and water polo followed by another parade through Bridgeton. In August, the *Bridgeton Evening News* carried an ad for a KKK show of "hand painted pictures" titled "The Future of America" to be held at the park. "Children Under Sixteen Not Admitted."

The White Legion didn't murder people, but they were still a violent, menacing group. The Klan had historically served as vigilantes in breaking worker-led actions. "Klan vigilantism sometimes expressly targeted labor unions, especially in cases where workers were not 'Nordic,'" notes Linda Gordon in *The Second Coming of the KKK*.

In California, the Klan aligned itself with the big growers against the farmworkers, not only those of Mexican descent but also the perfectly "Nordic" "Okies." In the 1930s the Klan openly aided the thugs used by the Associated Farmers and the California Citizens Association against farmworker unionization. Vigilantism strengthened the Klan.

≈⁊

THE SEABROOK MANSION on Polk Lane was a large Queen Anne–era farmhouse, onto which C. F.'s work crews had added an extension in back with a solarium, as well as making numerous other improvements. The house and landscaped gardens were surrounded on three sides by densely planted rows of yew trees that blocked the view from workers in the fields, but the property was hardly secure. Belford was then finishing his career as a student at Princeton, from which he would graduate in 1934, at the uniquely old age of twenty-five, and was already married with two children. Courtney was attending Lehigh in Bethlehem, Pennsylvania, a hundred miles north. Only Norma Dale, Thelma, and Jack, along with Clarence Jones, the family's cook, were in residence most nights.

Since C. F. was often in New York at the Engineers Club, or in Washington trying to keep the government from winding up the FSA loan, he decided to hire a live-in bodyguard to protect his family. He chose Jack "Red" Saunders, a small-time gangster and bootlegger from Brooklyn, to be the "watchman." Their paths might have crossed in Atlantic City, where Red was known. Prohibition had recently ended with the Twenty-First Amendment, passed in December 1933, putting Saunders out of work; he had reinvented himself as a professional strikebreaker. The farm was only about forty miles from the still-fashionable resort, and my grandparents were frequent visitors to the "World's Playground." C. F. was an acquaintance of political boss Nucky Johnson, who may have personally vouched for Saunders.

The colorful Red moved into the Polk Lane house and was welcomed by the Seabrook clan, who were charmed by his tales of a violent life lived beyond the law. Jack, still residing at home, became especially close to Red, who called him "Slapfoot" for the sound his flat feet made on the floor when he was shoeless. The older man instructed Jack in how to use a gun and gave him a .45-caliber pistol with an armpit holster to conceal the fact that he was armed. My father later recalled, "We all went armed. From the time I was fourteen or fifteen years of age I never went anywhere without a pistol in my left armpit. That was just the way it was."

꿏

AFTER THE APRIL STRIKE, C. F. amassed a vigilante strike force, recruited from the ranks of small farmers, some of them the second-generation Italian immigrants whose fathers had worked for the company twenty years earlier. Politically, it was not in these small farmers' interest to back the Leviathan that was likely to swallow their land at a future bank auction. The land transfers recorded in the Cumberland County Record Vault show page after page of transactions involving Seabrook-backed entities in the mid-1930s. Nevertheless at least thirty farmers were issued axe handles, the farmer's blackjack, and made special deputies by Upper Deerfield Township.

The local chapter of the White Legion also pledged to support C. F. The Klansmen weren't landowners like the vigilantes; they were mostly Deep South Jersey locals. But ideologically, C. F. and the Klansmen agreed on matters of religion, white supremacy, organized labor, Communism, and the international Jewish banking conspiracy.

Work on the farm continued through the spring and early summer spinach season, followed by the pea and bean harvests. In the third week of June, the weather turned hot. Starting on June 20, the temperature topped 90 degrees for seventeen days in a row. By June 30, it was 102 degrees in Philadelphia, the highest June reading since records began in 1870.

Toward the end of the month, management announced layoffs of about 125 workers. As usual, nearly all the furloughed workers were Black. The company also announced that wages would be reduced to eighteen cents an hour again, despite the April contract. Courtney told a reporter that the cuts were necessary because the cabbage that had been planted in April, when the strike was settled, was now selling in New York for less than the cost of producing it. As a result, *The Morning Post* reported, "Officials of the farm insist they are unable to meet the high rate of wages and said it is possible the federal government will institute receivership proceedings because of a $225,000 loan grant and on which payments are delinquent."

On the morning of Monday, June 25, Arthur Remmert, a Seabrook crop duster, was already aloft, preparing to dust while there was still enough dew on the crops to dissolve the fertilizer. (The "dust" contained substances later banned by the EPA, including DDT.) In a picture taken from the plane, the workers' committee of CAWIU Local No. 2 and their supporters, along with a second, noncommunist affiliated group, can be seen marching toward Farm Central along the highway. The two-story houses for the "Americans" are in the foreground, and the barracks where the Black workers lived are in the distance. The countryside looks scorched.

An earthbound photographer captured workers dressed in their overalls, walking toward the administration building, to demand that management honor the April contract. Black and white men are in front, women and children are right behind. One of the leaders is walking with a cane. The body language of the marchers is relaxed. No one looks like they're spoiling for a fight.

The committee arrived at the administration building. As they stepped inside they were set upon by C. F.'s hired vigilantes, who blackjacked and pistol-whipped the men. The vigilantes escaped out the back door into a waiting "black limo," according to eyewitnesses. Shots were fired from the car, and lead was found on the porch of the office.

In response, 350 field and cannery workers walked out. On June 27, the *Bridgeton Evening News* reported, "A mass-meeting was held [last night] near the water tank, and the strikers heard speakers, both colored and white." For a segregated community like Seabrook Farms, the diversity of the strikers was itself an extraordinary act of defiance. On June 29, a picket line of workers carrying signs and chanting slogans formed along the concrete highway to Camden that C. F. built when he was highway commissioner, now called Route 46, outside the entrance to the plant. The farm, which had never had fences because C. F. disliked the sight of them, hastily erected barbed-wire barricades around the entrance to Farm Central, with a barbed-wire gate that guards opened only for company vehicles. Inside the gates were Seabrooks, supervisors, and workers loyal to the company, along with Red Saunders and his special deputies, and local police.

A truck emerged from this fortress and headed straight for the picket line. Mack Bradwell got in front of it, hoping to persuade the driver to come out and talk. But the truck, which had several men in the cab along with the driver, kept going and ran Bradwell over, injuring him and three women, one of them Vivian Dahl. Bradwell and the other injured strikers were taken to the Bridgeton hospital, only to discover, according to Dahl, that the company had sent word ahead to the attending physician, Dr. Pino, not to treat them.

Dahl was close enough to identify Red Saunders in the truck, along with another man. She also saw the driver, according to the coverage in the *Bridgeton Evening News*. When I came upon this article, preserved on microfilm in the Bridgeton Public Library, my heart sank. Vivian Dahl had named Uncle Courtney as the man behind the wheel.

As the truck sped away, the striking workers attacked the Seabrook loyalists, who were backed by Saunders's thugs. The *Morning Post* report says, "This was the signal for a general fight between strikers and workers. All manner of farm tools were swung and fists flew as scores of men tangled in battle." The police were unable to stop the fighting, which threatened to "tear the place apart," according to a farm spokesman. C. F.'s brother-in-law, Douglas Aitken, a Cumberland County assemblyman, appealed to New Jersey Governor Harry Moore to declare martial law and send in the National Guard. With the July Fourth weekend approaching, the governor had retired to his summer mansion in Sea Girt, which also happens to be New Jersey National Guard headquarters. But Moore, a Democrat, declined to intervene. Later, he said he was not going to send the Guard in against people who were only trying to make a living wage. This enraged C. F.

Colonel Norman Schwarzkopf Sr., the father of the future leader of Operation Desert Storm in Kuwait, was a World War I vet who created the New Jersey State Police in 1921 and had led the force since then. To the Troopers he was "the Commandant." In 1932, Schwarzkopf had become the chief investigator in the Lindbergh baby's kidnapping and murder. A few months after the Seabrook strikes, he oversaw the arrest of the kidnapper Bruno Hauptmann in September 1934.

Schwarzkopf agreed to dispatch seventeen state troopers to the scene to quell the rioting. The *Bridgeton Evening News* reported, "Warrants were issued for the arrest of Courtney Seabrook, a son of Charles F. Seabrook, who was driving one of the trucks, and for Constable Jack Saunders. They are charged with assault and battery." The following day, Sheriff Brown appealed to the township to dismiss Jack Saunders as constable, whom he had earlier deputized, on the grounds that he was "incompetent and unfit to be an official." But the Township Committee refused, because "the farm was a vital part of the township and that protection should be afforded to those in charge."

On June 27, Vivian Dahl called the Vineland police to report that she had found two cases of dynamite and some blasting caps in their garage on West Landis Avenue. Whether the explosives had been placed there to frame the house's occupants or to blow them up was unclear, although the papers noted that the percussion caps had been left on the floor of the garage where the Dahls' car could have rolled over them.

Saunders was soon back on the job. The sympathetic editor in chief of the *Bridgeton Evening News* devoted part of a column to Saunders. "Big Jack Saunders, the Deerfield Constable, who seems to be the center of attention . . . wears kid gloves constantly. . . . He allowed us to search them for 'brass knuckles' . . . and we failed to find nary a knuckle anywhere. . . . During the past week Jack has been in and out of the hoosegow . . . but it doesn't seem to worry him much."

༤ၟၟ

BY THE SECOND WEEK OF PICKETING, *The New York Times* had dispatched a reporter to cover the strike. Newspapermen from Camden, Philadelphia, and Newark were also present, as well as representatives of the regional publications. The *Bridgeton Evening News* was pro-Seabrook; the Vineland *Daily Journal* was pro-union (or possibly just anti-Seabrook). Photographers present included the photojournalist Walter Ranzini of the *New York Post*.

Among those following *The Philadelphia Inquirer*'s coverage of the strike was Esther Peterson, a young teacher at the Bryn Mawr Summer School for Women Workers in Industry, located on the campus of Bryn Mawr College, outside Philadelphia. The summer school, founded in June 1921, brought to the campus each summer approximately a hundred working women between the ages of eighteen and thirty-five, white and Black—textile workers, switchboard operators, secretaries—where they were exposed to all the cultural bounties an elite liberal arts college had to offer, from poetry to politics to theater productions. The school was run by Hilda Worthington Smith, a progressive educator, and was supported by a board of deep-pocketed donors who included John D. Rockefeller. Peterson taught economics and poetry to the worker-students and discussed labor politics with them. During the summer session in 1934, the strike at Seabrook Farms was a hot topic.

Toward the end of the second week, several faculty members, including Peterson and Mildred Fairchild, along with Leo Huberman and Colston E. Warne, authors of the August 1934 article in *The Nation*, decided to show their support for the workers by driving the forty miles to the farm "to be damned nuisances, if possible," as Warne later said. In her 1997 memoir, *Restless*, Peterson, who would one day serve as President Kennedy's assistant secretary of Labor for Labor Standards, writes,

I decided to join several other summer school teachers who were driving down to witness the strike. We went on the weekend and, it is important to note, we are acting as individuals, not representatives of the school. . . . The Seabrook workers lived in shacks. A trench—an open sewer—ran through the area where the children played. There was violence; tear gas was thrown into workers' homes, even though babies and children were inside.

In his first heyday, my grandfather could count on a friendly press. He courted reporters, to the point of having a dedicated room in the administration building for journalists to use. The man from *The New York Sun* marveled, "Where else does one find on a farm a press room for the convenience of visiting reporters and two press agents prepared to serve up facts and statistics?" Using the family story to get free publicity from journalists, instead of paying for advertising, was a strategy both C. F. and, later, Jack pursued very effectively. My father's notion of a journalist derived from his father's use of hacks to promote his business. He regarded my mother's and my profession as being fundamentally transactional.

But in the summer of 1934, C. F. lost his grip on the Seabrook narrative. Newspapermen could no longer be counted on to take the family's side. Walter Ranzini depicted the Seabrooks' use of force against the strikers in stark images of violence that were published in the *New York Post* and the *Times*. To counter the negative press, C. F. went on a charm offensive, making himself available for interviews, cracking jokes and backslapping, dressed in his lightweight Weatherill summer suits, looking cool and pressed, while the men of the press sweated in rumpled seersucker.

C. F. laid all the responsibility for the strike on radical organizers and protesters imported from Philadelphia. He mentioned Donald Henderson, an "outside Communist agitator," who he suspected was an agent of the Soviet Union. His own workers, C. F. insisted, were absolutely loyal to him.

In addition to schmoozing the press, C. F. launched his own information war on the strikers through daily paid advertising in the *Bridgeton Evening News*. When Henderson challenged my grandfather to a public debate, the old man responded with an ad:

> I DO NOT INTEND HOLDING [*sic*] A DEBATE with
> Mr. Henderson or any other labor agitator on the program
> of the Communist party. WHY HOLD A DEBATE before a
> limited number of people in hot weather like this?

The union took out paid advertising of its own:

> BLACK JACKS
> RUBBER HOSE
> BULLETS
> KANGAROO COURTS
> ICE BOX JAILS
> This Is Only Part of
> The Story of the Seabrook Strikes
> Strikers Will Tell You More at the
> MASS MEETING TONIGHT

In one of his newspaper ads, which ran in early July, C. F. alludes to an ongoing farmworkers' strike in Alabama in which the KKK had lynched a striker. He uses the dog whistle tag "true American," a term restricted to white Protestant "Nordic" people.

> AS A TRUE AMERICAN I hope that what is going
> on in Alabama in dealing with these Communists will
> not take place here at home in New Jersey.

Another advertisement read in part:

> The White Legion may soon give the entire nation a full-blown
> sample of its cure for industrial unrest—the rope and the fagot.

The African American Seabrook strikers hardly needed to be reminded of the role the Maryland KKK had played in recent labor disputes at crab packing houses on Maryland's Eastern Shore.

Matthew Williams was lynched in Salisbury in 1931, and George Armwood was lynched in Princess Anne in 1933. Bystanders cut parts from Williams's body as souvenirs, set it on fire, and hung his charred corpse from a lamp pole in Salisbury's Black neighborhood as a warning. Salisbury was less than a three-hour drive away from Deep South Jersey. Culturally, it was right next door.

The White Legion had already burned several fifteen-foot crosses in Bridgeton during the unrest and sent warnings to the workers at Seabrook demanding white and Black not mingle at organizing meetings. They threatened that the "Klan will ride again" if the strike wasn't called off. According to the *Amsterdam News*, early one morning "five carloads" of Klansmen turned up at the house the Hendersons and the Dahls shared in Vineland. The men surrounded the house, calling for Donald to come out. Eleanor's terrified calls to the police were ignored. The siege lasted for an hour and a half until finally a group of Black and Italian farmworkers chased the men off.

CHAPTER 15

BLOODY HARVEST

C. F. Seabrook built the first private swimming pool in Cumberland County. It was a family ritual, one that lasted into my time, for the Seabrooks to celebrate Independence Day at the pool, which had blue mosaic tiles along the water's edge and a changing cabana behind the diving board. Kids would swim and the adults would sit under the trees, drinking. When my parents brought us to these parties in the '60s, I would watch my uncles explode M-80s in metal trash cans to amplify the sound. I still remember the chest-thumping percussion—BOOM!!!—on those sweltering evenings, and the smell of gunpowder. That night in 1934, it must have sounded like war was coming.

By July 4, the 1934 "hot wave"—the term used by the *Times*—was into its second week. Labor tensions were roiling, but if the family wanted to cool off while the workers sweated it out, that was their prerogative. Jack, seventeen, was still a skinny, gangly looking boy. He didn't become really handsome until he was older, and his face filled out. He would have joined his older brothers at the party, and their sister, Thelma, probably brought her fiancé, Harry Barber. The other top Seabrook people were there too—Frank App, the agronomist, Mark Loper, the farm superintendent, and Red Saunders, who was serving both as the muscle and as chief narrator of the recent violent events, including Courtney's June 28 arrest for assaulting strikers with a truck. Before the strike, Courtney was generally viewed by his father as a mama's boy. But now he had risen in status.

A few miles away, the White Legion were holding a July Fourth

Konclave at Tumbling Dam Park, with a big burning cross as the finale. The Seabrook strike didn't come up that night in remarks at the event by Klan speakers, or in readings from the Klan bible (the "Kloran"), but the subject was surely discussed. The elder Klansmen remembered an incident in 1923 in Bridgeton, when, according to *The New York Times*, a group of "Italian immigrants smashed the Klansmen to the ground and beat them." The Seabrook strike would be a chance for payback, as well as a way to recover some of their former glory through vigilantism. The ethnic makeup of the Seabrook strikers was diverse enough to appeal to anti-Catholics, anti-immigrant nativists, anti-Communists, and anti-Black racists. The union offered an all-you-can-hate buffet.

The following night, the Klan held a meeting that C. F. Seabrook himself addressed. The assembled group pledged to aid Seabrook in "eliminating Communistic agitators among striking farmworkers at Bridgeton." At the meeting, "the leaders announced their intention of taking action in the Communist inspired strike at Seabrook Farms," the *Bridgeton Evening News* reported. At the same meeting, the Reverend Harvey Cann of Bridgeton delivered "an impassioned harangue against alleged Red activities in the nation at large and in the strike area in particular."

The old man told the group, in effect, to stand back and stand by. After the meeting, the *Bridgeton Evening News* reported, "Charles F. Seabrook . . . declared that [tomorrow] he has been assured that one hundred armed vigilantes will be on duty to protect workers from 250 striking employees." That night another fifteen-foot fiery cross blazed in Upper Deerfield Township.

❦

FRIDAY, JULY 6, was the hottest day of 1934. The Seabrooks couldn't wait any longer to harvest their beets, which were to be canned. To get them to the cannery across the highway, the company needed to move tractors from the shed at Farm Central into the fields, where scab workers were loading wagons with bushel baskets of beets. Dozens of

Saunders's "special deputies" were on hand to assist the tractor drivers, many of them armed with axe handles, the weapon of choice. A few were carrying shotguns.

The lead tractor was driven by a longtime African American Seabrook employee, James Gould, called Gouldy, who was not in sympathy with the strikers. The Gould family had deep roots in the area. The Quaker John Fenwick had founded nearby Salem, New Jersey, in 1675, an act commemorated at the John Fenwick Service Area, the southernmost on the Turnpike. His granddaughter, Elizabeth Adams, was said to have had a child with one of her grandfather's Black servants, a man named James Gould. Fenwick banished the family from Salem, and the outcasts supposedly founded nearby Gouldtown, one of the oldest free African American settlements in the United States.

As the tractors started across the road, the strikers began throwing rocks. One of the rocks struck Gouldy in the head and knocked him out cold. He was pulled to safety and taken to the Bridgeton hospital, where he was reported to be "suffering from a possible fracture of the skull as a result of being struck with stones and clubs." Maurice Park, the superintendent of the tractors, also needed several stitches in his head. The tractors retreated behind the recently erected barbed-wire gates.

Then, according to the *Daily Journal*, "the strikers turned their attention to the Seabrook offices and charged the building." The company "resorted to tear gas, which had the desired effect. The crowd retreated." In the ensuing melee a Black worker stabbed Jack Saunders and was arrested. The striker told the officers, "I didn't cut him deep." Saunders was taken to the hospital, treated by a physician, and then arrested on a charge of atrocious assault and battery.

❧

ON MONDAY, JULY 9, the whip came down. David Jaggers, the leader of the farmer vigilante group, offered C. F. fifty "shotgun deputies" to help "clean up" the strikers. "If they aren't satisfied with their pay, let 'em get out," he told a reporter. More than one hundred vigilantes showed up with axe handles. The company had enclosed workers' housing with chicken wire. Anyone tearing the wire would be assumed to be an agitator and subject to summary dismissal.

The day was significantly cooler: the thunderstorms of the night before had broken the "hot wave." C. F. was observing the action from the front porch of the administration building. Other directors of the company, including Uncle Bert and A. R. McAllister, along with C. F.'s brother-in-law, assemblyman Douglas Aitken, were nearby. Also milling around were some two dozen reporters and photographers, as well as observers from the American Civil Liberties Union and several faculty members from the Bryn Mawr Summer School, who wrote the piece I read sixty years later in *The Nation*.

Mrs. Frances Warne, representing the League of Women Voters, and Dr. Mildred Fairchild, a sociologist on the faculty of Bryn Mawr, were standing next to C. F. on the porch of the administration building that morning. Fairchild knew Seabrook; she had spent nine months in Moscow in 1929, while he had been living at the Savoy Hotel, organizing his ill-fated Moscow roadbuilding project. In an affidavit Warne gave to the American Civil Liberties Union, she wrote,

Mr. Seabrook said they were taking out the tractors and for Dr. Mildred Fairchild and myself to come into the office as the gas would make us sick for two weeks. Dr. Fairchild and I both said to Mr. Seabrook that things were so peaceful there was no need for gas, that we would stay on the porch. This was about eight o'clock a.m. Within ten minutes thereafter a man, who appeared to be in the employ of Mr. Seabrook, came to Mr. Seabrook and said, "It is ready." Mr. Seabrook replied, "We will not use it now." It was apparent to both Dr. Fairchild and me that Mr. Seabrook and his employee were referring to the throwing of gas bombs at striking workers who were picketing on the highway in front of the office.

Without the cover of the gas bombs, four tractors were driven out of the warehouse and headed for the beet fields, where gangs of scabs, brought by Seabrook trucks from Philadelphia, were beginning to pick beets. On each Seabrook tractor stood three men with long clubs. When the tractors started across the highway, the workers attacked. "As the strikers attempted to rush the tractors," the *Millville Daily* reported, "the crews swung their clubs and the drivers steered them into the throngs. Terror-stricken, the mob ran from the path of the ponderous machines, but they took up the fight with bricks and stones." The tractors eventually managed to make it across the highway and into the fields.

Soon after, Sheriff Brown arrived at the farm and officially deputized about thirty men, including C. F., Belford, and Courtney, and distributed shotguns and axe handles to the "deputy sheriffs," who wore white shirts and white fedoras. Photographs also show uniformed "Special Officers," who carry sidearms. C. F., through Aitken, appealed for a second time to Governor Harry Moore to declare martial law; the governor again declined. The Seabrook Fire Department turned their hoses on protesters to keep them away from the gates.

Shortly before noon, a truck loaded with scab beets in baskets came down the highway and rolled up onto a scale to get weighed before entering the processing area. The "deputies" in their white fedoras stood guard. West Indian women in spotless white cannery uniforms surrounded the truck and began throwing handfuls of beets onto the road. The fedoras wrestled the women away from the truck, manhandling them as part of what the *Delaware News Journal* called a "vicious hand to hand battle." (In 16mm footage of this encounter, which can be viewed online, a woman can be seen throwing what looks like a gas bomb away from her home.)

A Black striker tried to seize a revolver from Samuel Prince, a Special Officer, according to a report in *The New York Times*. Harry Shapiro, a hatless, sunburnt vigilante farmer, put the man in a choke hold and recovered the gun. (Walter Ranzini captured the moment in a searing photograph.) When the women saw what was happening, they attacked. In an account published the following month in the Marxist publication *The Working Woman*, Vivian Dahl quotes a New Jersey state trooper's description of the melee:

A beet truck was coming down the road. Scab beets . . . As the truck drew up to weigh in, the women saw red. It was three colored women who started pulling the beets off the truck. It didn't take long for one of those rich farmer vigilante friends of the Seabrooks to swing his pickaxe handle. Smash, down on the eye and forehead of Ella Roberts, young colored girl who never missed a day on the picket line and in volunteer relief duty. That started things. For an hour and a half the women, colored and white, joined by their husbands and children, put up such a battle as the cops and deputies and what nots never saw. Battling against scabs the valiant strikers wore out the cops and deputies.

Management launched tear-gas bombs. Mildred Fairchild writes of the action Uncle Belford allegedly took part in,

I had supposed the battle dying down when tear and nausea gas bombs appeared on the scene, apparently from the company general offices. The bombs were thrown first in the street, then as the workers retreated to their homes, directly around and beside windows and doors of the little houses, completely surrounding them, so far as one could tell, with fumes. Wives and little children and at least one infant were in the houses at the time.

The wind blew the tear gas back in the faces of the vigilantes, cops, and the observers standing with Warne on the porch. Eleanor Henderson, choking on tear gas, was arrested by Sheriff Brown himself. That afternoon a caged truck took the protesters into Bridgeton, where they were jailed. In all, twenty-seven people were detained. Justice of the Peace J. Ellsworth Long set up a court in the Seabrook administration building and tried strikers there. They were kept locked up in an unventilated icebox, according to the *Amsterdam News*.

❧

BY THE NEXT MORNING, the State Legislature had passed Aitken's resolution compelling the governor to send the National Guard to protect the farm. A second resolution ordered an investigation into the Communist ties of the leaders of the Seabrook strike. Later that day, July 10, FDR's Secretary of Labor, Frances Perkins, alarmed by the newspaper stories and photographs, dispatched a federal mediator, John A. Moffitt, to negotiate a settlement. Moffitt, who had settled the famous silk mill strike in Paterson, New Jersey, twenty years before, arrived at the farm and immediately went into conference with C. F. and a Bridgeton lawyer named David L. Horuvitz, who had been hired by a national labor organization to represent the strikers. Most of the union leadership had been arrested the day before and were still detained.

By 2:00 p.m. a settlement had been negotiated without any of the union officers present. On the main points, the workers seemed to have won. Wages would be restored to April levels. Management agreed not to punish striking workers. Outside the office, Horuvitz read the agreement out loud to the workers and their families. He went "over and over" the key provisions, according to the *Times*'s front-page story, urging the workers to accept them and go back to work the next day. "I have done all I can for you and if you do not accept this agreement I can do no more," he said. "If you want bloodshed, gas bombs, and your homes ruined, as took place yesterday, you can turn down this agreement, but I advise you to accept it, for it is clearly in your best interest." The *Times* continued, "The crowd had seemed sullen and embittered before the meeting began, but they showed obvious pleasure as the settlement was read. The workers' faces brightened and they cheered and applauded Mr. Horuvitz."

Although Donald Henderson had been banned from negotiating the settlement, along with the union leaders, he was on hand to hear it read. After Horuvitz finished, Henderson "leaped on the soapbox and boldly spoke to the crowd." The *Times* reported that "the agitator was coatless [and] wore a blue shirt, open at the neck, and a loosely knotted blue and red tie." Henderson urged the crowd to reject the settlement, which had been negotiated when the officers of the union were unlawfully jailed. After Henderson's plea, Horuvitz jumped back on the soapbox and cried, "Now boys, tell me, man to man, do you really want to go back to work?"

"Yes," came the booming reply, and the crowd moved toward the office to clock in.

"Is the strike over?" asked a policeman.

"Yes," many called out.

"No!" Henderson cried. The crowd closed around him. "Throw him out of here! He's caused enough trouble!" someone called out. "Let me at him!" shouted another worker. In some reports, the mob was said to be prepared to lynch Henderson. Six policemen, along with vigilante Harry Shapiro, were required to escort Henderson safely through the crowd.

꿎

THE OLD MAN SHOWED the whip the very next day. Despite the terms of the agreement, most of the Black strikers were fired. Henderson had been right to try to reject the contract FDR's man had negotiated—management had no intention of honoring it. According to one report, of the two hundred and fifty workers, only three were rehired. Black workers were evicted from Seabrook properties. C. F. resolved to find other sources of labor, which, years later, led to the company recruiting Japanese Americans from incarceration camps during World War II, a "model minority" that would never challenge the old man's authority. Vincent Salmon, who had joined the scabs during the strike, got to keep his job. However, "It wasn't a comfortable working situation," he said.

Lester Granger returned to the Elk's Hall a few months after the strike and spoke to some of the Black workers. Many of them were on the newly established New Deal policy of federal unemployment assistance, or welfare. Although they had lost their jobs in the strikes, Granger described "a feeling of satisfaction among Negroes, strikers and non-strikers, that the demonstration was made, no matter what the immediate results may be."

A group sat in the colored Elks Hall and, chairs tilted back against the wall, summed up the situation.

"Did we win the strike? Brother, I don't know, and that's a fact," said Jim Mills. "I know we didn't lose it. We ain't got nothin' now, maybe, but we didn't have nothin' befo' so how could we lose?"

"The way I look at it is like this," said another man, a towering truck driver. "I've been hanging around this town a good while— too damned long. I've never seen a colored man get anything for his work but a beating. He works his head off all day long, and all he's got is enough to eat on. If he don't work, he's no worse off, because the relief won't let him starve anyhow.

"I say, if we can't get anything for working, let's see what we can get for fighting. This ain't the only town in God's country. If we can't make it here, we'll let these pecks have the town. But we'll make 'em sweat for it first!"

Authorities were told to keep an eye out for anyone associated with the Hendersons or the Dahls. Colonel Schwarzkopf "issued an ultimatum to agitators [that] they would be summarily ejected if they did not leave voluntarily" within a twenty-four-hour time frame.

Charges against the Hendersons, Dahls, and others who had been arrested were eventually dropped, except for William O'Donnell, a former state trooper who was arrested for using inflammatory language against local officials. (He had referred to some of the vigilantes as "dirty bums.") When he was given a six-month sentence for disorderly conduct, O'Donnell went on a hunger strike in protest. The county let him see his wife in an "infirmary cell" after twenty-three days, so that they could celebrate their twentieth wedding anniversary.

In July, a "workers' court" held a mock trial of C. F. Seabrook, John

A. Moffitt, Dave Jaggers, Justices of the Peace Leslie O. Downes and Ellsworth Long, and Jack Saunders, on a Sunday morning before four hundred people, including Esther Peterson and other Bryn Mawr faculty members, at the Moose Hall in Bridgeton. Charges include terrorism, inciting riots, intimidation, and collusion. Among those sitting in judgment were Huberman and Warne, along with Mildred Fairchild, Alexander Fleisher (of the Philadelphia Child Health Society), and the authors John Spivak and Ernest Hallgren. The accused were convicted on all counts, and a symbolic warrant for their arrest was issued.

Donald Henderson returned to national organizing, and at first rose to bigger things. He became president of the United Cannery, Agricultural, Packing, and Allied Workers of America (UCAPAWA), which claimed one hundred thousand members in 1939. But he was not popular with his fellow officials or with the rank and file. "You didn't work *with* Don Henderson, you worked *for* him," one remembered. The Hendersons moved to Chicago, a more central location for labor organizing, and it was there that Eleanor died, of poisoning, on June 11, 1941. The coroner concluded that she had taken the poison by accident.

With the rise of McCarthyism, labor unions were thoroughly investigated for Communist Party ties. Henderson was repeatedly subpoenaed to appear before committees in both the House and Senate. In 1952, when he was national secretary-treasurer of the Distributive, Processing, and Office Workers Union of America, Henderson appeared before the Senate Judiciary Committee. He took the Fifth when asked about whether he had ever belonged to the Communist Party, even as Senator Arthur Watkins of Utah, the committee chairman, brandished a copy of the 1931 *Daily Worker* article in which Henderson announced his membership in the Party. After a final appearance before Senator Joe McCarthy's Un-American Activities subcommittee, in 1953, Henderson disappears from published records.

The year 1934 was the turning point for Seabrook's frozen food business. The company showed a big profit at the year's end, the first in the three years since C. F.'s return to farming. Contracts with General Foods were multiplying. The infrastructure upgrades put in place by Belford, which included a new power plant, were finally paying dividends. The plant was soon packing 60 percent of Birds Eye's frozen vegetables, by far Seabrook's largest client. Wages rose, and the workforce increased. By 1941, when 90 percent of Seabrook production was frozen vegetables, there would be two thousand employees in construction, factory, and field work. That year, a new union, the A.F.L.-affiliated Union Local 56, Meat and Cannery Workers, successfully negotiated a contract with a new Seabrook leader whose view of organized labor would prove to be far more progressive than his father's. That leader was twenty-three-year-old Jack Seabrook.

CHAPTER 16

REVENGE OF
THE NUBIANS

After such knowledge, what forgiveness?

—T. S. Eliot, "Gerontion"

O N THE FRIDAY EVENING AFTER THANKSGIVING, LISA
and I gathered with my parents in the Pine Room for cocktails. I had resolved to tell them what I had learned of the strike. I was
young and righteous and now, for the first time, the writer son had sort
of something on his father. At least I had information he didn't have.
Or did he?

I needed my wits about me, so before we got too deep into the cocktails, I said I had something to talk to them about. In the course of my
research into the Seabrook story for my father's project, I had come
across some interesting information, and was thinking of writing my
own story. I said that I wanted to focus on the Seabrook reunion and
the Japanese Americans who were returning, as adults, to the place
where they had been children. I wasn't asking for permission, I said,
but as a courtesy I was giving them a heads-up. I invited my father's
participation, in the form of an interview at some point, although they
wouldn't be able to read the manuscript in advance, I told them.

From the Pine Room, I could hear the staff setting the table in the
dining room, including the proper stemware for the evening, which
would feature two different wines. After a silence, my mother said, "I
think it's a terrible idea to write about your family."

"I know you feel that way," I said tensely, "but it's my story too, and
I have a right to it."

"What kind of story?" my father asked. He seemed inclined to favor the idea. In the old days the brand would have killed for this exposure. The family angle was always the Seabrook's special narrative sauce.

I was across from my parents. Behind them, directly in my sight line, were the two Nubians, with potted Ficus plants on their heads and green tendrils curling down around their muscular ebony shoulders. I felt that weight. My family's history was a burden I could feel in my shoulders. The big eyes of the Nubians looked right at me.

I said, in as conversational a tone as possible, "I wanted to ask about the 1934 strike." More silence. "I came across some information about it when I was doing research."

"Ah!" my father said.

"Well, yes, 'Ah!' indeed. I wondered if you were there that day."

"Oh very much," my father said. "And I can tell you the strikers weren't Seabrook employees. They were people from Philadelphia and Newark who the Communists brought in on buses. Squatters."

"What about the final day, when the vigilantes put down the strike? Were you there then?"

"Of course I was there." He had worn the "snub-nosed" pistol sack Jack Saunders had given him, he said, in a holster under his armpit. He recalled how a plainclothes state trooper had handed him a spoke from a wagon wheel and showed him how to use it as a club. "I can remember the sergeant saying, 'Never raise your club, because some damn photographer from *The New York Times* will take a picture of you. Keep in low and jam the guy in the crotch. Then, when they take the picture, it will look like the guy is bowing to you.'"

"And did you try that?"

"Yes, and it worked."

Bullshit, I thought. It was impossible to imagine my father engaging in the violent melee. That just wasn't who he was. So why was he pretending to place himself both on the battlefield and on the wrong side of history? Wasn't he the Seabrook who, seven years later, would help the workers achieve their union?

"Did Belford set one of the workers' houses on fire with a bomb?"

"Where did you hear that?"

"I read it in *The Nation*."

He looked at me reproachfully. "And you believed it?"

I was aware that I was tiptoeing toward a line here. I was glad that I wasn't too buzzed yet to walk it. My father had been willing to tolerate this literary gambit of mine up to a point, but undermining our family's success story—one that he had a hand in creating—was another matter. Investigative journalists and the Seabrook family had an unpleasant history, of which I already knew enough and would eventually know more. Journalists are nosy, and they're potentially dangerous. I was supposed to be doing public relations for the family, not investigating it.

I wrote the piece anyway. A lot of it was favorable to the Seabrooks. I only touched on the farmworkers strike. It was hardly the searing exposé it could have been, had I known what I know now, but I did quote from *The Nation*'s account of the final, bloody day, including Belford's alleged bombing of the worker's house.

Belford Seabrook, son of the proprietor, himself threw a bomb into a house then occupied only by an Italian mother and two very small children. He had previously shouted to his men: "Get this woman; she talks too much." The bomb, hurled through the window, landed on a bed and set the sheets ablaze. The rooms were so filled with smoke and gas fumes that the place was uninhabitable for more than two days.

No one in the family was happy about that. My mother was most vocal about her displeasure. My father, as always, guarded his true feelings. When their Philadelphia and New York friends told them they'd loved the article, their attitude softened considerably. Carol was diplomatic as always. In the end, I was let off with an unspoken "don't do it again" (I did) by everyone except for Lizanne. She regarded what I'd published about Belford as an absolute betrayal from which there could be no recovery. In her view, I had reenacted the original family trauma, in which C. F. betrayed his father, by betraying my grandfather and uncle.

Lizanne was named after Grace Kelly's sister, and she had exquisite Grace Kelly looks. Her early childhood had been difficult. Our father and her mother divorced when Lizanne was four, and she moved to the Upper East Side. Anne used her as a pawn in her fights with our father. They couldn't afford a better apartment, and she couldn't have a dog, because her father didn't give them enough money. Perhaps because of the uncertain loyalties of her childhood, Lizanne tended to see the world in black and white. Talking to her, you walked a minefield of potential faux pas: one wrong step and you were a bad person. Lizanne would rage about small things people had done or not done to her, and perhaps it was the same rage that our grandfather had, and our father knew it when he saw it. After she died, we learned she had been diagnosed with borderline personality syndrome. If our father knew about that, he never told us.

Carol had gone on to Swarthmore and University of Pennsylvania Law School, and had a brilliant career as a tax and estate attorney, which made her an invaluable asset and adviser to our father. Lizanne, in contrast, had done a few years of college, dropped out, and married an impecunious upper-crust Brit, Johnny Lethem, with whom she lived in a basement flat in Sloane Square. Her husband's family had a castle in Northumberland called Chipchase that wasn't far from Hadrian's Wall, where orange-flavored gin was served by Lizanne's in-laws at breakfast.

Johnny, who liked to gamble, thought he'd married an heiress, because surely a man who drove a coach and four horses for a hobby must be immensely wealthy. When he realized that much of our father's wealth went toward appearing to be wealthier than he was, and that whatever money remained wasn't available, he didn't stick around. Lizanne returned to New York and tried to start a career on the non-profit side of banking, but that didn't go anywhere. She was a fixture at the Regency Bridge Club on Lexington Avenue, a few blocks from her East Seventy-Ninth Street apartment. By the early nineties she had stopped speaking to her mother, and her relationship with Carol was chilly at best, which was awkward because they lived on opposite sides of the same street, just a block away from one another. Lizanne had been snooty to my mother from the start, and was constantly feuding with her and our father.

Lizanne was outraged that in my piece I had called attention to the family's response to the 1934 strike, and especially the part about Belford. When I tried to speak to her about it, she threw Lisa and me out of her apartment.

Janet Malcolm begins *The Journalist and the Murderer* by declaring "Every journalist who is not too stupid or too full of himself to notice what is going on knows that what he does is morally indefensible." She continues,

> He is a kind of confidence man, preying on people's vanity, ignorance, or loneliness, gaining their trust and betraying them without remorse. Like the credulous widow who wakes up one day to find the charming young man and all her savings gone, so the consenting subject of a piece of nonfiction learns—when the article or book appears—his hard lesson. Journalists justify their treachery in various ways according to their temperaments. The more pompous talk about freedom of speech and "the public's right to know"; the least talented talk about Art; the seemliest murmur about earning a living.

Joan Didion concludes her introduction to the nonfiction stories collected in *Slouching Towards Bethlehem* with "one last thing to remember" about the practitioners of nonfiction storytelling: "writers are always selling someone out." Whether or not the journalist is explicitly "investigative," every story involves trying to get at the truth about what happened by asking questions, and sometimes that means trading on intimacy with one's subject to get the information to tell the story. A journalist has a duty to follow the story wherever it leads; your only real loyalty is to the truth, as you understand it.

But what if your family is the story, and telling the story truthfully means exposing the family?

Later in 1995, Lizanne was diagnosed with bone cancer and had part of her hip removed. Her prognosis wasn't good. Our father, without ever saying it, somehow made it clear that he felt Lizanne, by being so difficult, had brought the cancer on herself, because Seabrooks don't *get* cancer. Being a Seabrook, Lizanne knew exactly what he was thinking, and perhaps her rage helped fuel her miraculous recovery. In any case, once she was well enough to manage on her own, she wanted nothing more to do with any of us. She disowned us. She changed her name to Brooke. Worse, she had a lawyer send a letter demanding money from our father, and then a second letter, alluding to the murky origins of his post–Seabrook Farms wealth.

Dad shared her letter with the rest of us, along with a memo about how he planned to respond. He explained that because of Lizanne's going outside the family and threatening him, along with her evident desire to no longer be a Seabrook, he had decided to remove her from his estate, so that she couldn't make trouble for the rest of us after his death. He would settle a sum of money on her on which she could live comfortably for the rest of her life; Lizanne was never extravagant. This was all very practical, and I can't say I objected, but the surgical way Dad had excised Lizanne from his affairs was a reminder for the rest of us that there were practical limits to his love. The whip was there.

Father and sons at a working lunch in the 1950s. Left to right, Belford (BLS), Jack (JMS), C. F. (CFS), and Courtney (CCS).

OLD BULLS AND YOUNG BULLS, 1939–1954

And he [Zeus] was reigning in heaven, himself
holding the lightning and glowing thunderbolt, when
he had overcome by might his father Kronos.
                                    —*Hesiod, Theogony*

CHAPTER 17

GROWTH UNITS

IN 1937, DURING HIS SOPHOMORE YEAR AT PRINCETON, Jack Seabrook attended a round of winter house parties in Erie, Pennsylvania, the home of his roommate, Bill Wilson. There my father met a beautiful eighteen-year-old debutante named Anne Schlau-decker, a friend of Wilson's girl, Jeanne Sully. Anne was Jack's first real girlfriend. Over the next two years, they saw each other as much as his studies and work on the farm allowed.

Anne was from a Catholic family, and made it clear there would be no sex before marriage. So, in April 1939, in the sort of impulsive act I could easily imagine myself making, but which is hard to reconcile with the careful, calculating father I knew, the couple eloped in Elkton, Maryland, where it was possible to get a marriage license overnight.

After his Princeton graduation in June 1939, when his father had disappointed him by not attending, Jack returned home and requested a meeting with C. F. to talk about his future. Pauline Lober, C. F.'s secretary, said the CEO and chairman would have time to see him on the morning of July 4, which was weeks away. It would have to be early because, in spite of the holiday, the boss would be hard at work all day. Jack turned up at his father's office before seven.

As far as C. F. knew, his son was merely engaged; Jack didn't have the nerve to tell his father that he had eloped. Up to this point, the youngest son had been the golden boy, consistently getting the highest marks in school, excelling in his work at the plant, never quarreling with his older brothers or father. That morning, Jack told C. F. a story about how he had the engagement ring made, from his own design, by one of the Seabrook blacksmiths, saving all that money spent by fools on marked-up, store-bought rings. He knew that would please the old man.

Jack said that they hoped for a September wedding; his father replied that he would be overseas, but if Jack was willing to wait until he returned from an upcoming trip to Europe, he would attend. That trip would be scuttled when Hitler invaded Poland on September 1, triggering war in Europe, a sudden, shocking upheaval in world order that would also transform the power balance among the Seabrook brothers and their father, in ways that would not please C. F.

ONE DAY, when I was around ten, rooting around in the basement, I came across a shoebox containing old letters from my father, written to Anne in the summer of 1939, when she was home in Erie telling similar lies to her Catholic parents about being engaged. She must have sent Jack's end of the correspondence back at some later point in their acrimonious relationship. The letters were written in a tone I had never heard him use in our family, full of gushy endearments like "my darling baby who I love so much." Was this my father? He sounded like a different person, one better matched with the ungainly penmanship.

His letter of the night of July 4, 1939, the evening after his long-awaited chat with C. F., and five years after the poolside party during the strike, is written on yellow legal paper—already his preferred writing surface. His hand is shaking with excitement. After boasting to his bride about how he handled his father with the ring, Jack relays the astonishing news that his father informed him at the meeting that he had chosen him, the youngest, to "take his place in the business." C. F. had explained, Jack wrote, that "I would have to learn fast, because most men don't undertake a job like that until they were at least 35 because bankers don't like to deal with young men but that under the circumstances, I would have to do it unless he went outside the family for someone, and he didn't want to make an outsider the chief executive. He said I would have to learn in 10 years what it took most men a lifetime to learn because he only had about 10 years left. Then he cautioned me about being brash and so forth."

He follows this with a startling declaration. "I will rule them." Is he talking just about his brothers here, or does he plan to rule his father too? It's a flash of the enormous ambition that Jack normally keeps hidden.

C. F. had also offered Jack a place to live, he tells his bride, which happened to be one of the best properties he had acquired during the Great Depression. The large house with its mansard roof was known as the Ballinger house, after the wealthy landowner who had built it in the late 1800s. "As for the number, size, and arrangement of the rooms it is perfect for our wants I think," Jack writes. His wants, that is. The house won't satisfy Anne's needs at all. She has already made it clear she doesn't much like Jack's father or his family, who she finds dull and provincial. Unlike Harriet, Belford's wife, or Mae, who Courtney married in 1935, Anne isn't keen to live the life of a Seabrook woman on the farm; she'd much rather be in New York City going to parties.

"Now I know honey that you would rather live in the city," Jack continues, "but this will please you much more than anything I have seen yet in the city. Then of course I have always wanted to live in the country because some day I hope to have horses."

C. F. despised horses because they represented the past. The "mysterious powers" that hover around us, in Carnegie's Engineers Club address, did not include horsepower. When C. F. had accumulated a large enough fleet of tractors and trucks to dispense with horsepower on the farm, he sold the animals and horse-drawn machinery in a big auction in 1920. At a time when the equine population in the U.S. was peaking at twenty-five million, Seabrook was practically a horse-free town. All except for C. F.'s youngest son.

Jack, who had started riding a horse as a practical way of getting around the huge family farm, was beginning to develop the interest in driving that would eventually lead to Nimrod and Jack Seabrook's prominent role in the world of coaching. For his industrialist father, gasoline engines represented power. But for Jack, horses and coaching were a way of transforming the raw power of machines, from which the family derived its fortune, into the soft power of class, which gained Jack entrance to social circles that shunned his grasping father.

At the end of the letter Jack returned to the wedding and the matter of religion. The fact that Anne was a Catholic was bad enough; that Anne's mother wanted them to be married by a priest in a Catholic church was worse. Jack seems to think he can somehow skate through this schism. "I must talk to Mother sometime about your religion because Dad says she is worried I will become Catholic." But at least, he added, his anti-papist father recognized that Catholic priests had their uses in his autocratic regime. "He of course is in favor of them because the priests help control the Italian labor here and fight communism."

In September, Jack was with C. F. in his office when Mark Loper, who ran one of the company's two farming divisions, burst in, distraught. He could no longer cope with his job, he declared, and he was quitting for good "that very day," Jack recalled. When C. F. told Loper he couldn't quit because he hadn't trained a successor yet, Loper said, "Jack can do it." C. F. snorted and said it would take two years to train the boy. Loper said he would give Jack two days. The following week, twenty-two-year-old Jack took over Loper's job at a salary of forty dollars a week.

"C. F. didn't want to be a farmer himself," he wrote, "and he never wanted any of his sons to be a farmer. However, it was typical of C. F. prior to his 1941 illness to think, because we were his sons, we could do anything." Left unsaid (because it went without saying) was, "And he was right."

※

JACK SEABROOK WAS hastily and unwisely married, with a new house that his wife hated, especially when he was away. Now he, JMS, the third of C. F. Seabrook's three sons to join the C-Suite, was the monogrammed peer of his brothers, BLS and CCS. He had a big new job managing hundreds of field workers, with a war looming. For Jack's first week on the job, C. F. got up at five in the morning and sat at the breakfast table with his son, going over the details of the spinach harvest, until finally Nana told him to leave the boy alone, he would be fine. He got an office in the administration building, and a secretary, Betty Gaunt, a beautiful young woman and a devout Methodist who would remain with him for the next forty years. She never married. Was she secretly in love with him all those years?

Jack was a full-time farmer from 1939 to 1941. He oversaw planning when crops were planted, cultivated, and harvested, guided by the company's head agronomist, Dr. Frank App. It was essential to time harvests so that crops ripened sequentially, allowing management to deploy equipment and labor on one crop at a time. But the number of days from sowing to harvest varied widely, even with identical crops. A field of peas that took eighty days to mature in the spring might take only fifty-five days later in the summer. Too often, the company was overwhelmed during the harvest and had to pick all day and night, under floodlights, to keep up.

To plan more efficiently, Jack recruited the distinguished American climatologist and geographer Dr. Charles Warren Thornthwaite in 1946. He knew of Thornthwaite's work on climate classification through his youthful interest in soil chemistry. At Seabrook, he funded Thornthwaite's world-class Laboratory of Climatology. There he devised his thermal "growth units" system, one of his most important contributions to applied climatology. Thornthwaite, forty-seven at the time, became the first of Jack's surrogate fathers.

Growth units were a way of determining precisely how many days a particular crop would need to ripen. Calculating growth units required factoring in the place, the time of year, as well as the average temperature, precipitation, and rate of evaporation. Thornthwaite deduced that the climate at Seabrook Farms produced 7,500 growth units in a year, unevenly distributed across the calendar in a bell curve, with the most units per day occurring during the summer months. Accordingly, if an Alaskan pea plant, which Thornthwaite calculated required 1,680 growth units to reach maturity, was planted on March 4, the crop would be ready for harvest on June 5. By 1950, all crops at Seabrook were planted using Thornthwaite's climatic calendar, a practice he called "fitting crops to the weather." Contract farmers were equipped with climatic calendar slide rules, called "cropmeters," to guide them. If contractors didn't adhere to Thornthwaite's system, Seabrook reserved the right to refuse to buy their crop. Growth units were, more precisely, labor units. The system allowed the Seabrooks to predict long in advance when labor would be at a premium and plan accordingly.

✼

JACK BROUGHT THE SAME data-driven thinking to the company's union problems, which flared up again in 1940, when Belford learned that the Congress of Industrial Organizations (C.I.O.) was targeting Seabrook for a new labor action. Jack thought that instead of using force, as their father had done, they should negotiate. Concerns about the coming labor shortage, in the event that the U.S. was drawn into the war, gave union organizers leverage. A union could guarantee a supply of farmworkers. The American Federation of Labor (A.F.L.), the C.I.O.'s less radical competitor, promised to deliver workers through its partnership with the Southern Tenant Farmers Union.

The A.F.L. included among its affiliates the International Brotherhood of Teamsters, which had been trying to organize Seabrook's truck drivers and warehouse workers for years. The Cumberland Automobile and Trucking Company—Seabrook's trucking subsidiary—was already paying tribute to organized crime in New York City, according to my father, so that its trucks could pass unmolested through the Holland Tunnel, which had opened in 1927.

Jack perceived the pro-labor climate of the period and realized the farm needed to accommodate it, even if that set up a clash with his father. Perhaps he also felt some sympathy for the workers' cause—he had played with some of them growing up. In the arrangement the sons proposed to their father, the company would allow the Teamsters to unionize its drivers and warehouse workers, if another A.F.L. union, the Amalgamated Food and Allied Workers, would organize its plant workers and provide seasonal wage protection for farmworkers. Jack took the lead on these negotiations. He relished horse-trading with the union leaders, especially a young Romanian-American named Leon Schachter, who was the head of the Philadelphia branch of the Amalgamated Food and Allied Workers Union, Local 56. Jack and Leon became friends, and later served together for years on the board of the New Jersey Migrant Labor Commission. Schachter later said, of his dealings with my father and Belford, "the Seabrook family . . . was not medieval. It did not meet Local 56's organizing drive with blind, frenzied counterattack," which may have been a reference to the way C. F. had settled matters in 1934. "Once it realized that its employees wanted a union, and that the union was coming, [the family] was willing to abide by the workers' decision and try out the new force." Under the terms of the two-tier system that Seabrook management and the union agreed to, only full-time employees could become union members, but seasonal employees were granted "provisional" rights that were supposed to protect their jobs and wages.

Jack told a reporter a few years after the union contract was signed, "I think, actually, that the average farm laborer requires . . . a much wider range of skill than the average industrial laborer does. Conditions on a farm are such that the job content changes constantly. You can't break a farm job down into a series of repetitive, easily supervised operations like you can a factory job. I'm an engineer; I've run quite a few factories and I've run quite a few farms. I've never seen an honest job evaluation yet that didn't come to the conclusion that the farm job ought to be paid more than the factory job." In Seabrook, New Jersey, this amounted to wild-eyed radicalism.

In the summer of 1941, the entire Seabrook plant became an A.F.L. closed shop. Four thousand workers were guaranteed full-time employment at wages no lower than fifty-five cents an hour and a week's paid vacation—an unheard-of concession. Seabrook Farms became the first farm on the East Coast to offer farmworkers collective bargaining rights. His sons persuaded C. F. that the A.F.L. would deliver the needed hands in the event of a draft. The old man later grudgingly acknowledged of the union, "I don't think we've suffered from it," or at least, "We haven't suffered from any wildcat strikes." In other moods, he raged against the new force that posed a direct challenge to his control. But an even greater threat would soon find a way into C. F.'s brain.

CHAPTER 18

THE "STROKE"

T HAT OCTOBER, C. F. SUFFERED A MEDICAL EVENT that my father described in his speech as "a very serious stroke." The family rallied around. Nana wanted to care for Charlie, but he instructed her to locate Leila Small, the Australian nurse who had supposedly saved his life fourteen years earlier when he contracted dysentery in the Crimea. Nurse Small, who was living in the United States at the time, flew to C. F.'s bedside in New Jersey, and over the ineffectual objections of Nana, moved into the house and took over C. F.'s care, allowing no one to see the patient. According to my father, she described C. F. as being "close to death."

A few weeks after Nurse Small's arrival, according to Jack, a major investor in the company came to New York to talk to C. F. about "some matters involving large sums." Jack was delegated to go to New York and meet with the man, who represented a sizable Midwestern bank, as his father's surrogate. "I was called into the sick room where Miss Leila Small . . . hovered threateningly," he wrote. Small was a big woman. "The nurse, not C. F., told me I was to go to the Racquet and Tennis Club alone and close the deal on the best terms I could make. Her tone implied any deal I would make would be unfavorable." C. F. then weakly spoke from his bed. He said that the men Jack was going to meet all drank martinis, as did everyone else in that club. "I was to join them, but I was to keep my head," my father wrote. "I knew he wasn't worried about my capacity, so I decided the admonishment was Miss Small's idea." Capacity was never an issue for Seabrooks.

In November, C. F. and his retinue—Nana, Thelma, and Nurse

Small, along with a driver, housekeeper, and cook—relocated to an apartment in Coral Gables, Florida, where the old man could better convalesce. Thelma later wrote to her husband, Harry Barber, who served overseas, about the idyllic setting: "Florida is a very beautiful place. Coral Gables is a small city of Beautiful Homes, very select, absolutely no Jews allowed."

Thelma's path wasn't easy. It fell on her to care for her father when the old man was sick, but her gender excluded her from taking part in the business, even though she was the only one who had actually gone to business school. Her anti-Semitism is depressing but it was practically a filial duty in her father's household, and hardly his alone: genteel anti-Semitism was as common as chintz in the social circles that the Seabrooks aspired to.

సౌ

WITH C. F. AWAY, Belford took control. But when Japan attacked Pearl Harbor on December 7, 1941, bringing the U.S. into the war, he wanted to join the military immediately. The army thought that Belford's experience in running the Seabrook vegetable factory could be useful in organizing wartime supply lines. General Douglas Mac-Arthur was interested in bringing him to Australia to help with food distribution in the Pacific theater.

Jack wrote that Belford "felt he had a right to leave, especially since the country needed him." But C. F. became fearful that all three sons would leave him for Uncle Sam. He had no concept of sacrifice for a greater cause than the family business. The old man returned from Florida in the spring of 1942, even though he was still obviously unwell, to use his influence with the local draft board to obtain farmers' exemptions for his three sons. Belford refused his, which infuriated his father. Both Jack and Courtney complied. Nana said that my father had been keen to enlist too, and that C. F. had pleaded with her to make Jack stay.

Local families began petitioning C. F. to sign farm exemptions for their boys. The old man was happy to oblige, but the draft board refused to honor them. When C. F. found out the board was accepting exemptions signed by Belford, but not him, he was enraged and demanded his son sign the exemptions that he had requested, which Belford refused to do. In his biographical timeline, he wrote, "My father returned from Florida in March of 1942 and attempted to resume the management of his business affairs. I don't know whether it was a result of his stroke or not, but he talked irrationally about my conduct of the business and the manner in which I had operated the company." Belford's rubber- and gasoline-rationing policies at Seabrook, for example, which included the use of bicycles instead of automobiles to get around the farm, drew the old man's scorn. When C. F. saw a photograph of Belford riding a bike in the *Bridgeton Evening News*, he was apoplectic. Seabrooks didn't ride bikes. (My father never even learned how.) Also, according to Belford, C. F. "violently objected to gasoline rationing as it applied to himself, and he became enraged when his driver had to abide by gasoline rationing when filling up at the pump."

But Belford's worst offense by far was enlisting. In the summer of 1942, he accepted the army's offer of a commission. He wrote, "By this time the war had gotten rather desperate. Bataan had fallen and many Seabrook employees were in uniform. I felt that I should also offer my services to my country, and I did." His father went to Herb Letts, chairman of the draft board, to prevent Belford from being made an officer in the army. But since Belford had volunteered, the draft board had nothing to do with the matter.

Had C. F. indeed raised one of his children to be a psychiatrist, as my father's 1994 kicker would have it, they might have been able to resolve the conflict. Instead, C. F. threatened to take back the stock in the company he had given Belford in 1933 as a reward for engineering the new quick-freezing production facilities. This was the first time the old man deployed his soon-to-be-familiar threat of disinheritance. "He insisted that I endorse 50 shares of stock in Seabrook and Baitinger which he had given me for services rendered in 1933," Belford wrote. "He freely admitted that he had given those shares to me, but now he insisted that

I sign them back to him if I was going to 'abandon' him by joining the service." But BLS was not the type to back down.

> *July 31, 1942*
> *Dear Dad,*
> *After giving the matter very careful consideration, I have about concluded to enter the Armed Forces of the United States, providing satisfactory arrangements can be made in regard to my personal obligations, and for the taking over of my duties as an officer of the companies.*

Jack took over Belford's job as head of the plant, while continuing to run one of the farming divisions. Although Jack assured his brother that his job would be waiting for him when he returned, from this point forward, he would effectively be running both halves of Seabrook Farms.

❦

THE JMS JR. PAPERS contain pages of medical reports from C. F.'s doctors, describing his condition during the war and after. Not one mentions a stroke, but that could be for liability reasons. A doctor in Philadelphia diagnosed the problem as a selenium deficiency, which had caused a muscle in C. F.'s neck to spasm. Courtney said that his father had had a heart attack. Nana said it was a mild stroke that temporarily affected her husband's speech, but that he recovered quickly.

In a timeline of her husband's decline that she later prepared for lawyers, Nana stated that C. F. began to abuse phenobarbital after his 1941 illness. Phenobarbital is a barbiturate that preceded benzodiazepines like Valium and Xanax as a popular antianxiety medication. Symptoms of abuse include irritability, delusional beliefs, and psychosis; combining the drug with alcohol magnifies these effects, and long-term abuse can result in permanent cognitive impairment. When he returned to New Jersey, C. F. seemed to require the little red pills to function with his former confidence. Multiple reports speak of the old man swallowing pills by the handful, often mixed with alcohol.

Only my father seems to have believed C. F.'s ailment to be potentially fatal. He told a doctor who examined C. F. around this time that he doubted that his sixty-year-old father had long to live. According to this doctor, who later testified for C. F.'s side in a competency hearing, his patient's death was a prospect that Jack seemed to welcome. Was Jack just trying to do his best for the family business? Or was the stroke his way of justifying the sidelining of his father? The war had upended the old order, and he'd gotten a taste for leadership and his own negotiating abilities in the union deal. Perhaps he believed he knew better than his father how to run a modern company.

C. F. and his entourage returned to the Coral Gables apartment for the winter of 1942–1943. Jack led three more rounds of financing during the war, which increased the number of bankers on the board and aggravated the growing power struggle with his father. Nurse Small continued to control access to the old man. She wouldn't even allow Jack to speak to his father on the telephone about business; it was too much of a strain, she insisted.

Jack also used the war to justify another reform of his father's system: for the first time Black workers would be allowed to work indoors. A reporter from the *Courier Post* interviewed my father, who had recently turned twenty-six, at the farm on April 29, 1943. Young Jack sounds a lot like a hot-eyed liberal, a do-gooder like those my father mocked at the dinner table. "I admit I have been bitten by the desire to do something for the Negro," he says. "But regardless of sociological aspects, this is only good business. We certainly don't refuse to sell our products to anybody because he happens to be a Negro. Our stockholders are interested, not in an employe's [sic] color, but in the quality of his work." The article notes that the superintendent of the dehydrating operation is Thomas Brown, a Black college graduate. "Many of the employees and shift supervisors under him are white. . . . It has been said this couldn't be done." Among the loudest of the naysayers was Jack's father.

CHAPTER 19

SEABROOKS AT WAR

W ORLD WAR I HAD BEEN THE MAKING OF C. F. Seabrook's original vegetable factory, and World War II had a similarly transformative effect on its second incarnation. Wartime propaganda promoted food production as an act of patriotism: "Food Will Win the War!" became a slogan of the War Food Administration shortly after Pearl Harbor. Beginning in 1942, the quartermaster general—the military's grocer—asked the nation's food producers for a 525 percent increase in production during the war years. For three or four years running, Seabrook Farms sold the government its entire year's production in advance, plus that of some five hundred local farmers the company contracted with.

Seabrook Farms was particularly well placed to meet the military's demands because of its assembly-line production methods. Just as Ford had swiftly retooled its factories to produce tanks and jeeps instead of tractors and cars, so Seabrook pivoted from quick-frozen food for General Foods to frozen and dehydrated food for the U.S. Quartermaster, while still packing the Birds Eye brand for the home front. Stateside consumers were encouraged to choose frozen vegetables over canned goods in order to preserve metal for the war effort, accelerating the general public's acceptance of the new food technology.

In the early summer of 1943, Mona Gardner, a writer from *Coronet* magazine, visited Seabrook Farms during the pea harvest. A vegetable blitzkrieg, the pea harvest involved 150 tractors with mowers, 410 trucks, 150 viners, and 4 airplanes. All ten of the company's divisions— farming, processing, packing, production, raw product, prepared

C. F. Seabrook with steam shovel, building a railroad spur at the farm, ca. 1915. My grandfather was on the leading edge of the coming of machine power to agriculture. By 1920 the mules in the background would be replaced by trucks and tractors. First published in the *American Magazine*, May 1921.

Though his passport listed "Farmer" as his profession, C. F. hated the drudgery of farm work and thought of himself as a builder. His heroes were men like Henry Ford, Andrew Carnegie, and Henry Bechtel.

Front page of *The Seabrooker*.

The first influx of Black farmworkers arrived in 1920, part of the Great Migration out of the Jim Crow south.

A fleet of Fordson tractors at Seabrook ca. 1920.

The smokestack towered over the vegetable factory. Conceived by C.F. and built by Jack Kelly, it was a symbol of the potency of both men.

JMS, already the farm manager at twenty-five, with a truck from the Seabrook fleet. In the 1934 strike, the fleet was weaponized.

Black workers lived in dilapidated housing and were the first to be let go in slack seasons. In June 1934, they went on strike.

y Hope For Union Farm Wages

ation Against Negroes And Foreign Born Workers

The union membership was remarkably diverse for Deep South Jersey, where Jim Crow segregation endured long after the 1930s.

On July 9, 1934, sixty people, both striking workers and police, were injured in rioting during the beet harvest. Here a group of strikers grapple with police, after the women pulled "scab beets" off a truck.

A group of protesters walking toward the plant as seen from one of the morning crop dusters.

The strike was an unprecedented challenge to C. F.'s absolute power. He was outraged Black and white workers had struck together.

Retribution was swift. A county judge set up a courtroom in the Seabrook offices and tried and convicted protesters on the spot.

After the rioting, management launched a tear-gas and smoke-bomb counterattack. Flames from a bomb allegedly thrown by Uncle Belford ignited the house of a woman with small children.

After World War II, Jack Seabrook brought in Dr. Charles Thornthwaite, the inventor of applied climatology. Here he stands next to Jack outside his lab at Seabrook Farms, 1951.

C. F. broke the 1934 strike, but his sons negotiated union agreements with the trucking fleet and the plant and field workers—a major breakthrough for farm labor in the Northeast.

The company first froze vegetables for the Birds Eye brand, but eventually sold them under its own label.

Jack Seabrook, on the right, with the Duke of Windsor (center), cutting asparagus and discussing wartime labor, 1943.

Under Jack and his brother Courtney's leadership, Seabrook Farms embraced 1950s consumer culture. Ernest Dichter, the "Sigmund Freud of the Supermarket," was enlisted for psychoanalytic insights into Seabrook's customers' inner desires.

You could grow them f in your c back yard

Seabrook Foods are fre they're quick-frozen r

Plump and full of fla Seabrook Farms quic cook up firm and tas flavor is sealed in by right after picking in in the middle of the f Seabrook Farms. Cho you'll get the same w and fresh-picked tast

CUT GREEN BEA

Seabrook Farms

QUICK-FROZEN FOO

look for SEABROOK

The logo on the water tower nodded to the company's history as pioneers in overhead irrigation.

Jack was eight inches taller than his father, and matinee idol handsome. Here he inspects crops in his growing wardrobe, which would one day fill a whole floor.

JMS invited New York pals down to the farm for riotous weekends in the country, where Bollinger champagne was served at every meal.

My father's horsedrawn family picnics in the buggy were the best part of his coaching, which became increasingly grand after his break with his father.

pending welcome dollars, flock to Jamaica during Winter months.
dge (top) are Mr. and Mrs. John Seabrook. of N. J.. and daughter.
MIRROR MAGAZINE. April 29 (Copyright, 1951. King Features Syndicate. Inc.)

After the war, JMS and his first wife, Anne, began wintering in Jamaica as members of the new "jet set." Lizanne, here an angelic four-year-old, had a difficult adult life.

No one knew more about JMS's secrets than Betty Gaunt, his personal secretary for almost forty-five years.

Thanks to lobbying by JMS, *Life* magazine featured Seabrook Farms in a January 1955 special issue devoted to food, cover-lined "Mass Luxury." Yale Joel, known as "the photographer of the impossible," managed to get several thousand employees in one shot by using a company crane. The Seabrooks are on a loading platform in the center right.

Starlet Eva Gabor was my father's girlfriend for almost two years, following his divorce from Anne. Here she proves her value to the brand in a 1952 publicity photo.

Hints of Eva's later role, as the city sophisticate among country bumpkins in the 1960s sitcom *Green Acres*, are present in this photo. JMS was not a turtleneck guy; I assume that Eva tried to style him.

Eva and Jack had a genuine connection. Jack's daughters liked Eva and thought she was going to be their stepmother.

The Gabor sisters, along with their mother, Jolie, far left, formed the proto-Kardashian era of pop culture. C. F.'s infatuation with his son's girlfriend would lead to a boardroom blowup. My grandmother, Norma Dale Seabrook, is far right.

E. A. Toomey showed a talent for writing as an undergrad at Columbia Christian College. Here she and a classmate collaborate on a radio play.

On joining United Press in New York, Liz was given her own column, "Women's View." In 1955 she followed Marilyn Monroe into a party.

The Stork Club was in its heyday in 1956, when Liz wore the Hope Diamond there one night for a story.

Toomey, standing in the back in a white coat, traveled with Princess Elizabeth and Philip on their 1951 tour of North America, which concluded on this rainy day in Washington, D.C., with an address by Harry Truman.

One chilly day in November 1954, Grace Kelly came to Seabrook for one of Jack's picnics.

Elizabeth Toomey broke the story of Grace Kelly's engagement to Prince Rainier, and she was one of the journalists who crossed the ocean with the wedding party in April 1956.

Liz shared a stateroom with Jinx Falkenberg, the original Miss Rheingold, who became a pioneer of morning television.

Jack was also on the ship as a guest of the family. His romance with Liz took place against the events leading up to the Marriage of the Century.

Liz first visited Seabrook with two gal pals as chaperones in May 1956. All three committed a terrible violation of coaching etiquette: They were hatless. JMS looks pained.

Liz wasn't sure about whether she should marry Jack, and turned his first proposal down.

But Jack persisted, and they were married on October 6, 1956, at the Madison Avenue Presbyterian Church, with a reception at the St. Regis.

As a woman, Thelma, bottom right, C. F.'s only daughter, wasn't allowed to work in the family business.

Coaching afforded Jack Seabrook, a subtle but deadly serious social climber, access to men with fortunes far greater than his own.

Titled "We Know Our Place," this 1958 image appeared in Slim Aaron's collection "A Wonderful Time," a defining document of midcentury American glamour.

Liz traded her hard-earned independence as a career woman for motherhood and the life of a country chatelaine.

Aaron Shikler's 1969 portrait of JMS with the Nimrod hung behind his seat at the dining-room table. He was the first American since Arthur Vanderbilt to be elected to the exclusive Coaching Club of Great Britian.

JMS married his personal brand to Nimrod just when the biblical strongman's name was becoming synonymous with "dork." He had the name of our street changed to Nimrod Road but pranksters kept stealing the sign. It's Seabrook Road now.

NIMROD RD

Inside Bernard Weatherill, Civic and Sporting Tailors, with bolts of cloth for clientele including Walter Annenberg, Dalí, and JMS. New York, July 1964.

foods, manufacturing, engineering, research, and purchasing—had to operate in sync not only with each other, but with the rapidly ripening crop. First the tractors dragged mowers through the pea fields, laying the vines into windrows. A "loader" ran over the windrows and spewed them onto the flatbed dump trucks, which drove over to a viner, a huge, very loud machine that separated the pea pods from the stems and leaves. The latter were fed to the company's thousand-head herd of beef cattle; they turned it into fertilizer for future crops. The unshelled peas were then loaded onto elevators and lifted four stories high, to be fed into hoppers and then, successively, to a sheller, a chaff cleaner, a stone remover, and a size grader. At the end of that sorting process, the peas went through a steam tunnel to blanch them, and then a chilled brine solution to stop them from cooking further. The heavier peas sank in the brine, and the lighter ones—which would be packaged as "Extra Fancy Grade"—floated on the surface. From there, flumes of water carried the vegetables further downstream to moving conveyor belts where female plant workers stood by to remove any remaining refuse. In C. F.'s view, women made better sorters than men.

Then the peas entered the quick-freezing part of the process. Those destined for Birds Eye–branded individual packages went into the "freezing trays" that were kept at 37 degrees below zero. The bulk stuff for the government was shunted into the enormous 10-below-zero cold room capable of accommodating twenty million pounds. If the peas came from nearby fields, about two hours passed from harvest to freezing. Working day and night, in floodlit fields, Seabrook could process a million pounds of peas every twenty-four hours. "But when the pea season is over, does all this efficient machinery stand idle?" Gardner wondered rhetorically. "By pulling a few levers, and pressing a battery of buttons, it is converted for lima beans, or spinach or any one of 11 other crops."

At the government's insistence, three enormous dehydrators had been installed at Farm Central, paid for in part by additional sales of securities. It was impossible to keep food frozen on many battlefields, especially in the deserts and tropics. Dehydrated vegetables, on the other hand—beets, potatoes, turnips, and rutabagas—were ideal for soldier's grub. In June 1942, the quartermaster ordered 1,250,000 pounds of dehydrated beets from Seabrook Farms. The Seabrooks and their contract farmers planted all the beets they could. The Seabrook peach and apple orchards, which had never been profitable, were ripped out to plant more beets. Nearby Sunset Lake, the public bathing area where the Klan had had their camp, turned bloodred from the processing plant runoff. It remained that color throughout the war.

≈

IN A LETTER C. F. WROTE from Coral Cables to his personal lawyer, Leo P. Dorsey, in the winter of 1943, he complains about Jack's integrating of the plant. He wonders why "it became necessary to put negro women workers in the plant and mingle them with the white women workers, which drove away many of our best women employees." He goes on, "I have no prejudice against negro labor, and have always used negroes on the farm. I like them very much for farm and field work. I do not believe, however, (speaking now of women) that they are as good at factory work as white women, and I know they work better and are much happier outside in the fields and in the sunshine. Besides, the class of trade that purchases quick-frozen foods is very particular about the conditions under which it is handled and produced." In other words, nice white people won't want to eat Seabrook frozen food if they know it was handled by Black workers.

The letter continues, "Now that we have gotten into this predicament, I am not recommending that we eliminate negro workers altogether from the factory. I am hopeful, however, that we might be able to use them only in groups on certain projects, perhaps dehydration, and to use the men as porters, platform men, car loaders, warehousemen, etc. I had information before I left that a very bitter feeling is being built up in Bridgeton and the community against the Seabrook organization because of the use of negroes to the exclusion of white people, particularly negro foremen, and I have received letters from friends, who have no connection whatsoever with the company, with reference to this matter. It seems to me that the boys have gone 'all out' in trying to do everything differently from the way it was done before." He concludes by prophesying that there will be "a final showdown with the boys as to who is going to run the business when I return. I think they should gradually be prepared for this; otherwise, it is going to come as a very severe shock to them in April."

Three days later C. F. wrote to his corporate lawyer, Albert R. McAllister: "Knowing how sincere and honest you are, I am sorry I must say this, but I feel it is my duty to tell you that I have a feeling the boys are not sincere in the cooperative attitude they apparently have adopted. I believe it is their intention to lead you and Dorsey to believe they will continue to cooperate with me when I return, but after having them plot against me for fourteen months in an effort to destroy me, I cannot put too much faith in their sincerity of purpose now. You and Dorsey may have performed some miracle, and I hope you have, but when two boys will connive against their own Father while he is too ill to know what is going on, as they have been doing, I am reluctant to believe they have been cured in so short a time."

❧

AS THE SEABROOKS' MAIN WARTIME CLIENT, the federal government had an incentive to recruit workers for the farm and plant. During the 1942 planting and harvest seasons, the Farm Security Administration (FSA) brought both white workers from the Appalachian region and Black workers from northern Georgia, as well as another group of Black migrants from Belle Glade, Florida, transporting them to and from Seabrook Farms.

During the Great Depression, the Civilian Conservation Corps had built several camps around Cumberland County. For the 1942 growing season, white migrants from Appalachia lived in one of these camps, called simply "Field No. 16." Although these workers had been promised free housing, the company charged them $2.75 a month for a double room, and $2.00 for a single ($38 today). When a worker from Tennessee complained, company officials told her that charging rent was the best way to keep out Black tenants, because they couldn't afford to pay.

The FSA housed Black migrants in the government-built camp known as Big Oak, located several miles from the plant, which had accommodations for almost a thousand workers, mostly in prefabricated buildings and tents. Photojournalists hired by the FSA, including John Collier Jr. and Arthur Rothstein, photographed migrants arriving in the middle of the night in a driving rainstorm, in the back of flatbed trucks with a canvas tarp over it. One woman had to be hospitalized with pleurisy. Single men were put in the FSA's army barracks–style tents, while families got the prefabricated "hutments." The photographs, now in the National Archives, depict hard, hot work in the miserable buggy conditions of summer in Deep South Jersey.

The Seabrooks' concerns about wartime labor shortages soon evaporated. Thanks to the combined efforts of the A.F.L. and the federal government, the company now had more workers than it could accommodate. A PhD student named Margaret Gordon, who visited Seabrook during the war years for her Atlanta University School of Social Work dissertation, "A Study of Migratory Labor at Seabrook Farms, 1941–1945," described conditions at Big Oak. The camp was surrounded by a five-strand barbed-wire fence. There were no adequate cooking, laundry, or bathing facilities, except for wash tubs; drainage was poor and water sat stagnant in ditches; garbage was collected irregularly; clean water was limited; and tents were not screened in, so there was no protection from flies and mosquitoes. The absence of lights at night was a hazard. To get to the privies, families had to get through a maze of tent ropes and pools of water. Families worried about children falling into the privies.

The federal government had promised to build additional housing, but wartime shortages of construction materials delayed the project. Knowing how much his father enjoyed building, Jack asked C. F. to take charge of getting the project completed. The old man was indeed energized by this assignment, not least because he would get to charge rent for, and eventually own, structures taxpayers were funding. Leaning on his connections in government and industry, C. F. did manage to procure the material to finish the job by spring 1944, when the scouts from the Japanese American incarceration centers out West arrived.

§

AMONG THE FIRST GROUP WAS George Sakamoto, a former fruit orchard worker from Newcastle, California, near Sacramento. Like one hundred thousand other Japanese Americans on the West Coast, he, his wife, Rose, and their infant daughter had been forced from their home by Executive Order 9066. That May, signs had gone up in the Sakamotos' neighborhood announcing that all people of Japanese ancestry had seventy-two hours to report to an assembly center, taking with them only as much as they could carry, on authority of a new federal agency called the War Relocation Board.

The Sakamotos were sent to the Los Angeles assembly center, which was the Santa Anita racetrack. For five months incarcerated families lived in horse stalls and showered in the big open area where lathered-up racehorses were rinsed down, until the "relocation centers" were ready. In October, they were moved to ten centers in remote areas of California, Arizona, Idaho, and Arkansas. The Sakamotos were incarcerated in the Granada War Relocation Center in Colorado, known as "Camp Amache" to residents. Rose's father was sent to Tule Lake.

The federal government had begun to rethink its incarceration policy almost immediately after implementing it, sensing correctly how future Americans would view this shameful episode in national history. The new policy was to empty the camps and resettle the inhabitants somewhere away from the coast of California, until the war was over. In December 1943, Sakamoto and a small group of other young men were given twenty-five dollars each by the War Relocation Board and told to head east and scout for prospective employers who might need large numbers of workers.

In the smoking car on the train headed east from Chicago, Sakamoto picked up a discarded copy of the January 1944 issue of *Reader's Digest*. It contained a condensed version of Mona Gardner's "Assembly Line Farmer" article, in which C. F. talks about the company's desperate need for wartime labor. The piece begins with an anecdote from the spring 1943 asparagus harvest. At the peak of the harvest, the plant had lost the ability to make steam, which was necessary for blanching the vegetables as well as for sterilizing the equipment between runs. Processing came to a halt, and trucks full of freshly cut asparagus spears were backing up outside the plant. The entire crop was in danger. Someone got C. F. on the phone—he happened to be in Utah—and in a three-minute conversation, the old man devised a solution: back up two New Jersey Central locomotives with full heads of steam onto the railroad sidings next to the plant, and connect the boilers to the plant. "The crop was saved," Gardner reports.

On arriving in New York, Sakamoto and his group caught a train to Philadelphia, where they asked around about Seabrook Farms. They were directed to Bridgeton, took a bus there, and walked the five miles to the farm. The men were immediately put to work in the processing plant and given beds in a barracks-style building. When the local authorities heard about their presence, Sakamoto recalled, "we were questioned by the FBI, Naval Intelligence, those people were swarming us . . . wanted to know how come we are here."

WEST COAST JAPS ENJOY WORKING ON JERSEY FARM

COLLEGE ATMOSPHERE GIVEN TO SEABROOK COLONY BY U.S. NATIVES

JAN 26, 1944.
The dozen or so American-born Japanese who arrived this week at Seabrook Farms, near here, are a far call from the war-crazed legions of the Pacific empire. Only their features and their skin resemble anything Oriental.

JMS HAD REACHED OUT to the Philadelphia Society of Friends about the possibility of recruiting African American day laborers from the city—workers the Seabrooks wouldn't need to house—provided that the company could get enough gasoline to transport them. However, Jack was concerned that the 1934 strikes might have left some lingering ill will in the community. He sought out the Friends for advice.

The Society of Friends had been one of the only religious or civil rights organizations in the United States to express outrage over Executive Order 9066. In *Years of Infamy*, Michi Weglyn writes, "The Quakers made their presence felt, many driving the long hot miles to even the most out-of-sight concentration camps to bring gifts, camp needs, and the precious reassurance that there were white Americans who cared." The American Friends Service Committee had two people working full time as liaisons between the government and private industry to resettle people.

Although Jack had come to inquire about recruiting local labor, the Friends told him about large numbers of Japanese American workers from the camps out West, who would soon be available. With the Friends' help, the Seabrooks sent recruiters around to the camps and placed ads in camp newspapers. The recruiters said that the Seabrooks personally promised every man and woman a job at the going wage, a house with heat and utilities, and decent schools for their children. In return, workers committed to staying in their jobs at Seabrook for at least six months.

Before leaving the camps, incarcerated Japanese Americans had to answer and sign a "loyalty questionnaire" to prove their patriotism. It included the question "Are you willing to serve in the armed forces at a moment's notice, on combat duty, whenever ordered?" Anyone who refused to sign the questionnaire was sent to the high-security Tule Lake Segregation Center. Since only those who signed were eligible for release, Seabrook Farms was assured of employing Japanese Americans whom the government and military had vetted.

Jack was right to be concerned about his father's reaction to this plan. When C. F., wintering again in Florida, saw the newspaper article about Japanese Americans at Seabrook, "he went ballistic." But by April 1944, when a delegation arrived from Jerome Camp, an incarceration center in Arkansas, to inspect the facilities, the old man had changed his tune. He realized that not only were the relocated Japanese Americans skilled workers—many of them had previous farming and gardening experience in California—they were also highly motivated to prove their patriotism by working hard and not complaining about the fifty-cents-an-hour pay and the bare-bones accommodations for which they paid rent to Seabrook Housing Corp. And their loyalty to the old man was absolute. For their part, Jack and Courtney were delighted that their father's interest in the housing of his new semicaptive workforce distracted him from meddling with their plans for the company.

C. F. personally led the visitors on a tour. He promised them first dibs on the government housing, which was nearing completion: thirty-five new buildings, divided into two hundred apartments for families and dorms for single men. Never mind that the living spaces had been promised to Black workers like Mack Bradwell, who had been with the company since the 1920s, and who were still living in tents and shacks at Orchard Center and Big Oak. The new arrivals were moved to the front of the queue.

One member of that group, Ellen Noguchi, later Ellen Nakamura, was most impressed with the place and with C. F., who, she later said, "made every effort to make sure we were well taken care of. After visiting Seabrook for ten days, I could hardly wait to get back" and tell the others about what she had seen. Of C. F. she said, "He was a little man, but he had a lot of noodles." Eventually almost two thousand people, many of them, like the Sakamotos, families with small children, came to Seabrook from the camps between 1944 and 1946.

When Rose Sakamoto and their children eventually joined George at Seabrook, they lived at 922 MacArthur Road, in one of the new government-built bungalows. Both parents worked alternating twelve-hour shifts from April to November, six days a week. During the pea, bean, and spinach harvests, they worked Sundays too. (Less perishable vegetables like potatoes, asparagus, and beets could be harvested without such haste.) Pay started at forty-nine cents an hour and rose to fifty-five cents. When the farming ended, Sakamoto recalled in a 2001 oral history, laborers were put to work as carpenters and bricklayers, or insulating cold-storage areas. If they were mechanically minded, they might overhaul motors in the machine shop. C. F. also hired his workers out on contract construction jobs, where they labored alongside men making twice what the Seabrookers made. "In other words, we were making about half so Seabrook did pretty good on that contract," Sakamoto said, implying that the company pocketed the other half of the wages the labor recruiter paid Seabrook for the men.

Someone in the C-Suite recognized the value of a feel-good story and concocted a plan to use Japanese American Seabrookers as ambassadors for the brand during the off-season. Workers were bused up and down the Eastern Seaboard as far south as Georgia, and to cities around the Midwest, including Detroit and St. Louis, where they spoke to retailers about Seabrook products and how they were produced. "Some places were curious why a Japanese is trying to do all this kind of work for Seabrook at wartime," Sakamoto said. But discussions were "always friendly."

Asked whether he felt C. F. Seabrook had exploited his workers, Sakamoto said he considered him "a friend" because he had used his influence in Bridgeton to make sure everyone treated the Japanese Americans with respect. Friendly Seabrook newspapermen wrote positive stories about the new arrivals. The White Legion backed off. "He didn't tell them what they had to do," Sakamoto said of the local community, "but he suggested that we be treated like any other Americans."

CHAPTER 20

THE MIRACLE-PACK

T HANKS TO WARTIME DEMAND, SEABROOK FARMS HAD
become one of the largest processors of frozen vegetables in
the East. By war's end, the company was packing 65 percent of the
nation's frozen lima beans, 35 percent of its frozen broccoli, and 40 percent of its frozen spinach. (As much as any other producer, Seabrook
was responsible for making lima beans popular in the mid-Atlantic.)
Almost eight thousand people worked for the company, and about a
thousand leaseholders paid rent to Seabrook Housing Corporation,
which was wholly owned by C. F.

But size, always my grandfather's favorite metric of success, counted
less in the postwar era. Geographical proximity to population centers
was the reason Arthur Seabrook's truck farm was in the Garden State
in the first place, and that had informed young Charlie Seabrook's idea
of a Fordist, vertically integrated vegetable factory, a huge machine
with thousands of moving parts. But frozen food, which had afforded
C. F. a second chance at industrial farming, had also undermined the
advantages of vertical integration and "just in time" logistics. A frozen
lima bean was a commodity that could come from anywhere and be
stored in a warehouse for months. What really mattered to modern
consumers was a post-Fordist concept: the brand.

Jolly Green Giant, founded in California's Central Valley in 1951,
excelled at branding. The company's brand imagery featured a bean-
green Adonis sporting an off-the-shoulder Roman tunic of pea plants.
It was created by Leo Burnett, the Madison Avenue advertising firm
behind Charlie the Tuna for StarKist, Morris the Cat for 9Lives, and

the Keebler Elves. In creating the Seabrook brand, the family itself became the mascot. Behind the brand's products lay the family's stirring backstory of bootstrapping, hard work, and entrepreneurial genius. My father wrote, "The fact that there was a real family named Seabrook who owned and ran these extensive scientific farming and freezing operations was used to develop a form of publicity even more effective than our paid advertising." He added, "We could never match dollar-for-dollar the General Foods advertising budget, but, through this more subtle approach, we could still compete on an equal basis in many areas. Food editors, society writers, radio hosts, wine societies all gave us free plugs." And in handsome "Spinach King" Jack Seabrook, as one series of ads for Western Union dubbed him, the brand had an Ivy League brand image—a sleek mid-century fashion plate instead of a bare-chested hunk in a pea skirt.

Courtney and Jack worked with C. F. on the brand story. My father wrote that he and his brother wanted to place the company's origin in 1875, when A. P. first started truck farming. But C. F. wanted to begin the story in 1912, when he took over the farm. C. F. eventually compromised on 1893, the year his father bought Poplar Brook Farm, as long as they didn't mention A. P.

The consumer society had the "boys" thinking outside the box in other ways. A rapidly changing frozen-food business would soon begin to offer such novelties as frozen concentrated orange juice from Florida, and prepared frozen entrees, complete with sauces. The Seabrook brothers were keen to expand into that trade. They explored producing goods in Florida and on the West Coast, where the labor costs weren't as high as they were in a unionized shop in New Jersey, and where better weather made for more growth units in the calendar. West Coast companies like Jolly Green Giant could make the same products the Seabrooks made with less overhead, including nonunion labor, and ship goods east on the new Interstate Highway System that the federal government was building. To Jack, under pressure from the bankers to cut costs, packing on the West Coast was an appealing prospect. But to C. F., whose relationships with local politicians and government officials were rooted in the land, buildings, and roads of South Jersey, the idea of moving to another place was unthinkable.

❧

BELFORD SPENT THE WAR YEARS IN AUSTRALIA, organizing food supplies for Allies fighting in the South Pacific. He left the army as lieutenant colonel in August 1946, but he did not return to the family business right away. Eventually his brothers convinced Belford to come back, which he did in 1947 as executive vice president in charge of production, with a seat on the board. However, as my father writes, "Belford was never again willing to assume any leadership position of the type he had held from 1932 to 1942. . . . Although I was ten years younger and originally was definitely the 'kid brother,' Belford became my most loyal supporter, especially after I was elected executive vice president in 1951."

After his return from Australia, Belford bought a house in nearby Alloway, where he planned to move his family. When C. F. heard about this, he became so angry that he sent a work gang to dig up all the rhododendrons planted around the house where Belford and his family had been living in Seabrook, saying the bushes belonged to him. Terrified, Belford's wife, Harriet, called her husband in his office. "I asked my father for his explanation," Belford wrote, "which was that I had stolen them from him in the first place and now that I was moving to Alloway, he was removing them before I could move. My father was never reconciled to the idea of owning my own home."

As Belford's role in the company diminished, Courtney's increased. As a young man, Courtney Seabrook had been the Fredo of the three brothers. He was given Koster Nursery to run in the same way the middle Corleone got the hotel in Vegas, as a consolation prize. But Courtney came into his own in the postwar era when he oversaw branding and packaging. He became the Seabrooks' top brand ambassador, hosting dinner parties with excellent food and wines for journalists and important clients with his wife, Mae, which Jack could never get Anne to do. C. F., in a rare compliment, once called Courtney "the best sales-man in America." Courtney also became a driving force in the National Association of Frozen Food Packers, a trade organization, attending meetings and hosting several, including the 1956 annual meeting in the Rainbow Room in Manhattan, at which Kay Thompson, the author of *Eloise* and a glamorous friend of Jack's, served as emcee.

Courtney's brand imagery incorporated the piece of wooden sid-ing from the Beebe Run tenant farm, where young Charlie Seabrook had carved his name. C. F., who had seen Henry Ford's signature styl-ized on the hoods of every one of those Ford vehicles the farm owned, wanted Courtney to design a logo that featured his own signature, as he'd carved it as a boy. Courtney also came up with the company's motto, which was later featured on every package—"We Grow Our Own So We Know It's Good, and We Freeze It Right on the Spot"—with C. F.'s signature serving as a guarantee. As the packaging evolved, the feeling of movement of the food spilling out on a plate replaced the static picture of corn on the cob, or a mound of peas.

In 1953, DuPont engineers invented Mylar, known chemically as BoPET (biaxially-oriented polyethylene terephthalate). As a packaging material, Mylar's great advantage was that it could be both frozen and heated without coming apart. Also, it was transparent; the drawback of canning vegetables and fruits was that consumers couldn't actually see the food until they opened the container. Courtney proposed using Mylar in a new line of boil-in-the-bag frozen products. His inspiration was the French method of cooking "sous vide," in which a glass jar with food sealed inside is placed into a pot of boiling water. Vegetables and entrees could be cooked in sauces first in Seabrook Farms' industrial kitchens, then packed in Mylar pouches and quick-frozen. All the mod-ern housewife needed to do was to open the box, drop the pouch into a pan of boiling water, wait ten to fifteen minutes, and *voila*. "Fearfully I Served It," reads the headline of a print ad for Seabrook's Miracle-Pack Broccoli au Gratin, below a photograph of a meek-looking hausfrau tim-orously proffering a casserole. "Now he's a confirmed vegetable eater.

No question about it, Seabrook Farms Miracle-Pack Vegetables have man appeal!" The company's frozen creamed spinach, also sold in the Mylar Miracle-Pack, eventually became the brand's signature product.

Jack had no talent for graphic design, but he brought his narrative skills to the brand story. Jack also spent time cultivating media power brokers. Among his contacts was Sally Kirkland, a well-connected Oklahoma-born editor at *Life* magazine. He routinely took her and others to 21 to pitch Seabrook-related stories. As his marriage to Anne began to fall apart, he spent more time quasi-professionally carousing in the city.

✦

OVER TIME, the real family and the branded one blurred. Intimate personal relations got mixed up with public-facing togetherness. Instead of family values shaping the brand, marketing values came to shape the family. Though C. F. resented the rising importance of the brand to the company's success, he swiftly saw how to twist it to his advantage. A son's worth was a commercial calculation that measured his value to the company. As the men devoted all their energy to the family business, the women were left to nurture the actual family.

Any relation who didn't live up to the branded version of the ideal Seabrook family was subject to C. F.'s withering criticism at family gatherings. My father wrote, "At most family parties there was tension, because C. F. would be sarcastically critical of some family member, a daughter-in-law who was hard of hearing or a pre-teen grandson who happened to be overweight." C. F. was in the habit of mocking Mae, Courtney's wife, who was embarrassed by a hearing loss, and didn't wear a hearing aid. On social occasions, C. F. would speak softly and then enjoy watching Mae's discomfort, "proving" her vanity. This casual cruelty made the command-performance events—like the holiday gathering at C. F.'s—nerve-racking. Carol tells chilling stories of Sunday lunches at the grandparents, where one false move could land you in Grandad's crosshairs.

But could any Seabrook have lived up to the branded version of the family C. F. had in mind? Jack was the golden boy, and yet his father resented his son's social success. The more Jack came to embody the modern brand ideal in his own style of living, the more critical of him C. F. became, especially as Jack's deteriorating marriage and active New York nightlife diverged more and more from the wholesome farm family that the company marketed. And if Jack fell short of fulfilling the role of a Seabrook, what hope was there for anyone else?

CHAPTER 21

KILL YOUR
DAH-LINKS

A NNE HAD NEVER WANTED TO BE A FARMER'S WIFE.
She was stuck with the Seabrook clan in South Jersey, with
two children, born in 1942 and 1947, to keep her away from the life she
desired in New York. And even though Carol had all the right qualities to be my father's successor in business, primogeniture demanded
a son.

To cheer Anne up, in 1947 my father began to take the family to
Jamaica during the winter months. The company flew them down in
its Beechcraft Twin, or they traveled by commercial air service from
Miami, which had begun after the war. The family would arrive soon
after New Year's and then Jack would leave Anne and the girls at their
rented villa on the North Shore, near Montego Bay, while he went
back to work. He had obtained his pilot's license and sometimes flew
himself back and forth. Carol would be taken out of Hopewell Township School and put into a convent school in Jamaica, where she was
taught by nuns. Jamaica was still a British colony and dollars were
scarce on the island, and the fact that the Seabrooks seemed to have a
lot of them made them popular with the cash-starved Brits.

The island had served as a British naval base during the war, and
its infrastructure had been greatly improved. After the war, the North
Shore became a fashionable retreat for a new international social class
dubbed the "jet set" by the Russian-born gossip writer Igor Cassini, the
author of the "Cholly Knickerbocker" gossip column, which was syndicated in Hearst newspapers. Anne far preferred the company of these
witty, dissolute Brits to the folks back home. Noel Coward was in his

Montego Bay villa, writing plays and screenplays. Ian Fleming was just up the coast in Goldeneye, turning out Bond novels. (In the process of creating his shaken-not-stirred hero, Ian Fleming smoked seventy cigarettes and drank a quart of gin every day; he died at the age of fifty-six.) In 1948, the British-Canadian newspaper baron Lord Beaverbrook, formerly Max Aitken, the owner of the *Daily Express* of London and later the *Evening Standard*, bought the spectacular eleven-acre property known at Cromarty, overlooking Montego Bay. Winston Churchill stayed with "Beaver" when he visited Jamaica. Later, Princess Margaret holidayed there, before moving on to Mustique, where her sister, the Queen, had given her a plot of land as gift in 1960, on Margo's marrying Antony Armstrong-Jones, the future Lord Snowden. Jack was a sophisticated young man, but among these thrillingly cynical Brits he was out of his depth. Like his father, he enjoyed socializing with nobility. But unlike these swells, Jack had to get up in the morning and go to work.

In his biography of Noel Coward, Philip Hoare quotes Morris Cargill, a local writer, on this postwar Jamaican society of expat Brits, a hard-living clique of sexual adventurers who didn't have anything much to do except play bridge, drink, and have affairs. Jamaica, Cargill writes, was "where English families sent their black sheep . . . and gave them an allowance. They were remittance men . . . [who] sipped a rum punch before lunch, and then slept after lunch . . . crawled out for another rum punch before dinner, and . . . crawled back to bed."

Among the leaders of the British colony was Nina Caroline Studley-Herbert, the 12th Countess of Seafield. She was a Scottish peeress who was the second richest woman in Great Britain, after the Queen. Jack and Anne hit it off with the countess and her husband, who had the Waugh-worthy name of Derek Herbert Studley-Herbert. In the summer of 1951, the Seabrooks spent almost two months visiting the couple's estate in Scotland. The heart of Robert the Bruce was buried in the chapel at Cullen House, their family's sixteenth-century manor house, which had seven miles of corridors for Jack and Anne to wander around in, and forty bedrooms where they might seclude themselves with other house guests.

194 THE SPINACH KING

Somehow C. F. heard rumors about both Jack and Anne's affairs with houseguests that summer in Scotland. When the couple returned in August, he demanded that his son divorce Anne as soon as possible, insisting that his personal lawyer, Leo P. Dorsey, handle the matter. Jack dutifully went along with his father's hardball tactics against his wife and Dorsey's strategy for a speedy divorce. That may have been because by December, Jack Seabrook was very publicly involved with a movie star.

≈

THE GABOR SISTERS and their mother were pop culture proto-Kardashians. TV, gossip, sex, mama-and-three-daughters: the Gabors did it first. Eva Gabor was the youngest of three, who, together with their mother, Jolie, became fixtures in gossip columns and society pages, beginning in the late 1940s. As the talk show host Merv Griffin later said of the family, "It was as if they'd been dropped out of the sky." The sisters were frequently in competition, both for roles and for men. Zsa Zsa, the middle sister, married nine times; Magda, the oldest and least well known, had six husbands, including one of Zsa Zsa's exes, the actor George Sanders; Eva made five trips to the altar. Their nineteen collective marriages produced one child, Francesca Hilton, who Zsa Zsa said was conceived when Conrad Hilton, her estranged husband at the time, raped her.

Eva couldn't sing or dance, and her range as an actor—blond ingenue with Continental sophistication—was narrow. ("Like Sally Field doing a party impression of Marlene Dietrich," the journalist Bruce Handy wrote in *Vanity Fair*.) Her agent advised her to sleep with her leading men to get ahead. Gary Cooper, Errol Flynn, Robert Preston, Stewart Farley, and Paul Valentine were only a few of her liaisons.

When Germany invaded Hungary, Jolie and Magda fled to Prague. They eventually managed to get to New York in 1945. Among the things they left behind was their Jewish heritage.

Eva married her second husband, Charles Isaacs, an investment broker, in 1943. He made her a rich, chauffeured Beverly Hills hostess at
the age of twenty-four. She began an affair with Daryl F. Zanuck, the
head of 20th Century Fox, in the hope of getting better parts. Zanuck
secured Eva a role in *A Royal Scandal* (1946), starring Tallulah Bank-
head. But she was cut from the final edit. Eva also appeared in the
forgotten *The Wife of Monte Christo* (1946) and *Song of Surrender*
(1949), wearing brown-face to look like a South Pacific islander. After
that bomb, her film career stalled.

She divorced Isaacs in 1949 and moved to New York, where she
hoped to brighten her prospects on Broadway. She persuaded Richard Rodgers to cast her in the role of Mignonette, another blond
ingenue, in *The Happy Time*, a hit play by Samuel A. Taylor, produced by Rodgers and Hammerstein, that ran for six hundred and
fourteen performances at the Plymouth Theatre in the early 1950s,
and later became a musical. Eva moved into a duplex at 1033 Fifth
Avenue, subsidized by the hefty alimony that she was collecting
from Isaacs.

Meanwhile, Jolie had started a successful costume jewelry store at
699 Madison Avenue. By 1947, Jolie had made enough to purchase a
four-story brownstone on East Sixty-Third Street. She rented apartments to actors, designers, and writers; Holly Golightly's townhouse
in Truman Capote's *Breakfast at Tiffany's* is said to have been inspired
by Jolie's "Gaboratory," the site of wild, all-night parties that mixed
Hollywood and literary New York. At one, Errol Flynn allegedly
exclaimed, "I've fucked Eva and Zsa Zsa already, why not Magda?
Hell, why not the old gal?" Flynn supposedly ended up going home
with a man that night.

Jack's friend Sally Kirkland, to whom he had been pitching the
Seabrook story for years, may have introduced him to Eva. The star
was on the cover of *Life* in February 1950 (Zsa Zsa was on the cover
in the fall of 1951). A meeting at the Gaboratory was arranged, to
which Jack brought two dozen long-stemmed red roses. When Jolie

196 THE SPINACH KING

opened the front door and saw my father, she took the roses from him, flung them out into the street, and cried, "Who gives a damn about flowers!" Then, grabbing him by the lapel of his bespoke suit, and softening her tone, she purred, "But you, dah-link, can come inside."

✖

THE SEPARATION AGREEMENT between Jack and Anne was signed on November 28, 1951. Anne established residence in the Virgin Islands on December 1, which allowed for a quicky divorce. On December 10, 1951, the diary notes that Eva Gabor, a weekend guest at the farm, caught a ride back to LaGuardia on the company's airplane. (What, I wonder, was Betty Gaunt thinking as she transcribed this?) That day, Walter Winchell, still the dean of the daily columnists, broke the news: "Eva Gabor's current favorite is wealthy Jack Seabrook."

Eva weekended at Jack's house with a revolving cast of glamorous New York pals, who were intrigued by her country idyll with the grocery man's boy. Jack's New York friends regarded these country sojourns as "drying out" periods, only to discover that at virtually every event champagne was served. Down on the farm, Eva was sweet to Jack's daughters. Carol liked her, and assumed that Eva would be her stepmother. In some ways, Eva was more level-headed than Anne, who had conceived a plan to move the children to Mexico City, where they would be able to live in a style that Jack's stingy divorce settlement couldn't afford them in New York. Eva also did some product promotion for the company, dressed in what look like lederhosen. She even lent her acting talents to the Seabrook Farms Christmas pageant in 1952. Even fifty years later, former workers remember that on Eva's trips down to Upper Deerfield Township, she swam naked in C. F.'s pool, wearing only a bathing cap to prevent her platinum-blond hair from turning blue in the chlorine.

The columns had the couple headed for holiday nuptials, which thrilled the Seabrook workforce. On December 22, "Danton Walker" confided, "Eva Gabor's intended third husband is Jack Seabrook, millionaire farmer and food processer of Bridgeton, N.J." C. F. also seems to have found Eva's visits thrilling. He was smitten with his son's girlfriend and "took every opportunity to be in her presence," Belford wrote in his memoir. Eva presumably knew how to handle a randy old millionaire like C. F. Seabrook. What could possibly go wrong dah-link?

CHAPTER 22

BOY SCOUTS

W ITH MILLIONS IN OUTSTANDING LOANS TO SEABROOK Farms, the bankers on the board continued to press management to reduce costs, as well as calling for a moratorium on new construction. By 1951, those loans totaled almost $100 million in today's money. With the coming of Swanson's TV dinners in 1953, and other new frozen food products, competition for space inside supermarkets' burgeoning freezer aisles was growing. Adding to the bankers' sense of urgency was the lack of a succession plan. The banks recognized that Jack, who seemed to have been born to be a CEO, was fully capable of managing a modern, branded food company, and his father manifestly was not. It takes a different set of skills to run an established business than to start a new one. Jack was the logical person to follow his father, and it was to the old man's credit that he had foreseen this, back in 1939.

But C. F. still would not, or could not, cede power to his son. He wasn't about to listen to bankers and consultants tell him how to run his business. He wanted to keep building, buying more land, and adding more workers. A memo Jack wrote in 1965, in preparing to contest his father's will, portrays C. F.'s state of mind in the early fifties. "During the 1952–53 period, he became obsessed with expanding the freezing plant in direct violation of his agreement with the lending banks. As he poured money into fixed assets, he became afraid that the banks would find out through me . . . that he was in violation and decided that his only protection against this was character assassination."

C. F. complained to anyone who would listen that Jack wasn't the golden boy the bankers seemed to think he was. In a 1964 interview, board member Tom Milliman described C. F.'s humiliating treatment of his sons in meetings. "Now I'm not a Phi Beta Kappa man from Princeton," Millman recalled C. F. saying, in reference to Jack, "and I'm not a Princeton engineer," referring to Belford, "and I don't have any degrees from Lehigh," as did Courtney, "but I can tell you this," and, Millman said, he would wag his finger below the noses of his three sons, saying, "I know more about how to run a company than any of them." C. F. referred to them as "Boy Scouts."

Finally, in the fall of 1951, C. F. agreed to promote Jack to executive vice president. Belford supported this heartily. The board assumed this meant the matter of succession was resolved and Jack would become president before too long. But matters were far from settled.

❧

MARGARET SEABROOK, called Margie, was the oldest of Belford and Harriet's four children, and C. F.'s first grandchild. She attended Smith College, and in 1949 she and a group of other students spent their junior year in Mexico. There Margie met and fell in love with an older, divorced man named Xavier Sanchez, whom she announced she planned to marry. Belford wrote in his memoir, "My father objected to this and when my wife and I gave our approval, he hired a lawyer named Wallace Foster from Bridgeton and sent him to Mexico to investigate the 'Mexican N*****s,' as he called them."

Foster, who was Jack's classmate at Bridgeton High School and remained his bachelor pal for life, flew to Mexico with another man. They set up surveillance outside the impressive-looking villa of Federico Sanchez Fogarty, the father of Margie's lover. When the spies were spotted, the family invited them inside for a closer look. Foster and his assistant spent the next two weeks feasting on delicious Mexican food and thoroughly exploring the wines, mescals, and tequilas in the Sanchez cellar. Finally, stuffed and besotted, the investigators returned to Seabrook and reported to C. F. that he had no need to worry about these Mexicans—they were exceptionally cultivated people with excellent taste in all things.

The old man was unappeased. Perhaps he was mindful of what Salem's founder John Fenwick himself did when his granddaughter Elizabeth similarly abominated the family by marrying James Gould, their Black servant. Not only did C. F. threaten to disinherit Margie, "He threatened to disinherit me if I didn't stop the wedding," Belford writes. The wedding went on as planned, with a reception at Belford's place in Alloway. Jack drove the newlyweds from the church in a Rolls-Royce convertible. Nana attended, although her husband had ordered her not to. The old man stayed on Polk Lane, a venomous toad in his lovely gardens. As threatened, he disinherited Margie and the four children she had with Sanchez before they divorced in 1973.

❧

C. F.'s ANTISOCIAL BEHAVIOR wasn't limited to Belford's family. Thelma's husband Harry Barber also drew the old man's ire. As an established dentist in Bridgeton, Dr. Barber had his own career, separate from the family business. Barber had reluctantly consented to live in the Bridgeton mansion at 65 North Commerce Street that C. F. had purchased in Thelma's name for tax reasons. But he had refused his father-in-law's wedding gift of furniture for the place, because it "constituted improper interference in our affairs." The two men were at loggerheads, but C. F. was never one for direct confrontation, unlike Barber, who had served with bravery during the war.

Early in 1951, word reached C. F. that Harry Barber had taken up with his dental assistant, Mary King, and was entertaining her at the North Commerce Street house while Thelma was in Coral Gables with her parents. One of the domestic workers in the house claimed to have seen Miss King in a hallway, "swathed in a Turkish towel." C. F. demanded that his daughter sue her husband for divorce, charging infidelity and cruelty. She reluctantly complied. Then, on May 31, local police arrested Dr. Barber as he tried to enter his home. He was taken to jail, charged with trespassing, and released on $2,000 bail. Barber then sued C. F., Jack, and Thelma for wrongful arrest and defamation of character, asking for $2 million in damages.

The divorce trial reached the Bridgeton courtroom of Superior Court Judge William R. Burton in June 1952. Thelma was defended by C. F.'s longtime Camden lawyer, Judge Samuel Orlando, whose fee of $1,000 a day may have been one reason the trial dragged on for fifteen days. The judge heard testimony from the employee in the Barber residence who had seen the dental assistant wrapped in a Turkish towel. The dentist vigorously defended himself with receipts showing he couldn't have been in Bridgeton at that time. The Vineland *Daily Journal*, never friendly toward the Seabrooks, reported every salacious detail.

The judge ruled in Harry Barber's favor, throwing out all of Thelma's charges. It was an unmitigated disaster for C. F., who ended up owing a small fortune to Orlando for losing the case, and who now became the defendant in Barber's wrongful arrest and defamation suit against the family. The old man settled with Barber by agreeing to pay for the education of his three children with Thelma, one of whom, Richard Barber, went on to become a distinguished professor of oceanography at Duke University.

On the night of July 22, Jack "Red" Saunders, the Seabrooks' former watchman and strikebreaker, who had returned to work for the company as a truck dispatcher, was in the Bridgeton Elk's Club when Barber walked in. The two men got into an argument and began scuffling at the bar. "Saunders is alleged to have taken issue with remarks passed by Dr. Barber in connection with Saunders' work at Seabrook Farms," the front-page *Daily Journal* account says. The dispute continued outside. On getting in his car, Barber felt a pain in his arm, and realized he'd been "slashed from armpit to the elbow," the paper reports. Saunders was arrested the next day for atrocious assault and battery, and later released on bail. Cholly Knickerbocker picked the story up and printed it in his syndicated column. It became that day's fodder for the chattering classes.

C. F. seemed to be intent on prosecuting the morality of his family members, but given his own behavior it's hard to fathom what principles his stance rested on. It seems more likely that campaigns such as those against Margie and Harry Barber were attempts to exert his control over family members' personal lives to compensate for his loss of power in the boardroom.

CHAPTER 23

"A MARKED PLAYBOY"

S TARTING IN LATE 1952, C. F. SUSPENDED BOARD MEET-
ings for seven consecutive months, so that the banks' representatives on the board wouldn't see how he was violating their moratorium
on new construction at Seabrook. When the banks heard about the
new construction anyway, C. F. was convinced it was because their Ivy
League pal, his son Jack, had ratted on him.

Meanwhile, Jack's lifestyle became more and more lavish. Through
early 1953, Jack and Eva mingled with the jet set in New York, Florida,
and Jamaica, while continuing to host friends in Seabrook. The workers by and large did not resent the Seabrooks' profligacy, and many
admired it. The highlight of these weekends were the late-afternoon
horse-drawn carriage rides to a nearby spot Jack had established
as "the picnic ground." These seemingly casual picnics were in fact
highly organized affairs in preparation for which the staff followed
an itemized Picnic Checklist. At the picnic grounds the party grilled
steaks and drank chilled Beaujolais, which somehow tasted much better in this setting than anywhere else, and then drove back to the farm
in the moonlight.

For one daytime picnic, Jack invited Grace Kelly, of the Philadelphia
Kellys. In the same way that Henry Ford served as C. F.'s role model as
an industrialist, so John Brendan Kelly Sr., known as Jack, became my
grandfather's avatar as a builder. Kelly, eight years younger than C. F.,
was also an immigrant's son, from Ireland. Both had industrialized
their fathers' professions—in Kelly's case, bricklaying. Both men were
master builders and master self-promoters. In the 1930s, they collabo-

rated on the brick smokestack that towered over the Seabrook power plant, a symbol of the builders' potency.

Socially, the Kelly family was a useful yardstick by which C. F. could measure the Seabrook clan's status. Like the Seabrooks, the Kellys had risen quickly thanks to the patriarch's success as a builder. But as an Irish Catholic tradesman, Kelly remained an outsider in the eyes of the city's snooty Protestant elite, the same people who tended to look down on C. F.'s uncouth obsession with business. The Kelly children, on the other hand, were accepted into the same social circles that my father frequented, with other blue bloods of the Main Line.

Grace came with her older sister, Peggy, who their father always said was the talented one in the family. The weather was chilly. In a photograph taken that day, Grace is clutching her hands in her lap, sitting on the bench of a picnic table with my father next to her, looking casually debonair. They would have packed up quickly and gone back to Jack's house for a brandy soon after. There was talk of Jimmy Stewart, currently starring as Grace's leading man in *Rear Window*, who had been in Belford's graduating class at Princeton. But neither Grace nor Jack could have imagined how their own lives would change with the star's next Hitchcock picture, *To Catch a Thief.*

๑~~๑

IN THE WINTER OF 1953, my grandfather was in residence again in Coral Gables, while Jack and his brothers ran the company back in New Jersey. On learning that Eva Gabor was in Miami, C. F. called on her. When, in early April, Eva flew back to New York, C. F. followed her there and turned up at her Fifth Avenue apartment. He asked to come in, "only to be told by Miss Gabor to leave and not return," according to Uncle Belford, who alone among the brothers seems to have been outraged by his father's behavior. "This rejection of his devotion caused my father to develop a superlative obsession against Miss Gabor and other members of her family," Belford wrote. "As a result, he finally arranged for the board of directors to discharge Jack from the company."

But before the board of directors could meet, Jack was thrown from a horse and fractured a vertebra in his back. The accident was the lead item in Dorothy Kilgallen's April 21 column: "Jack Seabrook, the wealthy young frozen food tycoon oft linked to Eva Gabor, is in serious condition after being thrown from a horse on his New Jersey estate." C. F. came over to Jack's house the following day while his son was lying in bed, in a brace. "He was completely irrational," my father wrote, "raving and ranting and flinging his arms about. Actually, I had a wire recording of this scene, but unfortunately it disappeared during the 1959 move from Seeley to Salem." How he managed to secretly record his father while lying in bed with a broken back is hard to fathom, but if anyone could pull it off, it was Jack.

Instead of confronting his father over Eva, my father meekly assented to ending their relationship. Kilgallen's column for April 30, 1953, was headlined, "Jack Seabrook's Dates with Eva Gabor Are Off:" "The once-flourishing romance between Jack Seabrook . . . and Eva Gabor . . . has grown colder than his products . . . chums say [his family] didn't like the publicity."

On the West Coast, Hedda Hopper reported, "Eva Gabor's romance with Jack Seabrook of the frozen food clan was relegated to the deep freeze." Edith Gwynn's Hollywood confided, "Eva Gabor has iced Jack Seabrook and is back to Stew Barthlemess [sic]," the son of the silent movie–era star Richard Barthelmess.

Ending his son's affair with Eva wasn't enough salve for C. F.'s wounded pride, apparently. When the board finally met again, on May 18, 1953, the chairman publicly demanded Jack's resignation, excoriating my father in front of the other directors for being dishonest and incompetent. He said that Jack's playboy behavior was bringing shame on the family and the brand, and falsely claimed that the bankers had told him he must get rid of his son to save the company. Belford loyally stuck up for his brother at the meeting, saying that nothing C. F. was alleging was true. He added that even though he knew his father had the board votes on his side to force Jack out, he wanted his objections entered into the minutes. The minutes were later sanitized, however, "much to Belford's disgust," Jack wrote.

Jack offered to resign. "JMS resignation accepted," the diary notes. On revisiting this entry many years later, while working on his speech about his father, he annotated that entry, writing "actually demanded by CFS" in red ink.

Eva Gabor never returned to Seabrook, New Jersey. But can it be a coincidence that Eva is best remembered as Lisa Douglas, the cosmopolitan ingenue whose stuffy lawyer husband, Oliver Wendell Douglas (played by Eddie Albert), takes her to live on a farm? *Green Acres* ran for 170 episodes from 1965 to 1971 on CBS and lives on in a timeless TV-land that the Gabors helped create. Critics marveled at how natural Eva seemed in playing the part of a city swell living among country bumpkins.

✎

BY JUNE 1953, it was clear that the old man was having a mental health crisis. He was drinking heavily and continuing to abuse phenobarbital. Finally, Leo Dorsey convinced his client, who he unctuously referred to as "the Old Gentleman," to go to the Clifton Spring Sanatorium in the Finger Lakes region of New York. In late June, C. F. and his retinue traveled there on the company plane. Dr. George B. Watson, a staff psychiatrist, examined the new arrival. "The patient states that one of the reasons he has become increasingly nervous during the last few years is because of the fact that his son . . . has become a rather marked playboy." C. F. repeated the lie about the bankers forcing him to get rid of Jack. "This he did about a month ago," Watson continues, "but it has bothered him a great deal. He states that he has had to shoulder most of the work of the organization of the last 3 yrs., and he has not had a vacation." He was admitted and began a stay that lasted almost two months.

Sunday, July 5
Dear Dad,
Yesterday Mother had her July 4th party at the pool and
the whole family was there except for you and Margie.

We missed you and hope that you are feeling well. Mother
and I considered flying up to see you today but she finally
decided you might prefer to remain undisturbed for a
while longer. When you would like visitors, we could be
glad to come at any time.
Take care of yourself.
Love
Jack

Nana also wrote.

Dear Charlie,
I just received your letter this morning of course we
did not have mail delivery on the 4th which delayed it.
I am glad you are feeling better and hope you continue
to improve.

In that letter, C. F. had requested the return of Nurse Small, who had
been a source of anguish to my grandmother when the brawny Australian lived with the family during the war years, until C. F. dismissed
her in early 1944 over a dispute. "Was surprised that you feel you need
a nurse," Nana meekly wrote back, "but will try to get in touch with
Miss Small."

Around July 10, Jack got word that his father wanted to talk to him.
The diary notes: "C. F. has written me a letter which I will receive Saturday saying he is sorry for all he has done and wants me back." (If he did
write it, the letter wasn't among the JMS Jr. papers.) On July 13, Jack
flew with his mother to Clifton Springs. They talked with Dr. Watson.
That was the first time, he wrote, "we realized how odd [his behavior]
was. We also realized that C. F. had had no close friends in his lifetime.
Seen up close, he was cold and calculating, but in public he was highly
successful at projecting a warm, caring, friendly image to a large group."

There in the hospital, father and son had what sounds like the first
real heart-to-heart talk of their lives. C. F. explained that the reason

he had been so consumed with the idea that Jack and his brothers were trying to cheat him out of the business was that he felt guilty over having done exactly that to his own father, the kindly and trusting Arthur P. Seabrook, by paying him only $24,000 for his share of the farm, when Charlie knew it was worth much more. Jack's diary notes, "On Tuesday, July 14 (Bastille Day), 1953, CFS explained to JMS that he had had a very guilty conscience for 42 years about this transaction and that in times of stress when he wasn't himself, such as the 1941–44 period or the 1952–53 period, this memory haunted him and colored his relationship with his own sons." And yet, he wasn't wrong to fear that his sons would, in the coming years, try to take the business away from him.

On their return to Seabrook, Nana wrote again:

> *Wednesday, July 15th*
> *Dear Charlie,*
> *Just a word to let you know that our flight home was*
> *very smooth and pleasant. Jerry seems to be a very good*
> *pilot. I don't think you need to worry about Jack. He said*
> *he thought our visit to you was the best thing that ever*
> *happened, and one of the luckiest trips we ever made.*
> *He felt better and I guess we all did, after the talks.*
> *Much Love — Norma*

Even Belford, who may not have spoken to C. F. since Margie's wedding, wrote his father a card, after receiving a letter from him.

> *21 July 53*
> *Dear Dad:*
> *I was delighted to receive your letter yesterday and am glad*
> *to know you are now feeling better although I am sorry*
> *further treatment is necessary.*
> *I am looking forward to seeing you when you return home.*

Harriet, the boys, and Margie, all join me in
sending regards.
Sincerely your son,
Belford

During his monthlong stay at the sanatorium, removed from drugs and alcohol, C. F.'s delusions subsided, and he became calmer and more rational. He returned to Seabrook later in the summer, chastened and remorseful. Jack wrote, "When he came home in October, he was very contrite about his behavior and did all he could to calm the bankers who had been so disturbed by the May 18 incident." That good behavior continued through the November 5, 1953, board meeting, where Jack was formally reinstated. "I was elected first vice-president, a new title with the same duties as executive vice-president, but designed to save face for C. F." It was agreed Jack would be elected president at the next board meeting, on June 2, 1954.

My newlywed parents, on the right,
yachting in Miami with friends, 1957.

ACT V

THE PRINCE AND
THE REPORTER,
1954–1959

May 10, 1956

Dear Mother,

Remember when you told me the reason I was still single was that I expected some man to ride up on a white horse, and that never happened? Well, you won't believe it, but I have met a man who drives four white horses. He must be really strange, because nobody does that sort of thing these days. But he is sort of attractive so some friends and I are going to visit his farm and see for ourselves. More later. I've got to buy something to wear to a farm.

PS. I forgot to tell you the weirdest part. He wears a tall grey top hat when he drives his horses. Don't worry about me, Mom. I'll be careful.

Love, E.A.

CHAPTER 24

HURRICANE HAZEL

O NE IN THREE AMERICAN FAMILY BUSINESSES SUR-
vive into the second generation, and only one in ten make it
to the third. Although the idea of a family behind a business, even an
imaginary family, is a time-honored marketing strategy, especially in
the food sector, the enterprises that endure past the second generation
almost always recruit outsiders to manage them, as is the case with
Walmart, Kroger, and Tyson Foods.

The psychologist Kenneth Kaye devoted his career to studying the
dynamics of American family businesses, and the reasons why they
fail. Kaye identified several causes, including toxic relations between
the founder's children and the hired workers; the founder's habit of
both overtrusting and undertrusting his offspring; confusion of love
and money; the founder's inability to let go of power; and the self-
doubt that cripples the children when they finally do assume command. In a 1996 essay "When the Family Business Is a Sickness," Kaye
observed that in a surprisingly large number of family businesses in
the second generation or more, at least one member suffers from substance abuse. He muses on the similarities between addiction and the
all-consuming demands and rewards of a family-run enterprise. "Like
an addictive drug, the family business creates a 'high' with delusions of
grandeur and power, it creates a market for services that exploit those
delusions and thereby, unfortunately, feeds the addiction."

I corresponded with Kaye after my article about Seabrook Farms
appeared in *The New Yorker.* To him, asking how a family as dysfunctional as the Seabrooks could manage an extraordinarily functional

agricultural machine like Seabrook Farms is putting the question backward. He wrote, a "family-owned business can enable a dysfunctional family to maintain its dysfunction for decades, over generations," even after the business is gone, "resisting individuals' efforts to achieve healthier roles and relationships." He added, "Is the substance addiction a cause or a symptomatic result of family and business problems? In my experience, the business itself is usually that family's primary drug, and other dependencies follow."

❧

EARLY ON THE MORNING OF THURSDAY, OCTOBER 14, 1954, Sally Kirkland and her team from *Life*'s editorial department left New York for Seabrook to set up a day-long shoot about Seabrook Farms and the family. *Life* was doing a special issue celebrating American agricultural production and mid-century mass luxury, and Jack's lunches at 21 with Kirkland had paid off big-time. The magazine, then at the zenith of its cultural influence, had chosen Seabrook Farms, out of all the nation's food processors, to be one of the features in the issue. The staff photographer Yale Joel, known as "the photographer of the impossible" around *Life*, was assigned to shoot the piece.

The money shot in Joel's 4-page photo essay is a wide-angle portrait of the entire workforce, taken from a crane forty feet in the air, showing the Seabrooks standing together on an elevated platform, surrounded by five thousand workers grouped by departments, wearing uniforms and caps that designated them as plant or field workers, and in what role. Jack is in front of his father and brothers, clearly the leader, confidently astride the American Century, a dashing and commanding young man in an unbuttoned suit and a bow tie.

As the *Life* crew was packing up, Hurricane Hazel, a category 4 storm with winds measured over 140 miles an hour, was making landfall in North Carolina. It then took a rare inland turn toward the Northeast. The storm did not weaken as expected when it met a cold front over Pennsylvania; instead, Hazel got stronger. During the night of October 14, a gust at Battery Park in Manhattan was clocked in at 113 miles per hour—to this day the highest wind speed ever recorded in New York City. The hurricane went on to devastate southern Ontario and Toronto, where Hazel is still remembered as among the worst storms ever to hit that city.

The Seabrook Farms balance sheet was seasonally dependent. Large outlays of cash were necessary at the start of the growing season, for fertilizer, seed, and, most of all, labor. Periodic bridge loans, which were often needed to make payroll during these months, would be paid off as the crops were harvested, barring some unforeseen natural calamity. Late-year spinach—the third spinach crop of the year—was usually the harvest that tipped the balance sheet from red to black and provided much of the farm's annual profit. But fall spinach was vulnerable to both early nor'easters and the occasional tropical storm or hurricane that hit the Northeast.

Jack Seabrook was in Manhattan on the night of that historic gust. He had a company car and company driver and thought nothing of making the three-hour trip for an evening of partying at 21, El Morocco, Toots Shor's, and the Stork. The drive time was shortened considerably when the mother of all the state's toll roads, the New Jersey Turnpike, opened in 1951. The morning after the storm, Jack was supposed to take Carol, aged thirteen, and Lizanne, nine, to Idlewild Airport to catch an Air France flight to Mexico City. Anne had found a place for them to live there that was much more affordable than their life on Manhattan's Upper East Side; they could even have servants. The flight was delayed by the storm but took off that afternoon.

Jack then headed back into the city. He had planned a house party at the farm that weekend, and he saw no reason to cancel. His car stopped first at the apartment of his best friend, Louis Stoecklin, who was just getting up. Stoecklin, a handsome, urbane New Yorker with a George Hamilton tan, was a sales manager and brand ambassador for Seagram's. His job was to go out to nightclubs and order Bollinger, a Seagram's-owned champagne. Jack was a frequent wingman on these outings. Betsy von Furstenberg, a young heiress and actress known around town as La Von, rode with the pair as Jack drove back down the turnpike to see what was left of the farm.

Evidence of Hazel's destruction was everywhere. There were two big elms on the ground in Jack's backyard; the white picket fence around his house had blown down; and both the power and telephone were out. His father's house was also without power. Much worse was the brackish water that the storm surge had pushed in from the Delaware Bay, and that was now standing six inches deep in the spinach fields, temporarily changing them back to the shallow ocean floor that had been there in the Cretaceous Period. The water had obliterated the crop, and, with it, the company's annual profit. In addition, many of the farm's production facilities had been damaged, and the flimsiest of the workers' housing had been razed.

Saturday was the sort of gorgeous autumn day that often follows a hurricane. Jack was up early to survey the damage with C. F. and his brothers. The spinach crop was plainly ruined. The leaves had wilted and turned a greenish brown after their bath of brine. But one of the qualities the Seabrook men shared was a talent for carrying on as though everything was going splendidly, when in fact everything was falling apart. So they proceeded with their plans, which included a business luncheon at the Cherry Hill Inn and an afternoon at the Garden State Park Racetrack, which was owned by Eugene Mori, a director of Seabrook Farms. Jack had a deal whereby Mori paid him to drive his team of four Morgan horses around the racetrack to entertain the crowd between races. The following day, several more jet-setters showed up at the farm, including the model Janette Gage, in Belgian loafers, her escort, Dick Whitehall, and Gita Hall, a model and actress. Everyone rode atop Jack's horse-drawn carriage to the picnic ground. Thanks to Lou, the Bollinger flowed.

At the end of the weekend, Jack sent La Von and Lou back to the city in a Seabrook car, and then he got to work on saving the company.

⚜

IN OVERSEEING THE FARM'S FINANCES, C. F. relied on a small circle of outside advisers who had been with him going back to the 1920s, including Orlando, Dorsey, and a smooth-talking New York City accountant and professor of finance at Columbia University named Oscar Rogers Flynn. As vice president of finance, Flynn oversaw all the company's financial statements. He was, Jack noted, "extremely clever with figures."

But neither Belford nor Jack believed Flynn's fancy figures. Jack thought Flynn "was too glib, too quick with his explanations of discrepancies in his figures" to suit them. Flynn had valued the frozen product stored in the cavernous freezer-warehouse at more than $90 million today. The frozen lima beans and spinach were the only collateral that the banks had for their loans to the farm. The brothers had suspected that Flynn had vastly overvalued the product.

Once the banks realized the spinach crop was lost, auditors were dispatched to comb through the company's finances as well as its inventory. They discovered that Flynn, presumably acting on orders from the boss, had falsely reported operating profits. In fact, the company was losing money, and had wildly overvalued its surplus of frozen vegetables, figuring that the Arctic conditions inside the warehouse would discourage inspectors from checking. According to the audit the lender banks conducted after Hazel, Seabrook Farms was "close to being insolvent."

Several of the banks wanted to call in their loans immediately and force Seabrook Farms into bankruptcy. There was also talk of fraud. C. F., whose longtime practice had been to run the company as his personal piggy bank, was "badly frightened," according to my father, and "asked [Jack] to take complete charge and do whatever [he] could to prevent disaster." It required all of his financial acumen—he had some fancy figures of his own—as well as his Ivy League charm to prevent his banker friends from foreclosing right away. Reluctantly, they agreed to a three-person voting trust consisting of C. F., Jack, and Ben Sawin, the president of Provident Bank in Philadelphia, who represented the company's creditors; Sawin was another of Jack's WASP Hall of Famers whose portraits hung in his office. All major management decisions would require two-thirds approval from the three men, an arrangement that would pit my father and Sawin against C. F.

The voting trust would last for five years, at which time the three trustees could renew it for another five—but only by unanimous consent. There were various covenants and requirements, including that Flynn be terminated, that Jack make a full financial report in person to the banks monthly, and that the inventory be revalued realistically, which resulted in a pretax loss of $30 million in today's money. Jack would finally become president and chief executive officer of Seabrook Farms, a title he had long sought. The old man would be kicked upstairs. He could keep the title of chairman, and his $50,000 salary, for now, but he would withdraw from the management entirely, giving Jack free rein to implement essential changes. Jack would not allow his father to have an office in the administration building at Farm Central. He would find somewhere for him off-site.

Talks dragged on into late December, until finally, on Christmas Eve, 1954, the remaining banks agreed to the arrangement. That evening, the family convened for the annual Christmas Eve Bible reading and drinks party in the Seabrook mansion—one of those intimidating command performances. But C. F. was chastened. The patriarch gathered everyone together in the library and soberly announced his complete support for Jack as the new CEO. "He asked all the family to help me in any way they could," Jack wrote, adding that his father "seemed happy to have shifted the responsibility to me and actually pleased with the outcome." In a deposition taken in the matter of his father's estate, he remembered, "Mother was overjoyed. Belford started clapping, which was rather indelicate."

But after her husband went upstairs to bed, Nana took her three boys aside and cautioned them. She said that their father was still haunted by the way he had cheated his own father out of the true value of his half of the farm. She added that C. F. "seemed happy right now, but he could have another bad spell and view the voting trust as a way for 'the boys' to get control."

CHAPTER 25

THE INVITATION

THE *LIFE* PHOTO ESSAY ABOUT SEABROOK FARMS, headlined "Biggest Vegetable Factory on Earth," came out on January 3, 1955. The timing couldn't have been better. The story appeared the week after the banks had tentatively agreed to keep Seabrook Farms afloat. "I had worked for two years to get that story," my father wrote of this triumphant rendering of the brand story. "I had no idea it would have such a powerful influence on our customers at such a critical time. . . . In the days before television dominance, [*Life*] was the most potent form of publicity. . . . The story helped convince customers to stay with us, and we breathed easier."

General Foods was understandably outraged by the *Life* coverage. As the owners of the Birds Eye brand, and Seabrooks' former partner—now a competitor—General Foods was a major *Life* advertiser, often buying multiple four-color pages in an issue. Seabrook Farms received a 4-page editorial story that was far more effective as brand marketing than any paid advertising. Prior to publication, *Life* editors had kept the content of the story secret from the magazine's advertising staff, who might have tried to have the story killed.

Jack knew the piece was gold. The week after it appeared, he was elected CEO by the board. He and his team began a methodical review of every aspect of the company's operations. "It was obvious the plant and the bloated workforce were too big for our sales people," he wrote. He thought the workforce should be halved, ideally. He also ended new construction on the farm, shifted focus away from local expenditures, and expanded the company's growing and packing operations beyond New Jersey, to Florida and California. There was also the matter of C. F.'s salary, which the bankers now wanted Jack to eliminate, since his father wasn't contributing anything positive to the business. Jack, knowing how much this would upset their fragile relationship, resisted. Eventually, Belford agreed to give up his salary and take a leave of absence so that their father could stay on the payroll. C. F. was given an office at Koster Nursery, down the road from Farm Central. When C. F. asked for a desk from the company, he was turned down, the diary notes. It doesn't say why.

✺

ON SATURDAY NIGHT, FEBRUARY 11, 1956, C. F. and Jack were discussing business. His father had simply walked in as he was finishing dinner, a reminder that C. F. was the landlord and his son the tenant. Why did Jack continue to put up with this treatment, now that he was fully in charge? He would never win his father's approval, but he still wanted it. He had dumped Eva and cut back on his New York life. He had begun looking for a woman his father would approve of, with whom he could start a second family, and who wouldn't object to living with the Seabrooks in Deep South Jersey. You didn't meet those kinds of women in the Stork Club.

As they were talking, the phone rang. Jack's houseman came in to say that Mrs. Margaret Kelly was calling. Née Majer, Margaret was Jack Kelly's German-born wife, from whom their daughter Grace got her cheekbones and Teutonic coloring. Jack took the call in the kitchen, and after five minutes he returned to say he had been invited to "the Wedding"—Grace's upcoming marriage to Prince Rainier of Monaco, in mid-April, which was one of the biggest stories in the world. Mrs. Kelly had asked him if he would accompany Grace, the Kelly family, several bridesmaids, and some seventy of their Philadelphia friends on the SS *Constitution*, departing New York for Monte Carlo on April 4. Most guests were friends of Grace's parents, and a generation older than Jack. But there were the bridesmaids. And lots of press would be aboard: it would be a brand bonanza.

C. F. could have kicked up a fuss. After all, Grace's parents were closer to his age than Jack's. Were they excluding him because of his rough edges and lack of polish—his first-generation uncouthness? Or was he relieved to have the family represented at the "Marriage of the Century" without having to go himself, a trip for which he clearly did not have the strength or soundness of mind? The diary notes, ambiguously, "CFS seemed pleased at my going." That was as much as his successor could hope for.

CHAPTER 26

"DEAREST FAMILY"

E LIZABETH ANN TOOMEY WAS PROUD OF HER PIONEER
  ancestors. Her grandfather, Daniel Joseph Toomey, was an
Irish immigrant's son from Brooklyn who ran away from home as a
teenager, supposedly to escape an abusive priest. He ended up home-
steading a ranch in the Spearfish Valley, Dakota Territory, in 1877, at
the very end of the western frontier. He married the only schoolteacher
in the area, Vesta Noyes, and they had four sons and two daughters,
all spirited and sporty outdoor folk—hunters, golfers, and early avi-
ation enthusiasts. In 1911 Daniel Toomey purchased a flour mill and
produced "Toomey's Famous Flapjack Flour."

Beginning that same year, however, the Toomeys experienced what
"E. A.," as Elizabeth Ann was called, later described as "spectacular
sadness." First, D. J. Toomey's oldest son, Ed, shot himself at the top
of the steps of the mill and tumbled down dead at his father's feet.
They had quarreled about Ed's drinking—the family curse. In January 1918, D. J.'s daughter Maude went barnstorming with a visiting
aviator in Casper, Wyoming, and was killed when the plane nose-
dived into the ground; the pilot, a man named Cole, who was sitting
in the back seat, survived. (The newspaper account says, "One theory of the accident is that Miss Toomey, who wanted Cole to loop
the loop and do the tail spin, fainted when he was doing one of these
stunts and fell against one of the control levers.") Later that year,
Ralph, who was Vesta's favorite, was killed in one of the last big bat-
tles of World War I, on the day the Americans crossed the Hinden-
burg Line. D. J. and Vesta eventually moved to San Diego. Howard,

the youngest brother, ran the flour mill until he eventually succumbed to drink too, and the mill was sold.

E. A., born in Spearfish in 1922, was the younger of two daughters of Allen Toomey, the fourth brother, and Janet Cameron, a devout Southern Baptist from the Ozark town of Licking, Missouri. Isabel was the beautiful and talented one, everyone said. With her delicate, Pre-Raphaelite face, Isabel shone at the piano, and she sang with perfect pitch. "I didn't have to be outstanding as a child," E. A. wrote in a later autobiographical sketch. "My older sister was a genius. She also had naturally curly hair. Nobody paid much attention to me, which suited me just fine." But Isabel also suffered from what the doctors then called neurasthenia—anxiety.

In 1932, their father, Allen, was diagnosed with brain cancer at the Mayo Clinic in Minneapolis. The doctors informed Janet, who didn't tell her husband that he had brain cancer. But she did share the diagnosis with her young daughters. "For some reason difficult to understand," E. A. wrote, "the two young sisters were told about their father's condition when he returned from the Mayo clinic." In 1935, when she was thirteen, E. A. came down with rheumatic fever. She lay for months on her back staring at the pink wallpaper in her bedroom while a friend of her mother's sat with her and read aloud from the Bible. She eventually got better but was unable to play sports; her mother even forbade dancing and made her rest for an hour every afternoon. She recovered in time to bury her father, who died in 1936.

After Allen's death, Janet sunk into a long-lasting depression and clung to her daughters for support, especially E. A., the cheerful sister who never complained. In 1938 Janet rented out the family home in Spearfish and the three of them moved to Columbia, Missouri, with whatever they could pack into their Oldsmobile. Janet thought Isabel might like to go to the University of Missouri School of Journalism. They all lived in a one-bedroom apartment in Columbia. E. A. kept up a correspondence with her Spearfish sweetheart, a nice boy named Ralph Kamman, who addressed her as "Glamour Girl" and clearly wanted to marry her.

Janet took a job as a live-in dorm chaperone at Christian College, which allowed E. A. to attend the two-year college for free. She excelled in school, won first and second place in a college literary competition, and was the class valedictorian and president of the choir. As was her way, E. A. took no credit for these achievements. Isabel, who had spent one year at journalism school and dropped out to elope with a man named Duffy from New Orleans, was and always would be the star.

Ralph Kamman enlisted right after Pearl Harbor. He was stationed in San Francisco for training. In October 1942 he wrote to his girl that he was being shipped out to some place called Guadalcanal, where the fighting was supposed to be "pretty hot." He arrived in late October and wrote to say he would be seeing action soon. He signed off:

> Be good and take care of yourself, beautiful.
> Always, Ralph.
> P.S. Write and say a few prayers for me.

The news of Ralph's death, two days later, arrived before his letter.

❧

IN 1944, E. A. graduated from the Missouri Journalism School with a major in radio journalism. Her first job was as a wire editor with A.P. in Kansas City, a role that men normally filled in peacetime. The old-timers weren't friendly. She learned to prove a baseball box score and to edit the livestock report, working in the din of the teletype machines on the third floor of the *Kansas City Star* building. "To speak to a fellow worker," she wrote, "you had to walk close and shout."

In May 1947, E. A. moved to Washington, D.C., in search of a journalism job. She wrote Janet and Isabel as many as two or three letters a week. Because they were in different locations—her mother in Columbia, Isabel in New Orleans—she wrote to both as "Dearest Family," and typed the letters onto a sheet of carbon paper, with a blank page underneath, then a carbon and another blank sheet, so that she could send a copy to both, and keep the original.

E. A. had an introduction to a Missouri congressman, who was the father of a Kappa Alpha Theta sorority sister, and she got a job writing speeches for him. After two months, she was hired by the United Press's radio division.

"I knew I wanted to write features," she wrote, "but I had to get a foot in the door before my employer knew it."

"Liz," as E. A. was known to her colleagues, made a splash with a Sadie Hawkins Day story. In January 1948, she went to Capitol Hill to ask a bachelor congressman to marry her. She first asked Wisconsin Senator Joseph McCarthy, who was thirty-nine. "McCarthy took out his handkerchief and blew his nose," she wrote in a letter home. "Then with a kind of sickly chuckle he rose to the occasion with, 'Well, that might not be such a bad idea.'" More charming was thirty-year-old John F. Kennedy, a representative from Massachusetts. E. A. wrote, "He's as cute as he can be, and it's a shame I couldn't see him more often." Kennedy declined to comment for the record. "He said he had enough trouble trying to make the people back in Boston think he was a dignified legislator without talking about girls."

Liz Toomey soon caught the attention of the bosses in New York. She was given a job as a writer in U.P.'s main office, in the Daily News building on East Forty-Second Street. U.P. was trying to compete with the older and more established A.P. by running more feature and human-interest stories aimed at women. That would be Toomey's beat.

Her new boss, Bob Serling, whose brother Rod was the creator of *The Twilight Zone*, called attention to their new team member's charm and work ethic in a slightly leering 1948 internal memo.

All of us—especially feature writers—could learn a lot from watching Toomey at work. On features or after hours. Other writers would do well to follow her easy, informal style—"as friendly as a pat on the fanny" as one client, who knows her well, wrote in . . . Liz herself (she's Liz to her friends, Elizabeth Ann to her mother, a long low whistle to strangers) gives no particular reasons for her comet-like success. She modestly ascribes her climb to intelligence, cleverness, originality, beauty, and a style that's the closest thing to Shakespeare since his mother died.

As one of the few female United Press writers, Liz had to contend with everyday sexism in the office, such as this misogynistic style guide of U.P. adjectives for describing women:

> *attractive—a pig*
> *striking—a pig with big eyes*
> *comely—an average broad*
> *pretty—not worth a second look*
> *handsome—an Amazon*
> *buxom—fat with thin legs*
> *shapely—so-so*
> *stunning—does as much as possible with what she's got*
> *beautiful—acceptable in first row of a chorus*
> *gorgeous—worth a second look*
> *vivacious—nervous and talks too much*
> *exotic—a screwball*
> *alluring—has money, will travel*

Liz first lived in the Barbizon, the storied residential hotel for single women on the corner of East Sixty-Third and Lexington Avenue, until she and a colleague, Gay Pauley, found a place at 261 East Sixty-First Street, near the Third Avenue elevated train, which Liz rode every morning to work. U.P. promoted its new feature writer in print ads that showed the twenty-six-year-old standing outside the office, chatting with a cabbie, with the platform of the El in the background. The copy describes her as a "journalistic Geiger counter" who "writes her stuff straight." She kept the ad. She also saved Walter Winchell's column in which he wolf-whistled at the "doll-like" Liz Toomey, "the prettiest newspaper reporter in town."

In 1952, U.P. gave Elizabeth Toomey her own column, called "Women's View." She appeared five times a week in the *New York World-Telegram* and was syndicated in the hundreds of other large and small newspapers around the country that paid for the wire service. She explained her beat in a speech at the Missouri School of Journalism, where, only seven years out, she was now a distinguished alum and a role model for young women going into journalism. "My particular assignment is to cover things from a woman's angle. It may be an interview with a psychiatrist on some family problem . . . or a series of stories on a lady detective in the narcotics division of the police department."

There was also a steady diet of celebrity stories. She profiled Karl Malden when Elia Kazan's *On the Waterfront* was a hit in 1954. The following year she went to Paris to interview Christian Dior, who used the columnist's gams to demonstrate where the hemline should fall in his New Look. Marilyn Monroe was the subject of two "Women's View" columns, both based on interviews in New York, where the actress spent most of 1955 studying at the Actors Studio and falling for Arthur Miller. One evening, Liz accompanied Marilyn to a press event announcing her production company, held at the home of her partner in the venture, the photographer Milton Glaser. A U.P. photo of the event shows the fabulous movie star at her peak—it was the same year she filmed the subway grate scene in *The Seven-Year-Itch*. Next to her, trying to get his escort through the press crush, is Milton Glaser, elegant in French cuffs. And in the back, holding her notes for tomorrow's story, with her pen up so that she doesn't stick the tip into the starlet's ear if she gets jostled, is Spearfish's Glamour Girl.

"It isn't all so glamorous as it looks from the outside," Liz said in her talk at the journalism school. "But I have to admit that I wouldn't give up my job without a struggle."

So the granddaughter of Daniel Toomey, who had run away from Brooklyn eighty years earlier for the western frontier, wound up back East, at the frontier of modern media culture—a transactional world of movie stars, debutantes, business tycoons, sports figures, fashionistas, and the famous-for-being-famous. She learned how to operate in this demimonde without compromising her prairie-girl wholesomeness. She had boyfriends, but no one serious. In D.C., she had dated the Colonel, an older man. There was another fellow in Virginia, but she found his friends snobbish. A literary type in public relations in

New York who she did like had a nervous breakdown. Another guy took her out on a yacht on the Long Island Sound for a weekend, but a storm sunk the boat. Luckily, a Yale oarsman was on board, and he kept the lifeboat pointed into the wind for seven hours and eventually rowed them to the shore.

As Liz's career took off, the prospects of a husband and family dwindled. She met a lot of men, but they were hardly the type she could bring home to her mother, Janet. You didn't meet those kinds of men in the Stork Club.

⚜

THE BIGGEST SCOOP OF HER CAREER would ironically bring about the end of it. It came on a Wednesday afternoon, December 28, 1955. Liz was working on a story about the world's best-dressed women and trying to get a quote from Grace Kelly, who was tied for first place. Hitchcock's *To Catch a Thief*, starring Grace and Cary Grant, was still in theaters. It was while filming on the French Riviera that Grace had met Rainier III, ruler of the small European principality of Monaco.

Sometime after lunch, Liz got permission to call the actress. "By the time I telephoned her I had heard the rumor that she might marry the Prince of Monaco," she wrote in a Dearest Family letter a few days later. "I figured it was a ridiculous rumor, but thought I'd just check it with her while I had her on the phone." But to her amazement, Grace didn't deny it. Instead, she said only, "I can't say anything about that at this time."

"I explained that that sounded as if it could be true and I didn't want to misquote her, so wouldn't she like to deny it?" Grace repeated her statement.

On hanging up, Liz ran to tell her editor. Another writer was assigned to do a brief story saying that Grace didn't deny the rumor, for the Wednesday afternoon papers. That night Liz stayed late and wrote a longer story to run early the next morning. Later, on the morning of December 29, a bulletin came from Monte Carlo confirming the rumor. Liz was moved to the day desk and took over the day and night side writing of her scorching-hot dish.

When U.P. later ran a picture of their star feature writer interviewing Grace, a colleague sent her a note: "Liz, from what I see, the Prince married the second best."

✌︎☜

HAVING BROKEN THE STORY, Liz had earned a berth on the SS *Constitution* with the members of the press accompanying the Kellys and their friends from New York to Monaco. Her byline would compete with that of the columnist Art Buchwald, the actress Gloria Swanson (who was covering the event for television), and the *Chicago Tribune*'s Gwen Morgan, among many other well-known correspondents. British and European papers were also sending top talent to cover the weeklong event in Monte Carlo. The Marriage of the Century knocked the Suez Canal Crisis off the front pages. Thirty million viewers would watch the ceremony, to which MGM had secured the rights in return for letting Grace out of her studio contract. The studio's Oscar-winning costume designer, Helen Rose, was commissioned to make the royal wedding dress.

At 9:50 a.m. on Wednesday, April 4, 1956, Liz arrived at the West Side pier where the SS *Constitution* was scheduled to depart at noon. "So many times I go to piers to board ships for press conferences," she wrote to her family, "and as I walked toward the ship I could hardly believe I really was going to be a passenger." She had with her one big suitcase, a suit bag for evening dresses, a makeup case, a typewriter, and a Super 8 movie camera that the New York office had given her for taking moving pictures.

Guests were having champagne parties in their staterooms, while the press scrummed for position out on deck. At the 10:00 a.m. press conference, Grace wore a beige tweed suit with white gloves and a small white hat. A scuffle broke out as members of the press pushed and shoved for better views. In the newsreels, Grace looks terrified. Finally, all the uninvited press and the well-wishers departed and the last "Bon voyage!" was shouted into the mist as the ship slid away from the pier and headed for the sea. Liz wrote, "We stood on the sun deck just a little way down from the Kellys and threw paper streamers and waved. It was quite exciting, though the day was so foggy you couldn't see anything."

CHAPTER 27

THE PRINCE AND
THE REPORTER

FOLLOWING THE FEBRUARY 11 PHONE CALL FROM MRS.
Kelly, Monsieur J Seabrook booked a hotel in Monte Carlo—a
double room with a private bath at the Hermitage. Naturally, he
required proper clothes for a royal wedding, a matter about which he
knew as much as any protocol officer in the royal palace. In Monte
Carlo, there would be rich and powerful wedding guests to cultivate,
including Lord Beaverbrook, who had a nearby villa in the South of
France, and Aristotle Onassis, who mostly lived on his superyacht, the
Christina, in the Monte Carlo harbor. Among the invited guests were
Cary Grant, Ava Gardner, and the Aga Khan.

To pay for his trip, Seabrook Farms customers were asked to chip in
a few pennies per package of frozen vegetables, which were marketed
that spring under a "Send Jack Seabrook to Monaco" campaign. The
family and the brand were becoming ever more entwined. Jack also
managed to get Seabrook's advertising agency, Ayers, to fund a magnificent wedding gift—a $10,000 movie projector, to be installed in a
special screening room in the Palace.

On the morning the ship sailed from New York, Jack played host in
his stateroom to a cocktail party featuring magnums of 1947 Bollinger
that Courtney had delivered on board. Marshall Goldberg, Seabrook
Farms' Midwest wholesale broker, sent a case of Alexis Lachine Cha-
blis that became a favorite wine of Grace's during the crossing. Jack
appointed himself sommelier to the wedding party; cases of French
wine and champagne were piled up inside and outside his stateroom

throughout the voyage. He knew all about the right wines and the proper order in which to drink them and explained everything to the provincial but willing Philadelphians.

The journalists and photographers traveled first class, the same as the guests. Liz shared a stateroom with two women of the press. One was the Associated Press correspondent Cynthia Lowry, her main competitor; they had agreed to share all the information they gathered shipboard. The other was Jinx Falkenburg, a former tennis champion and pinup girl, who had been the first "Miss Rheingold" pin-up girl for the New York–based beer brand. Her morning talk radio show, "Hi, Jinx," began airing on NBC's New York flagship station WEAF in 1946.

Although the press went along with the marriage-as-a-love-match narrative in their dispatches, the general feeling among the reporters on the ship, Liz confided to her family, was that the wedding was a cynical arrangement. Monaco was a rundown principality that subsisted mostly on gambling and, thanks to Prince Rainier's efforts, served as a haven for tax exiles who couldn't afford to live in their own countries. The scuttlebutt was that Aristotle Onassis, who had extensive real estate holdings in Monaco, including the casino, had arranged the marriage to bolster the value of his investments. The prince, so this theory went, was the Greek shipping magnate's puppet. If Rainier failed to marry and produce a male heir, Monaco would revert to France, and Onassis would lose his tax shelter.

Liz was instructed to call the office from the ship's telephone at 10:00 a.m. and 4:30 p.m. East Coast time, every day, and to cable a story of two hundred words each night. Early in the trip, Liz, Jinx, and Cynthia got to interview Grace. During the photo session on the deck with the wedding party, Liz snapped pictures of Grace and her friends and family and tried to figure out how use the Super 8 camera U.P. had supplied. After that early interview, Grace was off-limits to reporters, but her father, Jack, basked in the attention of the shipboard press, playing ringmaster to the floating publicity circus. He had plenty of time for the pretty "colleen" Liz Toomey.

AFTER THE ACTUAL MOVIE STAR, Jack Seabrook and Liz Toomey were the most attractive people on the ship. They finally met on the second night out, at a cocktail party thrown by Mr. and Mrs. Matthew McCloskey in the ship's first-class lounge, the Tattoo Room. McCloskey was an Irish American who, like Jack Kelly, had used success in the contracting business to go into Philadelphia politics as a Democrat. McCloskey led Liz over to Jack and introduced them. As Liz was shaking Jack's right hand, she noticed that his left was holding the hand of one of Grace's bridesmaids.

They saw each other a couple of times during the crossing, but Liz was only interested in Jack Seabrook as a potential source, at this point. She was suspicious of what seemed to be his romantic interest in her. A French newspaper story about the wedding party had described Jack Seabrook as a *riche fermier, celebre bourreau des coeurs*—a "rich farmer, celebrated breaker of hearts." She kept her distance.

On the morning of April 12, the *Constitution* arrived in the harbor at Monte Carlo. The Prince came out to fetch Grace on the royal yacht, *Deo Juvante*. Grace wore an enormous white organdy hat and dark glasses, which the press hated because no one could see her face. E. A. described the scene to her family: "Rainier strode out to the gangplank to help her aboard, and he reached out his arms as if to kiss her. But Oliver the poodle apparently came between them and the prince instead gave Grace something like an awkward handshake."

After that, Liz caught a ride on the back of a passing motor scooter to the foot of the palace hill, where police had stopped all traffic. From there she alternately walked and ran up the winding roadway to find the U.P. bureau, set up for the wedding coverage in a croupier's apartment overlooking the palace courtyard.

"Sit down and give us some color on the harbor scene," the bureau chief Gene Patterson ordered as she staggered in the door, sweating and breathless. Back in New York, they were sending "Now pls" messages, which was Unipresser shorthand for "Where's the story already?"

꿏꿏

BEING TRADITIONAL IF TIN-POT ROYALS, the Grimaldis detested publicity. Having agreed to let MGM film the wedding, the prince and his family felt they had fulfilled their obligation to public curiosity and arranged virtually no events in Monaco for the press during the nine days leading up to the wedding ceremony. Reporters resorted to interviewing one another.

Might Jack Seabrook be a source of news? So far Liz had kept him at a distance, although he had been permitted to get her a nicer room at his hotel, the Hermitage. She took it for granted that a millionaire playboy like him was out of her league. She had read about his exploits in the columns: his romance with Eva Gabor, and more recently, with Ann Miller, who was starring on Broadway with Mickey Rooney in *Sugar Babies*, and with Doris Lilly, a young woman whose columns, later collected in *How to Marry a Millionaire*, were the *Sex in the City* of its day. How *Not* to Marry a Millionaire was more like Liz's approach.

On Saturday, two days after they arrived, Liz agreed to lunch with Jack in the Hermitage's restaurant. In her Dearest Family letter, she writes, "As I sat sipping wine in the excellent French restaurant, I was uneasily aware that this was not the place to look for the latest developments. If I got [a] 'now pls?' message for getting beaten that day, I could never explain it." Just then, Matthew McCloskey, the Philadelphia contractor, stopped at their table and leaned over to whisper, "My wife had her jewels stolen last night." Liz laughed. The story of a real-life Riviera jewel robbery, when *To Catch a Thief* was still doing business in theaters, was too good to be true. McCloskey insisted he was serious. "If you won't mention it to those other reporters," he said, "I'll take you over to my hotel room and you can see for yourself. My wife is there now describing the jewels to the police."

"I gave my companion a stunned look," Liz wrote, and "assured

McCloskey with a straight face that I'd be the last one to mention it to another reporter, and walked with him to the Hotel de Paris." Mrs. McCloskey was sitting in the old-fashioned, high-ceilinged hotel room describing the missing jewels in her $50,000 collection to the police. The nervous hotel manager was translating her descriptions to the French-speaking policeman.

"I slid quietly into a chair and began taking notes. The timing was perfect. It was close to 4pm in Monaco, six hours earlier in New York, which meant I could make all the Saturday afternoon editions." For several minutes nobody paid any attention to her. Then the hotel manager paled and asked suddenly, "You're not a reporter, are you? The prince has ordered no publicity on this. I'll lose my job and so will the policeman." McCloskey said smoothly, "She is my secretary." Everybody relaxed.

After Mrs. McCloskey finished her account, Liz went down to the lobby and dictated the story over the phone to Gene Patterson. "You're kidding!" he yelled; he thought it was a gag. Less than an hour after McCloskey's whispered words in the restaurant, the story was on its way to New York. It created a sensation, and it remained an Elizabeth Toomey scoop for two days. McCloskey kept answering "No comment" to the hundreds of other reporters, and the police department denied everything.

"All I had hoped for was an exclusive story for the Saturday afternoon papers," Liz wrote. "But my exclusive lasted into the next day, one of the most delightful 24-hour periods I ever spent." It's especially delightful when one thinks of all the high-caliber male journalists such as Donald Edgar of Lord Beaverbrook's *Daily Express*, who had been made to go to Monaco against his will to cover what he regarded as an event best left to society columnists. And when the cat burglar struck again later that week, Toomey scored her second big scoop. She wrote, "The victim of the latest robbery was Mrs. Maree Pamp, Philadelphia, who reported all her jewels taken this afternoon from her room in the expensive Hôtel de Paris." Grace and the Palace were furious—at the press in general, and at Elizabeth Toomey in particular. The word went out that there would be no more contact with reporters until the wedding, still four days off.

༄

ON MONDAY, APRIL 16, 1956, Jack Seabrook turned thirty-nine. He had a birthday lunch in Monte Carlo that included the syndicated columnists Inez Robb and Liz Toomey. That evening he went to Lord Beaverbrook's villa, La Capponcina, in Cap d'Ail, where he finally got to meet the Beaver, then seventy-seven, the Anglo-Canadian newspaper baron whose villa in Jamaica Jack had driven past and gazed up at many times, and whose granddaughter, Lady Jeanne Campbell, he had dated in New York.

Among Beaverbrook's guests that evening were Onassis and Randolph Churchill, the famously querulous, lecherous, and dipsomaniacal son of Winston, who wrote a political column for the *Evening Standard*. Evelyn Waugh later said of him, after doctors found a benign tumor on Churchill's lung, "It was a typical triumph of modern science to find the one part of Randolph which was not malignant and to remove it." Beaverbrook's *Daily Express* had once written, in an obvious reference to the Churchills, *pere et fils*, that "major fathers as a rule breed minor sons." C. F. wholeheartedly embraced this adage, perhaps because his youngest son clearly disproved the rule. My father loved to quote it too.

During dinner, the subject of the proper clothes to wear to the 11:00 a.m. Thursday cathedral wedding came up. Churchill maintained that the only correct outfit was a gray cutaway "morning coat," such as the British royals and swells wear to Ascot, with striped trousers—and most certainly *not* the white tie and black tails that Rainier and the French contingent were planning to wear, which were evening clothes and an abomination to wear in the morning. Churchill "shrieked and screamed," according to my father, that the Kelly family and the other Americans were following the French in wearing white tie and black tails. "Even though Americans are a bad lot in general they couldn't let the Anglo-Saxon race down by wearing white tie like common Frenchmen," Jack quoted Churchill as saying. Upon hearing he planned to wear his own cutaway morning coat, with striped trousers, Churchill declared Seabrook was "one of us."

The guests debated the finer points of dress for hours, to Jack's delight. Churchill declared that if a man is under forty, he need not wear gray gloves, but if he is over forty "he must wear them." Beaverbrook observed that since Seabrook was thirty-nine that day, he did not have to wear gray gloves, but since he would now undoubtably have to sit up all night drinking with Churchill in the casino, he had better equip himself with a pair because "I would look a good deal older by Thursday."

Back in Monte Carlo, Jack shared his account of the evening with Art Buchwald, who produced a column about the controversy, "White Tie vs. Striped Pants," in the *Herald Tribune* two days later.

One of the most serious controversies in the history of twentieth-century diplomacy has broken out in the open over what is the proper attire to wear to the Prince Rainier III–Grace Kelly wedding. It all started at a dinner party for the press given by Lord Beaverbrook at his villa outside Monaco.

As his source Buchwald cites "Jack Seabrook, the frozen-food lima bean king from New Jersey, who was also at Lord Beaverbrook's party."

JACK SLEPT THROUGH Wednesday morning's civil ceremony, but did not miss the party on Onassis's yacht that evening, at which a five-piece band led by a recent Princeton graduate, Stan Rubin, played Dixieland jazz, and everyone danced, including Jack and Liz. Onassis was persuaded to fly the Princeton flag along with the flags of Monaco and Argentina, where he was a citizen.

The cathedral wedding was the next day. The bride wore 320 yards of lace, 25 yards of peau de soie, 25 yards of silk taffeta, and 100 yards of silk tulle. Somerset Maugham, Lady Diana Cooper, and

Conrad Hilton attended—Hilton represented President Eisenhower. Buchwald, who had wrangled an invitation by writing a hilarious column about the four-hundred-year-old feud between the Grimaldis and the Buchwalds, was seated directly behind the Aga Khan, who brought his girlfriend Magda—the oldest Gabor sister.

At the garden party afterward in the Palace courtyard, the six hundred guests dined on caviar, smoked salmon, shrimp, ham, salami, soup, jellied eggs, salmon with cucumber salad, and cold lobster, among other delicacies, and drank oceans of champagne. The prince and the new princess used Rainier's sword to cut the cake, pieces of which were packaged in white boxes tied with golden twine. Liz described the scene in a Dearest Family letter. "I saw Jack Seabrook carefully wrap two pieces of wedding cake in napkins, take off his top hat, put the cake in the hat and then put the hat back on his head. He said he wanted to send it to his daughters. The whole scene was so unreal that somehow the cake in the top hat fitted right in."

CHAPTER 28

MARRIAGE OF
THE CENTURY

A FTER THE GARDEN PARTY, THE ROYAL COUPLE LEFT
for a cruise on the *Deo Juvante*. (Grace was ill and spent the
first week of her honeymoon sick in bed.) Liz, her assignment completed, went on a sight-seeing trip around France and Switzerland with
Cynthia Lowry of A.P. Jack traveled to London to advance his knowledge of four-in-hand coaching.

Liz was certain that she'd never hear from the *bourreau des coeurs*
again. In fact, Jack seems to have already made up his mind that he
was going marry Liz Toomey. She was beautiful, smart, funny, and
talented. Crucially, her agreeable, uncomplaining nature and frontier
spirit would make her adjustment to life in Seabrook, New Jersey, easier than the first Mrs. John M. Seabrook's had been.

When they both were back in the U.S. again, in early May, Jack
began his campaign by inviting his Monaco companion for a "coaching weekend" in the country—standard operating procedure when he
was wooing. Liz agreed, thinking there might be a "Women's View"
column in it—the top hat, the four horses, and the lima bean prince
would make great copy, if she could only figure out the angle. She
brought along two gal pals as chaperones. On the coach, Liz and her
girlfriends were bareheaded, a gross violation of coaching etiquette,
which dictates that ladies must always wear hats. Jack, as the driver,
wore a gray top hat. (That was possibly the point of the exercise.)
In a photograph taken of the party atop the coach, he also wears a
pained expression.

May 18, 1956
Dear Mother,
We lived through a ride on top of a black and red coach
pulled by four white horses! Talk about once in a lifetime!
I never expect to do that again. What a dumb way to
spend your money!

I got a raise last week, and I'm treating myself to a new
hat. Jack says women always wear hats on a carriage.
Your loving (and still single) daughter,
Elizabeth

Liz was back on the farm over Memorial Day weekend, unchaperoned. Jack took her for a moonlit drive with two horses.

June 1, 1956
Dear Mother,
That moonlight carriage ride sounded romantic, but
wait till you hear. We just started out with two horses
and a small carriage. I was wearing my new pale tan
pongee shirt dress. Jack had just poured us each a glass of
champagne and started off down one of the pretty lanes
through the vegetable fields and phhhhhttt! The horse I
was sitting right behind had apparently eaten too much
grass and you-know-what sprayed right over me.

Presumably her suitor was also hit, but even if you spattered him with liquid horse shit, Jack Seabrook still had style.

Liz returned again to the farm for a riotous July Fourth picnic, which included a lot of drinking with Jack's friends, who were a mix of Princeton pals, local gentry, and his wingman, Lou Stoecklin. That night at the pool Jack's brothers set off fireworks in trash cans, which Jack explained was a family ritual going back to the 1930s. After the Fourth, the couple drove to Dorset, Vermont, for the weekend. The receipt, which Jack kept, is for a single room.

On another occasion, they went to a hunt ball in North Jersey and stayed with a Princeton classmate of Jack's. Their host had a party trick he pulled out after an evening of drinking. He put a waste-paper bin on each foot and his Princeton football helmet on his head and pretended to fall down the stairs while everyone screamed with laughter. Liz, a teetotaler's daughter with a family history of alcohol-ism, laughed along, but she didn't approve. Fortunately, unlike his friends, Jack seemed to have the self-discipline to regulate his intake. He became a little redder in the face, and a little merrier, but he was always in control. His capacity was never in question.

❧

ON ONE OF THESE VISITS, Jack introduced Liz to his father. He had already told her about their fraught relationship and C. F.'s erratic behavior in recent years, and how his father was hindering his ambi-tions for the company. "His father really is a mean man," Liz wrote home. "In fact, he seems to me to be a pretty distorted personality. Both Jack and his brothers think so too. It's a miracle they all grew up as healthy and happy as they did. It is a great credit to his mother."

The couple were together in New York on July 26, 1956, when the news broke that the Italian ocean liner *Andrea Doria* had collided with another ship, the *Stockholm*, and sunk in the middle of the Atlantic. Jack accompanied Liz to the U.P. office and observed her on deadline. He never forgot how she worked the phones to get information about the notables on board. "She could get anything with a telephone," he would later say with wonder.

Jack's first marriage proposal, made at 21 a few nights later, was not accepted, a fact not recorded in the diary. Why had Liz refused her prince? In the first place, the romance was very sudden. Even Grace and Rainier had courted for a year. Jack was in a great hurry because he wanted to have more children, and Liz would be thirty-four that June. Producing a male heir would surely please his father, because it would guarantee the continuance of the Seabrook dynasty.

To become Mrs. John M. Seabrook, Liz Toomey would have to

give up her independence—a rare thing for a woman to have in 1956. But maintaining that independence required filing a column four or five times a week, a constant source of stress. Plus, her mother needed money, and Isabel's family was also having financial difficulty; her sister now had two children, Adrienne and Bill Duffy, and she was pregnant with the third, Stuart. By marrying Jack Seabrook, maybe Liz could ease her family's troubles. Although she had no idea what Jack Seabrook was actually worth. He had nice things, but what belonged to him and what belonged to the company wasn't clear. She observed that, for the Seabrooks, being rich meant not so much having money as not needing to spend money on things ordinary people paid for. The company took care of almost everything.

Liz presumably knew what was expected of Seabrook women. It wasn't just hostessing and mothering; the Seabrook consorts were essential to keeping the men from tearing each other apart. They were the Chief Emotional Officers of the family. A Seabrook woman had to be strong enough to deal with the things that the men didn't discuss in the office, because they weren't business. For friendships Liz would know no one in Deep South Jersey except the other Seabrook women. And there was a lot of drinking, never Liz's thing.

She confided her fears about marriage in a letter to Isabel. "She is very much in love with Jack," Isabel wrote to their mother, "and she seems certain he is just as much in love with her. Her problem is this: she said that during the last 10 or 12 years she had built up a strong fear of being hurt if she were to marry." Isabel quotes from her baby sister's letter to her (which wasn't among her papers): "'If something happens and we don't get married, then I know it will not be because Jack wasn't sincere in his feeling for me, but because of my own lack of confidence in myself.'"

Janet Toomey hadn't met her daughter's beau yet, but she was already suspicious of him. Why would a man who could have any woman in the world choose the second-best sister from Spearfish, South Dakota? How many other women did he have? Also, Jack Seabrook came with significant baggage. He was the divorced father of two. His former wife was suing him for more child support, a bitter contest in which Carol and Lizanne were being used as pawns. He was in a toxic business relationship with his father, on which the entire company and its thousands of employees depended. In becoming Mrs. John M. Seabrook, Liz would find herself in the middle of all this.

Nevertheless, the second time Jack proposed, in the powder-blue Thunderbird convertible that he had bought earlier that year, Liz accepted. Janet's reaction to the news was not, "I'm so happy for you!" or "Hallelujah, our money troubles are over!" It was, "Why would he pick you?"

❧

JACK HAD BETTY GAUNT draw up a social schedule for his bride-to-be.

Sunday Sept 23 J. K. Robinson's Westchester PA Coaching Party

James (Jimmy) Robinson was an heir of the Wanamaker department store family from Philadelphia.

Thursday Sept 27 Evening reserved for a function in NY

As consort to the new spinach king, Liz's presence at Jack's side would be required at various frozen-food industry trade functions.

Friday Sept 28 Dinner at JT Dorrance in Gladwyne PA and benefit performance of "The Happiest Millionaire"

Jack Dorrance was the son of the founder of Campbell Soup, who had attended Princeton around the same time as Jack. Like Jimmy Robinson, he was very rich.

Although Liz Toomey had rubbed shoulders with the most famous people in the world in the course of her work, she was nervous about socializing with these Main Line Philadelphia aristocrats. Even before becoming engaged to Jack, Liz worried about not having the right clothes to wear to smart events. In her letters, she described the outfit she had worn to this or that event, asking her mother and sister for reassurance. Now she was marrying a man who had the right clothes for everything. At social events with wealthy Philadelphians, Liz remained in reporter mode, peppering people with questions about what they did, bemusing those who didn't do much of anything at all. Charming girl! And to think Jack found her on the ship!

Never one to waste time, Jack pushed for an early wedding. They settled on the first Saturday in October. Liz filed her last column in late September. "On Friday I went to the office around 11am and visited with people," she wrote, "then went to lunch with some of the office gang. I must say I had no qualms about what I had left behind when I went back. All I could think of was how pleased I was I didn't have to sit down and write a story."

On September 26, Dorothy Kilgallen made the impending nuptials the lead item in her syndicated column, placing it above the news about Elizabeth Taylor and Mike Todd's budding romance.

GOSSIP in GOTHAM:

A Romantic postscript to the Grace Kelly-Prince Rainier wedding will be written October 6 when Jack Seabrook, heir to the frozen foods fortune, takes pretty journalist Liz Twomey [sic] as his bride. They met aboard ship en route to the marriage in Monaco; Jack was a member of the Kelly entourage, Liz covered the story for the UP. Their courtship flowered during the front-paged festivities in Monte Carlo.

Thanks to Kilgallen's column, Jack and Liz's love story took on a life of its own. They were sought-after dinner guests at parties in New York that fall, including one given by Mrs. Cornelius (C. Z.) Guest, one of Truman Capote's "Swans." The table listened rapt as Jack retold the story of meeting shipboard, the jewel heist, and the night on Ari Onassis's yacht when they danced to the Tigertown Five and Onassis flew the Princeton flag.

Liz couldn't help but notice how Jack would change certain details to make the story better. In his telling, at various points in the crossing Grace would say, "You should marry that girl," which certainly never actually happened. Ruthless honesty, which was one of Liz's core virtues, compelled her to fact-check him, mid-story. "Now Jack, you're exaggerating again," she'd say, delighting the other guests. Liz supposed it was a generous kind of fib, a way of adding to people's pleasure in the story. But it took her aback to see just how easily Jack could tell these white lies. What else might he be fibbing about?

☙

THE WEEKEND BEFORE THE WEDDING, Janet came East to meet Jack and the Seabrook clan. A formal Seabrook dinner party was held in Janet's honor, attended by fourteen Seabrooks, at C. F.'s house. It did not go well. Janet was already deeply insecure around the Seabrooks, who may as well have been the Rockefellers to her. She was a teetotaling, fiercely religious woman. To her, the Seabrooks' conspicuous consumption in general, and of liquor in particular, was sinful. It was excruciating to be the object of all this feasting and boozing, sitting before the gold-rimmed Lenox plates and the Seabrook monogrammed silverware, unsure of which fork to pick up. Janet just wanted to go back to "Missour-a" as she pronounced the name of the Show-Me state. She did not return East that Christmas, although Jack, at Liz's urging, wrote Janet a long handwritten letter asking her sweetly to come.

Liz also met Jack's children, Carol and Lizanne, now fourteen and ten. Carol warmed to her quickly, but Lizanne was a tougher nut. She was as difficult as Carol was agreeable. Liz felt sure she could win her over; it would just take time.

Jack's bachelor party, held in an upstairs room at 21, was attended by his brothers and Thelma's new husband, Bob Sidur, along with a mix of South Jersey, Philadelphia, and New York friends. Also present were Lou Stoecklin and Wally Foster, Jack's high school friend, who was best man. The movie star Joseph Cotten also came; Seabrook Farms had sponsored a serial radio drama called *The Private Case Files of Matthew Bell*, in which Cotten voiced the main part, and the actor and Jack had become pals in New York and Los Angeles.

The black-tie event featured a naked woman who was brought into the room lying on top of an old bathtub filled with ice and bottles of Bollinger champagne. The bathtub was actually a horse-watering trough that Jack's nephew Jim Seabrook, Belford's second son, had brought up from the farm. Had Janet Toomey heard about the girl in the bathtub, she would have called off the wedding immediately.

Gay Pauley, Liz's roommate, threw her a bridal shower. Gay would be moving out of their apartment, and Jack, who had previously crashed at Lou's place, would be taking over the lease. Bob Serling, Liz's former boss from the U.P., wrote her a wistful note.

> *October 4, 1956*
> *Dear Liz:*
> *Mr. John M. Seabrook is the luckiest male this side of*
> *the Mississippi River. I'd include west of the Mississippi*
> *except that Arthur Miller might object.*
>
> *It goes without saying all of us here wish you and yours*
> *the very best—and me more than anyone else, I suppose,*
> *because I always thought you were something special both*
> *as a newspaperwoman and a friend.*
> *Lots of luck and happiness, Liz gal, which you so richly*
> *deserve. Bob*

This letter breaks my heart. "I wouldn't give it up without a fight," Liz had said of her career. And yet, in the end, like so many women of her generation, she hadn't put up much of a fight at all. She had come so far from Spearfish, South Dakota, to her life in New York, where she lived by her talents and wits, courted by the famous and powerful who hoped to feature in her "Women's View" column. She was giving all that up—and for what?

The wedding, on the afternoon of October 6, 1956, was small—twenty people in all, almost all family and friends of Jack's. Liz would have liked a bigger wedding, but she wasn't about to let Jack pay for it, and she couldn't afford one herself. She had consented to let him provide the champagne. The ceremony was held in the Dana Chapel of St. James' Church on Madison Avenue, with a reception afterward in the Library Suite of the St. Regis Hotel, on Fifth Avenue and Fifty-Fifth Street. C. F. and Norma Dale both attended, as did Janet, but Isabel was not there. At the wedding the old man was on his best behavior. Jack had Reverend Bair flown in on the company plane from Maryland, where he'd had another engagement, so that he could get to the Dana Chapel by 5:00 p.m. Jim Flanagan, a Philadelphia pal of Jack's, walked my mother down the aisle. The *Columbia Missourian* reported that the bride wore "a street-length dress of periwinkle blue, *peau de soie* styled with surplice bodice and bouffant skirt," and she carried "a cascade bouquet of white roses and lilies of the valley."

CHAPTER 29

"MODERN FOOD DREAMS"

L IZ QUICKLY LEARNED THE IMPORTANCE OF LOOKING
the part. In the spring of 1958, *Holiday* magazine assigned
writer Roger Angell and photographer Slim Aarons to do a story titled
"The Effete East." Jack, who was pals with Aarons from Jamaica,
where some of the photographer's most evocative portraits of Babe
Paley and Slim Keith were made, persuaded him to come to Seabrook
and shoot him and his bride. The photograph is included in Aarons's
collection, *A Wonderful Time: An Intimate Portrait of the Good Life*,
a defining visual document of midcentury American glamour. In the
photo, the girl from the Black Hills of South Dakota looks as if she is
to the manor born, posing with the talented Mr. Seabrook in front of
their stately home, with horses and carriage and coachman, and Jack's
Dalmatian, Tamburlaine the Earthshaker, at their feet.

But while Jack Seabrook excelled at living the life of the country squire, in the office he was a dynamic young executive who was
plugged in to the beginnings of the *Mad Men* culture of the 1960s.
In 1957, he and Courtney brought in the marketing consultant Ernest
Dichter, the "Sigmund Freud of the Supermarket," to do a study of
Seabrook's products, packaging, and advertising. Dichter, an Aus-
trian immigrant with strong entrepreneurial skills, was the founder
of the Institute for Motivational Research, a consultancy and market
research group based in a twenty-six-room "castle" on a mountain
in Croton-on-Hudson. Dichter offered clients, which included General Mills, General Motors, and American Airlines, a window into
their customers' subconscious minds, through in-depth surveys con-

taining hundreds of questions derived from psychoanalytic theory. Dichter told General Mills to remove powdered eggs from its Bisquick cake mix and require the cake maker to "participate" by using real eggs, because women didn't want a "total product solution." He advised Procter & Gamble that people who bought soap were subconsciously seeking spiritual ablution; hence the tagline "Be smart, and get a fresh start with Ivory Soap." Dichter was especially attentive to links between sex and food. Cake baking was about fertility. Asparagus was obviously phallic, and its rapid rate of growth put Dichter in mind of tumescence. Women didn't buy lamb because it wasn't as virile as steak. Dichter gendered products, claiming, for example, that Wheaties was a masculine cereal, whereas Rice Krispies was a "bubbling, vivacious, young woman."

Dichter saw his mission as helping Americans overcome their puritanical guilt about indulgence. He viewed consumption as a form of self-expression and fulfillment. "If the desire for freedom and discovery can be expressed through the glamour of a new convertible," he said, "I willingly accept responsibility for combining these two strong human desires." Marketing's role was to give what Dichter called "moral permission" to indulge in the pleasure of buying. "After the privations of the Depression and the war," writes Barbara Ehrenreich, "Americans were supposed to enjoy themselves, held back from total abandon only by the need for Cold War vigilance."

It's not surprising that Jack Seabrook, a man who liked to enjoy himself and didn't have a puritanical attitude about sex, would be drawn to Dichter. They met at the height of Dichter's fame, which coincided with peak Freud in American culture. Dichter's renown only increased after Vance Packard criticized his work in the 1957 bestseller *The Hidden Persuaders*. Instead of employing a psychologist to understand his customers, Jack might have been better off investing in a mental health professional who could help him and his brothers with their father. But Dichter was as close as the family got to an in-house therapist.

The institute conducted several studies for Seabrook Farms. Westchester housewives were asked detailed questions about Seabrook's new boil-in-the-bag Miracle-Pack lineup, which included Baby Limas in Cheese Sauce; Asparagus Cuts and Tips, Hollandaise Style; Potatoes and Peas in Cream Sauce; Creole Succotash; Delmonico Potatoes; and Chopped Broccoli au Gratin. Courtney had developed two different kinds of bags, one using Mylar, the other an opaque pouch of gold-colored foil. Respondents liked the Mylar bag for its transparency, which "created feelings of security in the quality of the product," according to Dichter's report. But foil allowed for baking in the oven and foil was "firmer to handle" than the slippery Mylar pouches.

As with his Bisquick work, Dichter found some women didn't want the Miracle-Pack to be a total product solution. One respondent thought the homemaker needed to be "offered an involvement, a partnership, which may increase her gratification." Dichter recommended the company "enable the housewife, through advertising and promotion, to participate in Seabrook Farms new experiments in frozen food advances . . . so that she can experience with Seabrook the sense of adventure and expectations which have become part of her modern food dreams." The priapic qualities of asparagus notwithstanding, frozen vegetables were difficult to sexualize. If anything, frozen food called to mind an anodyne fifties housewife in her spotless space-age kitchen, who prepares a meal for her husband without ever touching the food.

With the other group, Dichter tested a possible "Elizabeth Seabrook" brand for its Miracle-Pack products. The idea was to make Elizabeth Seabrook the Betty Crocker of quick-frozen vegetables. One interviewee thought the name conjured "a tall, slim, well-groomed woman—a professional dietician or nutritionist who has spent her adult life in some career, probably food, since a great many career women do go into that field." But another person thought, "Lizzie Seabrook would sound more rural and homey." Elizabeth Seabrook was a "society lady, and not at all the farm woman associated with food."

Was Jack trying to brand his bride? In a thoroughly branded family, perhaps this was the ultimate pledge of devotion. Or did he think of his wife as a Seabrook product—a consumable good? In any case, the real

Elizabeth Seabrook would never in a million years have allowed her new name to be used to sell Seabrook products, Miracle-Pack or not.

ॐ

COURTNEY REDESIGNED THE BRAND for the debut of Seabrook's line of prepared entrees, in 1958. He eliminated the ragged wooden board and added the power plant and water tower to the iconography. C. F.'s signature still appeared below his personal guarantee, "We grow our own—so we know it's good—and we freeze it right on the spot."

Jack licensed recipes from Luchow's, a German restaurant in New York, and from Maxim's of Paris. The Luchow's dishes included Lentil Soup with Frankfurters; Swedish Cocktail Meatballs in Dill Cream Sauce; Meat Patty Bavaria; and Hungarian Goulash with Noodles. From Maxim's came Beef Mulled in Beer; Veal in Champagne Sauce; and Filet of Sole in Wine Sauce. For packaging, Courtney commissioned a series of gouache paintings from the artist Miriam Troop, depicting regional dining: a Hungarian restaurant for the goulash; an Italian one for the turkey tetrazzini (a dish unknown in Italy, where poultry is an abomination in pasta); and a New York steakhouse for creamed spinach.

The prepared food was cooked at the plant in enormous vats by a diverse team of Seabrookers that included two Estonians, one Japanese American, one African American, and a white supervisor. Clarence Thomas Walker was the one African American chef on the team. He had attended Florida A&M as an undergraduate and found summer employment in Asbury Park, New Jersey, in the kitchens of the big resort hotels. He was recruited there to work at Seabrook, where he met his wife, a plant worker. In addition to following recipes, Walker, working together with an Estonian engineer named Barkley Vilms, came up with several recipes for new products, including turkey tetrazzini, chicken à la king, and the frozen creamed spinach that became Seabrook Farms' signature product. (Walker is said to have based his creamed spinach on the dish prepared by C. F.'s chef, Clarence Jones, in the 1930s.) Walker's daughter Sharon remembers how, when her dad came home after spending all day around industrial vats of food, his wallet would be soaked in sweat. Walker also cooked for parties that Jack threw when Eva Gabor was around in the early fifties, and Eva brought him to New York for her parties, after she and Jack broke up. "What happened at those parties *stayed* at those parties," Sharon said.

But although the business flourished under Jack's leadership, C. F. remained severely and irrationally critical of his son. Tom Milliman later recalled, "His terrific jealousy and increasingly abusive tirades against Jack seemed to distort his mind completely so far as Jack was concerned." Milliman says that C. F. would refer to his older sons, Belford and Courtney, by name in business meetings, but refused to say my father's name. He called him "you," or "that guy at the other end of the table."

❧

BEING ELIZABETH SEABROOK (the real one) was the assignment of a lifetime, and Liz pursued it with the same dedication she had brought to her journalism. After a honeymoon in Vermont, she moved into Jack's house and began, tentatively, making it theirs. Her new position as chatelaine entailed running the staff of three, as well as playing hostess, going to parties with DuPonts and Philadelphia society, and sitting next to Jack when he drove his coach.

"I must learn the trick of instructing other people exactly how to do things," she wrote to her mother and Isabel. She was used to doing everything herself, and judged that by her standards the servants were slacking. "I'd rather cook something or clean it myself than try to tell somebody else how I want it done," she wrote. But she didn't want to cause trouble. "I realize that in a life like this, where much of the everyday labor such as cooking and cleaning is taken care of by hired help, it is possible to be just as busy and, in a way, get more frustrated because much more is expected of you," she wrote. "I have days of feeling awfully overwhelmed with my new responsibilities, and feel there are so many things to do I want to just sit down and hide and not do any of them, because I never will get done. But so far I have worked my way out of such moods by gritting my teeth and doing one thing at a time." It didn't help her confidence that the staff had worked for the previous Mrs. John M. Seabrook and had also been around for Eva and subsequent girlfriends, a steady stream that had ended only with Liz's very sudden arrival.

Living in the servants' quarters was Harris, a Jamaican who had come to Seabrook Farms during the war as a guest worker and never gone back, and his wife, Mattie, a college-educated former plant worker who met Harris in Seabrook. Harris, who spoke a mixture of English and "Calypso patois," as Liz put it, served as a butler/houseman, and Mattie cooked. There was also Helen, who came in to do the laundry and help clean. Jack had a man named Jack Whitaker to look after his horses, and a local teen, Ginny Matthews, who served as a governess to Carol and Lizanne when they visited from New York. The girls each had their old rooms in the house.

In planning her first horse-drawn picnics as an insider, Liz happened upon a stack of copies of Jack's picnic checklist. She was outraged, writing to her family, "Can you imagine having a checklist for something as spontaneous as a picnic?" Spontaneity is for amateurs, Elizabeth. You've married a pro.

Liz wondered if there might be a room in the large house where she could write. Apparently, the only space available was in the attic, which had sloping eaves. When she went up to inspect it, she found, as she wrote to her mother, "the entire third floor was taken up with Jack's model train setup." His attic train yard was modeled on the Pennsylvania Railroad's 20th Street Yard, in Philadelphia, as it looked around 1950. The thirty-six-inch-high platform the track was attached to went around three sides of the room, with a bay in the middle, where the controls were. Shelves were filled with trains, and train parts and the room smelled of solder, sawdust, and oil.

That explained why Jack kept a stack of *Model Railroader* magazines in his bathroom, next to the toilet. He made it seem normal for a grown man to come home in the evening, eat dinner, pull on a pair of pin-striped engineers coveralls, and repair to the Train Room for a couple of hours. His father had actually built railroads, as well as created the warehouses and the vegetable factory that rail fed into. The son, who had inherited the same love of building and logistics, was modeling the father's epic accomplishments in 1:32 scale track, with factories and warehouses built of balsa wood. What was he thinking as he was building this elaborate setup? Was he angry at being diminished? Was he working out in his head how to manage the modern company as he reenacted his father's building heyday?

Jack agreed to move some of the extra track and tools to make room for Liz to have a desk. The "Women's View" column she had come to Seabrook to write only five months earlier had landed her under the eaves of the house's mansard roof, in a windowless attic. But Liz didn't complain. Instead, she thought, Gee, a playful man like this will make a wonderful father. She did not foresee that his train setup in their next house in Salem would be far too complicated for children to play with. It was strictly off-limits unless he was there, which he rarely was.

≈✿

"You will come to appreciate the fertility of the soil," Jack would say, when his bride commented on the monotonous aspect of the landscape, which was nothing like the Black Hills of South Dakota where she grew up. Behind the elms and flowering bushes that surrounded Jack's house, there was some privacy, although the servants saw everything. But whenever she went for a walk, it was along an open road next to rows of crops, with farmworkers in the fields watching her.

Not knowing a soul in South Jersey, Liz's social life, apart from Jack's friends, centered on her two sisters-in-law: Courtney's wife, Mae, and Belford's wife, Harriet. Mae was going deaf and drank a lot, and Harriet was battling breast cancer. There was also her mother-in-law, Norma Dale, who seemed to be completely overpowered by C. F. He treated her terribly, but she said nothing. Nana once confided in

Liz, "No one will ever know the person I was meant to be." Her only pleasures in life, as far as Liz could see, apart from her grandchildren, were playing bridge with several ladies from church; taking a summer rental in Ocean City, New Jersey, in July and August, to get away from the mosquitos; and attending viewings in funeral homes. C. F. later claimed his wife gambled recklessly on horses, which was absurd, although she did enjoy a trip to the Garden State Park Racetrack from time to time.

That fall, Liz tried to arrange a weekend at Seabrook with Cynthia Lowry and Jinx Falkenburg—a reunion of the cabin they shared on the *Constitution*. "It will be fun to have all of them, since Cynthia and Jinx were in on the beginning of our romance," she wrote. Jinx was married to John Reagan "Tex" McCrary, a Skull and Bones man who became a well-connected public relations specialist and had persuaded Eisenhower to run for president in 1952. The *Tex and Jinx Show* that appeared in 1957 was the first in the popular morning TV "breakfast show" format.

Unfortunately, when the day arrived, one of the McCrarys' kids was sick, and they couldn't come, so Cynthia decided to wait. Then, when the McCrarys' could come, Cynthia was away. Tex and Jinx drove down anyway. Jack had arranged for a horse-drawn picnic, but their son, Kevin, turned out to be allergic to horses. (In later years Kevin became a locally famous hoarder in a rent-stabilized one-bedroom on the Upper East Side.) The planned reunion had not been a success.

✖

MY MOTHER'S MOST IMPORTANT JOB as Chief Emotional Officer was keeping her father-in-law happy. At first, Liz seemed to succeed brilliantly at this delicate task. The old man was smitten with the Irish pioneer girl from Spearfish. Though he insisted she call him "Dad," Liz continued to address her father-in-law as "Mr. Seabrook." She was ignorant of the incident three years earlier, when C. F. had been similarly enchanted with one of his son's partners. One can imagine people whispering about that behind her back.

Dear Mother,
Jack is so pleased that his father seems to like me and
consequently is being much more cooperative with Jack
in the business. Jack says if I don't do anything else than
keep his father happy I have made a great contribution
to his life.

Her father-in-law would often drop by their house unannounced when Jack was away on business in Florida or California. (Jack was always traveling in those days; he carried a pocket-size airline guide listing all carriers and routes in the side pocket of his suit.) Sometimes the old man would arrive with a crew from Koster Nursery to plant rhododendrons, which Liz thought was a nice gesture, until Harriet told her what happened to *her* rhododendrons when she and Belford had dared to move to Alloway.

The old man was delighted when Liz invited a former U.P. colleague down to the farm, the Hearst columnist and author Bob Considine, who shared C. F.'s concerns about Communism and the Red Menace over dinner and brandy. Considine was accompanied by cookery columnist Charlotte Adams. Jack took them all on a coaching picnic. Both Considine and Adams later wrote columns, proving that Jack wasn't the only one who could generate publicity for the brand.

C. F. was so taken with Liz that he announced that the annual Seabrook end-of-year party would be moved up to December 1 and held in the couple's honor that year.

Dear Mother and Isabel, Mr. Seabrook seems to enjoy me
and approve of me and is being so nice to me. They are
giving a reception for us on Dec. 1. It is a 6:30 affair, buffet
supper with dancing and an orchestra and everything. It
is to be formal. They have invited 250 people. Can you
imagine having a house big enough to have a buffet supper
and dance for 250?

There was enough Lenox china and monogrammed silverware for everyone to dine first class.

❧

BOTH LIZANNE AND CAROL came for Thanksgiving that year—the first holidays that Liz presided over as chatelaine. It was unclear until the last minute whether Anne would even allow the girls to come. Liz was learning that Anne loved to make a drama of everything. Lizanne, aged nine, wasn't very nice to her new stepmother during her Thanksgiving visit. "She made several rather pointed criticisms of me," Liz wrote her family. Jack had given her a mink stole, and she wore it that weekend for the first time. When Lizanne saw that it had a bow on the back she said, "A bow on the mink stole—that's a pretty stupid thing to put on a fur." "I suggested she speak to her father about it," Liz wrote, "since he had chosen the stole, and she said no more."

Carol, on the other hand, was always agreeable. "Carol couldn't be sweeter. She is very affectionate and thoughtful of me. I would ask her when I wanted Lizanne to do something and she would go tell her to do it. Jack is certainly on my side in any such situations, so I am sure it will work out eventually." It would not.

But on the whole, Liz was content. "My new happiness continues without any letup," she wrote, which seems like a strange way to put it. "Jack is always sweet. We've had a few arguments, and I don't agree with everything he says by any means, and vice versa. But we agree on all the important things and respect each other's right to disagree on little things."

❧

JANET TOOMEY DID NOT COME East for the party. Liz implored her to, and Jack wrote separately. But her meeting with the Seabrook clan in September had spooked my dour Scottish grandmother. She fiercely disapproved of the alcohol and fine living.

The Seabrooks approached party planning with the same kind of rigor they brought to agriculture. Organizing a party was an applied science. Just as the company's climatologist calculated the precise number of growth units required to bring a crop to perfect ripeness by factoring in heat, sunlight, precipitation, evaporation, and time, so C. F. and his sons calculated the exact amount of champagne, vodka, scotch, beer, food, music, and time it would take to get the party lit. (Like business, party planning could not be left to women.) The calculation had been refined over the years into an algorithm for hedonic abandon. Cyrus, god of the harvest, was well served.

As these harvest celebrations evolved into grander showcases of Seabrook power, an ever-greater array of politicians and business leaders came to kiss the ring. On the night of the party, Liz stood with the family inside the entryway of the big house on Polk Lane, greeting bankers, judges, Philadelphia society figures, Governor Robert Meyner, and future Chief Justice Richard Hughes. Cocktails, dinner, and dancing followed. The last guests didn't depart until 3:00 a.m.

This party would be the last big bash C. F. ever threw. During the festivities, the patriarch seemed distant, tired, or possibly stoned on phennies. After putting on a good show in the receiving line, he wandered around the house, smiling at his guests but detached from the merriment. Liz thought he didn't seem to be having much fun.

CHAPTER 30

"A MESS OF POTTAGE"

J ANET WAS FINALLY PERSUADED TO COME EAST AGAIN in July 1957. On July 6, C. F. and Nana had the family to their house for dinner. Soon after they were seated, C. F. started in on one of his paranoid stories about how Jack beat him with whips and chains. Janet was astounded that the old man was permitted to spew such lies and hate, and the "boys" just took it. No one dared call him on it, or even seemed to think there was anything wrong with his behavior.

Janet was quietly disapproving most of the time, but when angered she could be formidable. She answered to a power higher than C. F. Seabrook. After listening to him rant, she spoke up and told C. F. to his face that he was lying, that Jack was a good son who was doing his best. Everyone was stunned. Liz sided with Janet—she was done with trying to please this crazy old man. C. F. didn't speak. Jack tried to smooth things over, but the die was cast now. Inevitably, he would have to choose between his father and his wife.

❧

BY 1958, after three years of leading the company, Jack had turned Seabrook Farms' finances around. Profits for the year were five times what they had been in 1957. In addition to introducing the new product line of prepared foods, Seabrook had a foothold in concentrated orange juice in Florida, an exciting new product, through a deal he had negotiated with Snow Crop, a Florida based label. C. F. thought this was a terrible idea, but the Board agreed to the deal in late '57.

Everything seemed to be going Jack's way. The only thing that stood between him and his own "modern food dreams" was the three-man voting trust, which his father would need to reapprove by 1959, before the five-year contract expired. C. F. was bound to cause trouble, and it would require some unpleasant dealings with Dorsey and Orlando, but only a lunatic would refuse to renew the agreement. Dissolving the trust would mean the banks would call their loans and bankrupt the company. C. F. had already gone bankrupt once. He wasn't going to let that happen again.

❧

C. F.'s INCREASINGLY ERRATIC BEHAVIOR may have been early signs of senility, or a "hardening of the arteries," as Alzheimer's disease and dementia were referred to then. His condition wasn't helped by heavy drinking and phenobarbital abuse. Steve Ressler, C. F.'s masseur for seventeen years, said that the old man gobbled the red pills, along with aspirin, during their sessions. The masseur would arrive at the house to give him his morning massage, and as he set things up in the basement, he would hear C. F. making his first drink. He didn't sleep much—he never had. He roamed the house at all hours.

He resisted all of Jack's innovations. In the mid-1950s, Jack had introduced a mechanized method of weeding spinach fields. The machine worked well, but it left a few weeds between furrows that workers with hoes would have gotten. C. F. complained bitterly to Tom Milliman about Jack's incompetence at allowing this mechanized method to replace the "fine gardening" he had always practiced. When Milliman inspected the spinach fields himself, he found no more than two hundred weeds in ten acres of spinach.

C. F. went back to Clifton Springs in November 1957, but the visit didn't seem to do him the good it had done him before. He checked himself out after four days, before he had properly detoxed, and got the company pilot to fly him home. Not long after he returned, Milliman had a night out with C. F. at the Centerton Inn, a local restaurant and watering hole. The lawyer who interviewed Milliman in 1964 in connection with the dispute over C. F.'s estate offered a précis of his account of this evening. "C. F. sat down and talked with TM at great length, seemingly very agitated, and in a high voice about the many, many failures of Jack in most intimate details concerning sales, farming, financing. C. F.'s face was flushed and he seemed to have been drinking. He displayed a fixation against any expansion of the business, calling it 'reckless' (when in fact, Milliman says, Jack's activities in this regard were the soundest sort of business judgment.)" The interviewer's report continued, "C. F. displayed a fixation as to farming methods, complaining again and again about the lack of 'fine gardening.'" Milliman assured C. F. that the "fine gardening of the early days was long, long past." C. F. further deplored Jack's relationship with the banks. "All of this was done in such fashion that everyone in the room could hear the tirade. And everyone listened."

Another boisterous night at the Centerton Inn was recalled by C. F.'s Estonian driver, Edgar K. Roehle, in his 1963 interview. The bartender encountered "serious trouble" in getting C. F. and his party, among them a couple of Atlantic City pols, to leave at closing time. "But he was firm and made them leave." C. F. declared that "he had more liquor in his basement than anybody could use," so they headed to Polk Lane. The rest of the household was asleep when the party arrived and repaired to the well-appointed basement rec room. The lawyer wrote, "EKR observed C. F. on the telephone dialing many, many times . . . calling up girls to come over." Finally, the wife of one of the politicians came to break things up, but that wasn't the end of the driver's evening. Roehle "went out to take care of some chores, came in and could not find C. F." He located him in the bathroom, passed out on the floor next to the toilet. Alarmed, he woke the German butler, Walter, and his wife, Helga, and "had her come down and see C. F. in this condition." Finally, he slung C. F. over his shoulder and carried him upstairs to bed.

This same driver also reported C. F.'s liaisons with a local Romanian woman he called "Princess," because she supposedly was descended from old-world royalty. The interviewer writes, "Almost daily he drove C. F. to the home of a Rumanian [*sic*] woman in Seabrook Village, where C. F. would stay for hours, sometimes all night long." The woman was also a frequent guest at his house. "Sometimes C. F. would chase Mrs. Seabrook upstairs so as to get her out of the way so as to facilitate his enjoyment." The driver called his treatment of my kind, long-suffering grandmother "dastardly."

In another interview, one of C. F.'s drinking pals, a Dr. Carll, describes an outing in New York City. The old man and two or three cronies were driven up to the Engineers Club, where they had a couple of rounds of drinks at eleven o'clock in the morning. They lunched in the grill room, where C. F. ordered a case of champagne for the table and the waitresses. After several hours of feasting and drinking, C. F. disappeared into his room with a waitress who was in the long-standing habit of giving him a massage.

When in New York, the old man became an almost daily visitor at Weatherill, which was located in the Fuller building at Fifty-Seventh and Madison. He would often be waiting at the door when Charles Weatherill arrived at nine in the morning, and then would fall asleep in a chair in Weatherill's office, sometimes remaining all day long. When C. F. was in Doctors Hospital in New York for a prostate operation, he called Weatherill and insisted that he come to the hospital with samples of waterproof material for a new suit that would accommodate his incontinence. Weatherill was stopped by a nurse at the hospital before he could see C. F. and instructed not to sell him any more clothes.

The 1963 interview with Lucy Emerson, the wife of Harold Emerson, a longtime Seabrook executive who died in 1958, alleges C. F. was a sexual predator. The lawyer, paraphrasing Emerson's remarks, writes that the old man "frequently slapped women on the rump or put his hands on their breasts, this being done openly at parties at the Seabrook house. C. F. did this to her [Emerson], [to] Vy Maxey, and it was intimated to many other persons. Locally called the 'T-t' man. Lucy Emerson heard rumors that C. F. was often in his office at night when he summoned girls from the night shift at the factory, frequently with wet clothing sticking to them. He would offer to let them get on the day shift (from the generally disliked night shift) provided they gave a quid pro quo." According to the lawyer's write-up of this conversation, the wives of Seabrook employees, even at the administrative and executive level, endured similar treatment to preserve their husbands' jobs and their homes. Emerson, the lawyer goes on, "said that anyone who objected would suddenly find themselves without a job and without a place to live and with a notice to clear out immediately."

ON AUGUST 1, 1958, Liz and Jack had a party for Carol and Lizanne, who would be attending the Rose School in Switzerland that fall. C. F. and Nana came over after dinner, and once they'd arrived, Jack quieted everyone for a major announcement. Liz was expecting a baby in January.

Jack had hoped this news of me coming would delight his father. Norma, overjoyed, repeated the happy news to her husband, but the old man seemed confused. Jack later said in a deposition, "It was as if he couldn't comprehend." He later pointed to this incident as proof that his father must have lost his sanity by that point, which served as justification for the fateful step he and his brothers would take the following March. But I think the old man knew exactly what he was doing. Not responding at all to the news was the ultimate passive-aggressive move.

In the birth announcement Betty Gaunt made for JMS Jr.'s arrival, I am shown emerging from a peapod, with the iconic power plant and water tower in the background: a newborn brandling. The package says I was "processed" at Jefferson Hospital in Philadelphia, and "distributed" by Dr. Warren Lang, OBGYN. My grandfather's guarantee is at the bottom. "We grow our own—so we know it's good."

C. F. HAD LEARNED ABOUT the importance of owning a majority of a company's voting shares from the bankruptcy of the first Seabrook Farms. Voting shares are instruments of corporate finance that allow the holder to vote on major policy decisions affecting the company; one vote per share is the custom. The Whites held a majority of the voting shares of the first vegetable factory, which gave them the right to declare bankruptcy. When C. F. returned to the farming business in 1930 and had new articles of incorporation drawn up, he made sure that he held most of the voting shares.

As Seabrook expanded under Jack with public offerings, C. F.'s ownership of the common stock of the company was steadily diluted. There were the four financings during the war, and additional floats afterward. "We were a public company with all the restrictions that went along with it," Jack wrote. "The three investment bankers and other outsiders joined the Board of Directors of Deerfield Packing Corporation. C. F., when he was around, chafed under the new requirements and never did master the S.E.C. rules, so I handled most of these details." Large blocks of common stock were owned by two insurance companies in the Midwest. The corporation's debt, at which Jack was steadily chipping away with cost-cutting and product innovations like the Miracle-Pack, was held by a consortium of fifteen banks, including Chase Manhattan.

After 1955, C. F. no longer had any control over how his son ran the company. Even the three-man trust the banks had created in the wake of Hurricane Hazel to manage the Seabrook's finances offered C. F. no real influence, since Ben Sawin and Jack always voted together against him. The old man vented about the situation to anyone who would listen, including an Estonian gardener who encountered C. F. one day while working at his estate. In a later interview he recalled that his employer harangued him about how "incompetent" Jack was and what a "crook" Courtney was, horrifying the gardener. A Seabrook Farms annual report toward the end of the 1950s contains this extraordinary statement:

> During the past four years, C. F. Seabrook has usually opposed the major moves of the management in such matters as personnel changes, the decision to enter the prepared foods field, the

Luchow contract, the Minute Maid Snow Crop contract . . . and the plans to acquire a California plant. . . . The nine other members of the Board of Directors support the management.

But though powerless to manage the direction of the company, C. F. had two remaining levers to pull. One was the three-man trust, which had to be renewed in January 1960. The other was the option to sell the company, which his voting shares entitled him to. In 1956, C. F. had arranged a meeting with Reynolds Metals to explore a possible sale. When word of this got back to Jack, he confronted his father. "When I asked him if he did really mean to sell," the diary notes, "he at first said yes. Said he was doing it for his heirs and to get his estate in order. When I told him I thought the price was too low and that his heirs would be better off if he left them the business rather than the money, he would only say that he hadn't sold yet. The conversation was very quiet. Neither of us got excited or showed any emotion." The next day's record of calls and meetings begins: "7:15 a.m.—CFS telephoned me and told me not to be too concerned about [his] trip to see Reynolds that he wasn't thinking of selling."

✦

IN MARCH 1959, C. F. arranged to meet with Ben Sawin at his office at the Provident Bank in Center City Philadelphia. He brought along Orlando and Dorsey, and let his lawyers do most of the talking. They explained to Sawin that because of their client's dismay over the direction his sons were taking the company, Mr. Seabrook had decided he was not going to renew the voting trust. Sawin pointed out that if their client refused, the banks would call their loans and the company would go bankrupt. The old man seemed unperturbed: So be it.

The next day, Sawin summoned my father to his office and told him that if his father didn't change his mind, the company would be bankrupt by the end of April. Sawin suggested that Jack leave Seabrook Farms and work for him. He offered his protégé a job on the spot as vice president. Jack said he'd think about it. Then the surrogate son and his surrogate father went out for a "4-martini lunch," the diary notes.

A few days after his meeting with Sawin, C. F. had a bad "spell." He threw food around on the walls of the dining room and soiled himself. The butler, Walter Sabbath, called Jack and said his father was in very bad shape and he should come right over. Sam Orlando was there when Jack arrived. He said "the old gentleman" was doing poorly, but seeing Jack would only inflame the situation. They called Dr. Garrison, one of C. F.'s local doctors, who after examining the old man told them that C. F. was "slipping his cable." Another of C. F.'s physicians, Dr. Yaskin, who arrived that evening, recommended taking Mr. Seabrook to Jefferson Hospital. The following morning, Courtney drove his father there.

Jack met with Geoffrey S. Smith, the chairman of Girard Bank, another of Seabrook's major creditors. Smith said that C. F.'s refusal to renew the voting trust was not the action of a competent man. To save the company, he told my father, the family should look into having their father committed, and have the court appoint a guardian to manage his affairs. Then they wouldn't need the old man's vote to extend the trust. This sort of thing happens in family enterprises, Smith assured my father. He recommended a small private sanatorium called Fairmount Farm, located in northwest Philadelphia, where another of his wealthy clients had sent Grandpa when he became difficult.

"A family business is the ultimate enabler," according to the family business consultant Thomas M. Hubler. In this case, protecting the family business enabled the sons to contemplate corporate patricide. But had it really come to this—that in order to appease the bankers they had to commit their all-powerful father?

Jack consulted with his brothers. Both were in favor of committing C. F.; that was the only way, they assured each other, to save what he had created. Jack advised his brothers and their mother to make timelines that detailed C. F.'s "spells" in frequency and severity. They didn't tell Thelma what they were considering because they didn't trust her not to alert their father.

C. F. wasn't happy with the care he was getting at Jefferson Hospital and was demanding to be moved. Jack saw their opportunity. Courtney would tell their father they had found a better hospital, and that they were going to relocate him there. Courtney, who had taken him to Jefferson, was the logical person to take him to Fairmount; if Jack drove him, the old man would be suspicious. Courtney got their father discharged and brought him to the Main Line location of "the Farm." There, orderlies led him away to be examined by Dr. George Wilson. Courtney filled out the temporary commitment papers and left his father.

※茶

WHEN ORLANDO HEARD that his client was being confined against his will, he filed a writ of habeas corpus against Courtney, Jack, and George Wilson, demanding C. F.'s immediate release. Nana flew back from Florida and went to see her husband at the Farm. She found him in a fury, ranting that Courtney was a mere delivery boy; he would never have initiated such a daring action. Jack was clearly behind everything, backed by Liz, who C. F. accused of orchestrating the splashy press coverage of his confinement, release, disappearance, and the $3 million kidnapping lawsuit that he, Dorsey, and Orlando subsequently brought against the boys. "How sharper than a serpent's tooth it is to have a thankless child," cries Lear when Goneril refuses to let him keep his retinue at her place. Charlie Seabrook, who had done his own father wrong, now felt that serpent's bite.

On March 23, the family met with lawyers at the Barclay Hotel in Philly to decide whether to pursue a competency hearing. Nana wanted Richard Hughes, later a two-term governor and then the chief justice of New Jersey, to be the family's lead lawyer. Belford as always went straight to the point. "Is he committable?" he asked. Hughes assured the sons that their father was committable, but the family would only prevail in court if everyone was united. Bob Sidur, Thelma's second husband, had already made it clear he wasn't on board, and Thelma was wavering. Nana dreaded having to testify against her husband. At one point she began muttering darkly about how she refused to be involved in "dishonorable" behavior, not saying whose behavior she was talking about. Liz assured her that the boys were only trying to save the company, and that if she herself felt anything dishonorable was afoot, she would certainly object. But would she have known?

Orlando succeeded in convincing a judge in the Court of Common Pleas in Philadelphia that his client was being "illegally held" by the hospital, and C. F. was released from the Farm on April 1. He had Bob Sidur drive him to the Engineers Club in New York, where he remained for several days, panic-stricken that his sons were going to throw him into "jail," according to witnesses there. He hired Albert Coe, a former FBI agent now with a detective agency, as a bodyguard. He claimed nurses and doctors at the Farm had tried to kill him. Dolly, the hostess in the Engineers Club dining room, listened sympathetically. In her 1963 interview, Dolly expressed "her distaste for the sons who tried to lock him up in a mental institution when 'he was just as sane as anyone.'"

On Friday, April 3, Jack went up to New York to bring C. F. home, but he was gone. No one knew where. He didn't show up on April 5, the day of my christening at Deerfield Presbyterian, or for the champagne toast back at my parents' house afterward, a secular baptism-by-Bollinger. In fact, the old man, who had been staying with Leo Dorsey in New Jersey, had flown to Florida and turned up at the Coral Gables apartment that afternoon, surprising Thelma, who alerted the family. Nana left for Florida the following day. She found her husband very bitter toward her and his extended family, especially Liz.

"If she comes up and kisses me again, I'll slap her face!" C. F. declared. He told Nana he was going to leave her. She replied, "Where are you going to go?" She later shared with Belford that this was one of the worst twenty-four-hour periods in her life. She read passages from the Bible out loud for most of the night, while her husband raved about how Jack and Liz were the architects of all his troubles.

A few days later, lawyers tried to serve C. F. with a subpoena notifying him of the upcoming competency hearing. When they arrived at the apartment, Norma had gone to the movies. The old man refused to answer the door, sensing something was up. Lawyers managed to serve him several days later by posing as deliverymen.

On April 16, the sons went public with their bid to have their father declared incompetent in New Jersey Superior Court and appoint a guardian to manage his affairs. "It is with deep reluctance that the family has entered into this action," a spokesman said, adding of C. F., "The preservation of his life's work is uppermost in their minds." The hearing was set for May 11 in Camden.

C. F. hired a new driver/bodyguard, Richard C. Folsom, who arrived at the Florida apartment on April 17. In his 1963 interview, Folsom said C. F. told him he needed to be guarded because his sons had succeeded once in having him locked up, and that they were preparing to do so again. Back in New Jersey, the family met on Polk Lane. Bob Sidur told Nana that she had to choose between her sons and her husband. She replied that she wouldn't take sides. Belford said that if Thelma and their mother backed out now, "this would bring ruin on the family and ruin on this community." Turning to his sister, Belford continued, "You are being a coward not to help C. F. in his hour of need. If the business goes down and all these people are ruined, people will hate him and this will last for the next twenty-five years." The following week, Judge Hughes received a note from Thelma saying she was unable to support her brothers' action. She alone stood by their father.

❧

THE BROTHERS PRESSED ON. C. F. threatened to have his boys, wife, and Dr. Wilson arrested for kidnapping. When C. F. finally returned home in early May, he told Nana that he was going to throw everyone out of the company who had anything to do with Jack and run the business himself. Albert Coe, the New Jersey watchman, moved into the house to protect him from "being put away by his children," as Nana characterized his thinking.

The competency hearing was delayed so that an independent panel of doctors appointed by the judge in the case could examine C. F. They arrived on May 13. The doctors talked to C. F. for an hour, broke for lunch, and walked around in the gardens, which were in full bloom. Wisteria vines trained as standards marched down the center of one section, banked on both sides by beds of hyacinths, tulips, snapdragons, rhododendrons, and chrysanthemums. The Koster blue spruce was plentiful.

The old man had been calm for the first part of the hearing, but after lunch he became aggressive and paranoid. The three M.D.s on the panel—Drs. Collins, Garber, and Spradley—were observed by Dr. Hayes, a physician Orlando had brought in to make an independent report.

Collins, writing for the panel, found that C. F. was "suffering from Chronic Brain Syndrome associated with Cerebral Arteriosclerosis and is in need of care and supervision, and in view of his advanced years together with his paranoid reactions to his family . . . he could be unduly influenced by others and I do not feel he is capable of managing his affairs or his estate." Hayes, the physician Orlando had hired, found C. F. to be a "thoroughly able and competent man."

~⁂~

C. F. SEABROOK WAS A MAN who had made a lifetime of bold moves, often ruthless, a promoter who had convinced Joseph Stalin he was a world-class road builder, whose life's work had been likened to Henry Ford's, who had broken a strike, sired a dynasty, and changed the eating habits of the nation, all without amending his views or behavior, except when his accountant had been discovered to be cooking the books prior to Hurricane Hazel. Now he faced the humiliating circumstance of waiting for some two-bit local judge to rule on his sanity, with his sons arrayed against him. But he had one last card to play.

While waiting for the judge in the case to render a verdict, C. F. told Dorsey to find a buyer for the company. He didn't care who it was, so long as the new buyer had had no prior dealings with his youngest son, and that they pledge to "throw Jack out and save the business" on taking over. A few days later, Dorsey told the old gentleman that he had found a potential buyer—Seeman's, a New York–area food distributor.

Like Seabrook Farms, Seeman's was a family business trying to transition into second-generation management. A controlling share had recently been acquired by John D. Fowler Jr., a Wall Street operator. Fowler had merged Seeman's with White Rose, a well-known food distributor in the New York metro area, and was looking to expand further. He offered to buy C. F.'s stock and voting shares for $3 million, about $32 million in today's money, half in cash and the rest within a year.

On May 17, my father met Fowler at the Carlyle Hotel in New York. Fowler told him that though he had promised Dorsey he was going to get rid of Jack and Courtney as a condition of the sale, he had "no intention of doing this as it is ridiculous," Courtney wrote in his timeline. Instead, Fowler begged him and Courtney to stay and offered to multiply their salaries. Jack said he would think about it, but he never had any intention of accepting, and Courtney declined too. Jack told his brother he didn't like or trust Fowler, who, with some sleuthing, he had discovered to be Jewish. Jews were tolerable when serving JMS's interests, but taking orders from one was too much.

By the following day, the deal was done. The enterprise that had begun on A. P.'s tenant farm in 1875 (or 1893, as C. F. preferred) and that three generations had built into one of the most extraordinary farming businesses in the world, passed out of family ownership in less than a week. His sons, who had worked for years with the assumption that they would inherit the business, now had little more than thin slices of equity in an enterprise owned by someone else.

C. F. wanted to put out a statement saying he had sold the business to save it from his sons, but Dorsey and Orlando talked him out of it. Nana came over to Courtney and Mae's for lunch with Liz and Jack. She told everyone that "C. F. has sold his birthright for a mess of pottage"; Nana knew her Scripture.

Four days later, Belford's wife, Harriet, died. C. F. did not go to the funeral in the Old Broad Street Church in Bridgeton. Liz wrote a Dearest Family letter explaining that it was all over. "We are all well and still grateful for our many blessings. But the business crisis has ended and sadly for Jack. The new owners took over yesterday and Jack moved his things out of his office and is now finished. He is taking it with his wondrous calm, though I know it is a great jolt to him."

❧

IN EARLY JUNE 1959, my parents went to London to get away from it all and to socialize with Jack's coaching friends. Jack also made a quick trip to Zurich, to meet with a banker. "I'm glad we came now, as I believe it is good for Jack to have the change," Liz wrote in a letter to her family. "He is still bearing up remarkably well, though he has terrible sinking spells I know. He never complains though. I have gone over and over in my mind the events of recent months and still feel it was inevitable." I was left in Seabrook in care of relatives and the help. "Little Johnny has broken out in a rash," notes Betty Gaunt in Jack's diary. "No one knows what's causing it. He seems fine."

On June 15, while Jack and Liz were still in London, the family agreed to drop the competency proceeding if C. F. would forgo the kidnapping lawsuit. The following week, the patriarch changed his will, rewarding Thelma for sticking by him and all but disowning his sons, as advised by Orlando and Dorsey. On August 5, my grandfather made the last of his ninety-six trips to Europe, with "Mac," a male nurse who served as his Jeeves-cum-Sancho Panza. They sailed on the *Queen Mary* with two trunks of Weatherill suits and made it to Claridge's in London, where more clothes were acquired. Then the two departed for Paris, where, upon arrival, they realized C. F. had left the trunks behind at the hotel.

On October 26, my mother was at home with nine-month-old me when a work crew of C. F.'s rudely barged in and demanded to inspect the house. Don McCallister, the Seabrook Housing Corp. manager, informed my mother that the lease was expiring at the end of the month and the landlord—her father-in-law—wanted them out. My father was in San Francisco seeing about a job offer, so my mother had to organize a hasty move. Our new home in Salem County was about eighteen miles away. It was a colonial brick farmhouse set amid fifty acres of open fields, wrapped around by tidal wetlands that flow into Delaware Bay. Jack had purchased the house and land as an investment some years earlier. When we moved out of the house in Seabrook, C. F. claimed that the walls had been smeared with Limburger cheese, and that oil had been poured down the well. So began our life in exile.

That November Thanksgiving didn't take place in the big house on Polk Lane. Belford asked the family to his house in Alloway, for his first Thanksgiving without Harriet. The C. F. Seabrooks stayed home.

AFTER C. F. EVICTED US, we did return on occasional Sundays to visit the mansion on Polk Lane. We would first attend church with Nana, who I loved, and who was always so gentle and kind. Then we'd have a big midday Sunday "dinner," a custom derived from our supposedly lordly English ancestors, in the formal dining room with the Lenox china and the confusing array of monogrammed sterling knives, forks, and spoons to eat the different courses that Walter served. My grandfather was home, but we never saw him. He was upstairs with his nurses. He'd had another "spell," Nana would tell my parents.

On one occasion when I was four, my father took me upstairs to meet my grandfather. His room was on the third floor of the house. When we got to the bottom of the stairs my father called out "Pop!" his voice booming in the tight stairwell. Pop? Was that what he called his father? "We're coming up!" He took my hand, which he hardly ever did except to practice shaking hands, and we walked up to the white room, painfully bright with sunshine. My grandfather was dressed in a dark chalk-striped suit, sitting on the floor, with no shoes or socks on. His feet were pink and shining, as if they had recently been rubbed with ointment. He was building something with Tinkertoys.

My father said, "Pop, this is your grandson. This is Johnny."

My grandfather looked up at my father and his mouth opened a little bit. Then his head lowered again, and he looked right at me, pressing his lips together into a thin line. He stared at me balefully, this boy who would grow up to investigate and expose him for who he really was, seeking transgenerational revenge for the harm he had inflicted on my father's soul. His lips remained shut.

My father nudged me. "Hi, Grandad," I ventured. No answer.

"Does he understand anything?" my father asked the nurse.

"Oh, I think he does," she said, "when he wants to."

My father considered this, then he squatted down so that his head was at my level.

"This is my son, Pop."

The nurse came forward with a tissue to wipe the line of drool from the corner of Grandad's mouth. I got the feeling he might grab one of my ankles, so I put my hands on my knees, in a defensive crouch. Dad encouraged me to sit. I put a dowel inside a hole and handed it to Grandad, and he took it. We played at being builders together, my father later remembered, for ten minutes.

The Henry Ford of Agriculture died in October 1964. A thousand people lined up outside the house on Polk Lane for the viewing, which was held in the library. Richard Hughes, now New Jersey's governor, who had represented the family against the old man in the competency dispute, delivered one of the eulogies, along with the remarks I had seen my father composing on his legal pad by the fire.

❧

I NEVER SAW AUNT THELMA AGAIN. I wasn't present at the one and only time she came to our house on a Sunday in early November 1964, about a week after the reading of C. F. Seabrook's will. Their father had left 60 percent of the $3 million he got for selling the company (which did not include his land and housing) to the Princeton Theological Seminary, Princeton Westminster Choir College, Deerfield Presbyterian Church, the Deerfield Board of Education, and the Bridgeton Hospital Association. Fifteen percent went to Thelma, plus $100,000; 10 percent went to

Nana. The boys got almost nothing. My father was particularly enraged that his father had named as executors his cronies Dorsey and Orlando, as well as Bob Sidur, and not him or his brothers. He was certain Dorsey and Orlando had manipulated C. F. into changing his will when he was no longer competent. The estate paid them hundreds of thousands of dollars for their time. Belford was apoplectic. In a letter he wrote to his sister, but that may never have been sent, he noted that "we have always felt that you were entitled to share alike with us, even though you contributed nothing to building and creating [C. F.'s] assets, but you certainly cannot justify the favored and sole position in his Will that you importuned your father into giving you to our total exclusion." He claimed in the letter that Thelma got more than a million dollars from their father. He concluded, "And so we hope you enjoy your day of infamy and your greed."

Liz had seen Thelma at Deerfield Presbyterian, and when her sister-in-law said that she and Bob still hadn't seen the house in Salem, Liz invited her to stop by after church some Sunday. She was somewhat sympathetic to Thelma's plight. After all, Thelma would have loved to help build up C. F.'s assets, but because she was born female, she was excluded from the family business. And Thelma *was* the only child to stick by her father, when her brothers tried to have him committed, and a part of Liz couldn't help but admire her loyalty, misguided though it was. What had her mother-in-law meant when she had used that word "dishonorable" at the Barclay Hotel that day? Had the brothers dishonored their father in trying to save his creation?

The following Sunday the Sidurs showed up unexpectedly. The discussion about C. F.'s estate "got pretty hot," Jack recalled in a deposition two years later. Larry Seabrook, one of Belford's three sons, "blundered into the middle" of the argument, he testified, adding, of his nephew, "Poor fool." That meeting ended in a legendary loss of temper by my otherwise unflappable father, with he and his brother-in-law shouting curses at each other, and Jack allegedly calling Orlando a dishonest crook. I didn't hear this outburst, but when the brother-in-law died a few years later I recall the dark promise my father made, to "piss on Bob Sidur's grave."

Jack Seabrook, with obligatory top hat and calfskin
driving gloves, prepares his team of Morgan horses
for "coaching" in Seabrook, New Jersey, 1957.

EPILOGUE

SEABROOK & SON

If *guilt* is the psychoanalytic word for not getting
away with it, what is the psychoanalytic word for
getting away with it. . . .

—*Adam Phillips, "On Getting Away with It"*

CHAPTER 31

THE COTTON PLANT

S HORTLY AFTER THE START OF THE NEW MILLENNIUM, my parents left South Jersey for Aiken, South Carolina, where they had been wintering among the horsey set for years. Henceforth the Palmetto State would be their permanent residence. The South Jersey place was maintained by a skeleton crew of Hileses, who continued to die in tragic ways: Billy in a car wreck in Salem; Norman slowly of drinking. Delores moved with my parents and lived in a small apartment on the property, which bordered the Palmetto Golf Club. The pleasant thwack of a well-struck ball could be heard while sipping whiskey sours on the veranda.

My siblings and I were in favor of the move. The winters were much gentler down south, health care was closer, and my parents seemed to have plenty of friends. There were good airline connections, including, for a period, a very handy United Airlines flight that departed Newark at 6:00 p.m. Thursday evening and left Columbia at 6:20 a.m. on Monday morning. It later turned out that David Samson, the chairman of the Port Authority of New York and New Jersey, had bribed the airline to continue to operate the money-losing route, known around Port Authority as "the Chairman's flight" and "Samson Air," because it allowed Samson to get from his house in North Jersey to his Aiken polo stables on his preferred schedule. In addition to 3,600 hours of community service and a $100,000 fine, Samson was sentenced to a year of confinement on his polo farm. It was a very Jersey affair.

Before leaving the Garden State, Jack arranged for the dispersal of his entire collection in a two-day auction in May 2002. His father had disposed of his work horses and horse-powered farm machinery in a big auction in 1920, when Jack was three, and perhaps the buried memory of this event eighty-two years earlier informed his decision. In any case, Jack had decided to put down the whip. At eighty-five, he no longer had the strength in his left arm to control the team, should they startle and bolt, and the only one of his children who had shown much interest in coaching was Lizanne, always the horsiest of us. But he didn't speak to Lizanne anymore.

The auction took place under a large white tent on a warm spring weekend. For the catalogue, my father commissioned a magnificent, museum-quality monograph, with photographs of each vehicle and a description of its provenance, as well as an introductory text by Tom Ryder, a noted authority in the coaching world, that told the story of Jack's fifty-year driving career.

My father attended every minute of proceedings, in Huntsman "Newmarket check" patterned suits dialed up from the Country Clothes region of the closet. Everything was on the block: the coaches, carriages, and sleighs; the sets of matching leather and brass harness; the colorful topcoats worn by the groom at shows; the coaching horns, lap robes, knee-length riding boots; and the polished holly wood whips, several of which ended up on display in the Coaching Room at his club, the Knickerbocker on Fifth Avenue. At first, we sat with him, in an area reserved for family, but it was too grim to watch pieces from our childhood that my father would gladly have left to us, if only we wanted them, go to strangers. I repaired to the bar at the back of the tent for my second but not last Bloody Mary of the morning. By the end, only my mother remained by his side, loyally.

JMS was silent for much of the sale, inscrutable as always, watching as admirers and fellow coaching enthusiasts picked his equipage clean for below the set minimums. The Nimrod was purchased by a consortium and given to the Preservation Society of Newport, Rhode Island, where my father had driven on many previous summers while attending the American Coaching Club's annual ball. It was subsequently purchased by a whip from the Midwest, who was looking to raise his profile in the coaching world.

On Sunday afternoon, after his coaching legacy had been completely liquidated, the family had lunch in the dining room. Jack was seated in his usual spot, the Shikler portrait of him with the Nimrod behind him. We were in our familiar places. He mentioned the figure the entire auction had netted, and after admitting it was less than he had hoped for, pronounced himself satisfied and picked up his wineglass for a self-congratulatory sip.

My mother, who had clearly been worrying about the question for the previous two days, finally came out with it.

"Didn't it make you sad, seeing it all go?"

"No," he said, in that judicious, CEO-of-his-own-pain tone that seemed to mask despair. After another sip, he allowed that he *had* felt a bit sentimental when the leather saddle bags we had used on family horseback picnics as children came on the block, and we hadn't bid on them.

"I did feel a pang," he admitted. "I thought one of you might want them."

⁂

AS MY PARENTS' HEALTH BEGAN TO DETERIORATE, I found myself on the Chairman's flight more and more often. I had imagined that during those long weekends in Aiken my father and I would finally get to the bottom of what had really happened back in Seabrook. Was the old man a demagogue, a classic strongman with a personality cult, who like all dictators clung to power even though it meant tearing apart his own family? Was he a sociopath, a malignant narcissist who could not tolerate anyone having power over him? Was he driven mad by the guilt of cheating his father, and the fear his sons would do the same to him? Did the 1941 stroke, and the pills he abused in his recovery from that murky event, explain his behavior?

I asked my father some of these questions, but I didn't get answers. "He was a tough character" was about as far as he would go in criticizing the man whose malevolent enmity toward him, it seemed to me, went far beyond mere toughness. Sometimes he would quote the proverb attributed to Lord Acton, "Power corrupts, and absolute power corrupts absolutely," but say no more than that. He was stoic. He wasn't interested in exploring alternative narratives of the demise of Seabrook Farms or the disintegration of their relationship. He treated these notions as flights of fancy by his writer son. After my *New Yorker* piece he was less inclined to share as much as he used to about family history.

My father's speech at the New Beginnings reunion in 1994 had become *The Henry Ford of Agriculture*, a short history of Seabrook Farms and biography of C. F. Seabrook, which he self-published in 1996. The book celebrated C. F. the visionary and builder, and only lightly limned his faults, blaming them on a medical event beyond his control. Even when the book discusses the boardroom blowup in the spring of 1953 over Eva, when Jack was fired for the first time, the author's perspective is that C. F.'s behavior was his prerogative as CEO and chairman.

Dad had a fall in the bathroom and broke his hip. On his return from the hospital, he was confined to a wheelchair, and although his physical therapist, Phil, assured him he would walk again, he never did. When he accepted this, he borrowed a rich Aiken friend's private plane and flew to New York with a dozen suits and several of the staff from Aiken. He and the suits were transported to Anthony Zanghi, the Weatherill tailor, who had closed the business in the early 1990s and become the master tailor at H. Herzfeld, the high-end New York haberdasher that hewed mostly closely to Weatherill's veddy British cut, before it too closed in 2012. Zanghi took my father's measurements while sitting, to alter the suits "for the chair," as he put it.

I thought the gentle weather might soften my father and open his heart a bit, and mine too. We had a lot in common, after all, when it came to being the sons of all-powerful fathers, and the sometimes crushing pressure to live up to their expectations. If only we could somehow turn the thing that seemed to divide us, the lingering distrust caused by my grandfather's actions, into a common bond. But I didn't know how to do that, and I guess he didn't either, or didn't want to.

Instead, living in the reddest of red states seemed to bring Dad and "the old gentleman" closer. Fox News, South Carolina politics, and a deep streak of contrarianism that had always been there now seemed to dominate his personality. In the long, soft Aiken evenings, my mother arranged cocktail parties to give her husband something to look forward to. At these affairs he conducted himself like a Southern planter from bygone days, scion of that rice-planting, slave-owning Seabrook his father had claimed as our crossing ancestor. His guests would start out laughing at his politically incorrect remarks as he probed their tolerance with increasingly provocative sallies about, say, the need to keep the Confederate flag flying over the state capitol, which was a heated political issue around South Carolina in the aughts. Some of the guests, all much younger than he, seemed to regard Jack Seabrook nostalgically as a gentleman of "the old school," like Strom Thurmond, the long-serving South Carolina senator who had voted against the Civil Rights Act—an association Jack embraced. His more liberal guests (who tended to be my mother's friends) sat stone-faced as he leaned into Jesse Jackson and Al Sharpton, until even his Republican pals began to squirm nervously, and my mother would cry, "Oh Jack, enough!" and shut the conversation down.

I would excuse myself to refill my hastily thrown together old-fashioned—a triple shot of bourbon on ice with a teaspoon of sugar and a wedge of orange and bitters that burned on the lips. At some point it occurred to me that my father had turned into his father. If that could happen to him, it could happen to me.

※

IN AIKEN, the staff now included the home health-care service that my parents had contracted with for twenty-four-hour care, a rotating staff of regulars who hung out in the kitchen with Delores, waiting to be summoned by an electronic chime that sounded when my father pushed the button on the small buzzer that sat on the corduroy-upholstered arm of his La-Z-Boy recliner. Delores held court there as the others watched the small, ceiling-mounted TV tuned to Jerry Springer or Dr. Phil. As was the case in Jersey, the humanity in the house was always in the kitchen, and I escaped the dreariness of my parents' routine by spending as much time there as I could. But as my presence also inhibited conversation, I never stayed as long as I would have liked.

Before leaving New Jersey, my father had supervised the packing of his wine cellar in wooden crates, which were loaded into a large horse van and driven south to Aiken, where he had converted part of the basement into a paneled, temperature-controlled cellar. All that was left behind the sliding bookcase and the false wall was that old Seabrook & Son safe. I thought it was sweet, in a way, that my father had hung on to this useless hunk of metal for so long, purely for the sentimental reason that it was the safe where Seabrook & Son kept those first unimaginable profits that A. P. and Charlie earned from overhead irrigation. Of course, it was far too heavy to move.

One day the staff got Dad loaded into the NIMROD3 coupe and I drove from Aiken over to Seabrook Island, on the coast, in an attempt to satisfy his absurd notion that, despite my research in England and meeting with my beaky fifth cousin Colin, the South Carolina Seabrooks were our real crossing ancestors. On the way we pulled up outside the Edisto Presbyterian Church, where some of the Seabrook plantation masters are buried, including Whitemarsh Benjamin Seabrook, who was born on Edisto Island, educated at Princeton, and became the governor of South Carolina in 1869. This Seabrook was also the author of *The History of the Cotton Plant*, a book in which he advocated keeping slaves in stocks.

"You know, Dad," I said, as I nosed NIMROD3 through streets overhung with Spanish moss, "I'm really sure these Seabrooks are not our Seabrooks."

"Yes, you've said that," my father replied. He just smiled. He couldn't care less.

MY FATHER WAS DECLINING, but my mother's heart was failing faster. We entered the roller coaster of late-stage congestive heart failure, with big emotional lifts and dips almost daily. She joined a prayer group in Aiken. She also busied herself with my father's obituary, a macabre impulse, but she knew how much an obit in *The New York Times* mattered to him. In a way she was still working on the "Women's View" column she had in mind when she came down to the farm with her hatless girlfriends in May 1956.

When Courtney died in 2003, at the age of ninety-four, the *Times* wrote an obituary with the headline "Pioneer in Frozen Vegetables." The obit rightly gave credit to Courtney's many contributions to the company's success, and his leadership in the nascent frozen-food industry. The piece did not mention the strike. My father seemed pleased by the obit, but he must have realized it meant the *Times* was less likely to run an obit for him. And if the paper did, would the writer focus on his Seabrook Farms career, or on what happened afterward?

My mother died of congestive heart failure in August 2005. When I went to wake my father at 4:00 a.m. to tell him she was gone, he said, "Oh no!"—the only expression of genuine dismay I can recall him ever making. It was as if up to that point everything had happened according to plan.

After she died, most of my parents' Aiken friends dropped my father. To me, this was a shock, although in retrospect it was not surprising, given the way he had been provoking guests for years with increasingly racist or sexist sallies. It turned out some of his most frequent guests and apparently closest friends had only been coming because my mother was around. A few even staged an intervention when none of us siblings were there, coming over to the house to scold him for what they perceived was his less-than-generous treatment of Delores and others on the staff. Jack himself relayed all this to us in his CEO-of-his-own-pain voice, pretending not to care.

❧

DURING MY STAYS IN THE PALMETTO STATE, which I would take in rotation with Bruce and Carol, my father and I would go through the nightly ritual of discussing the upcoming meal and what wine would go best with it. What about an outstanding Meursault, if fish or chicken were on the menu, or a sturdy claret with beef? Once I blurted out, "Hell, why not open the biggest bottle you've got, Dad?" (I was already loaded at this point, on two generous Maker's Marks.) He shook his head vigorously and closed his eyes in horror at this drunken vandalizing of the natural order of things.

Nightly I made my unsteady way down the basement stairs to fetch yet another bottle of his wine. Standing among all the glorious bottles my father would never drink, I felt some of the beauty and grace that I had imbibed as a child begin to leak out of me. He was dying, and the rituals that went with the cocktails and the wine would die too. My legacy was the leftover booze.

In Aiken, decanting seemed pointless. After I brought a bottle up from the cellar and uncorked it, I went through the motions of pouring Dad a glass. He'd refuse; he'd lost the taste for wine, among other former pleasures. So I just kept the bottle next to me and slopped it into my glass, sediment and all.

After dinner, his regular evening health-care worker Donnie would get him out of the wheelchair and back into the La-Z-Boy in the study, an operation that required the core strength of a linebacker. Then it was either *Law and Order* or more Fox News. Finally, he would push his button, a distant chime was heard from the kitchen, and presently Donnie would appear and say, in a husky Southern voice, "Yes sir, you rang?" and repeat the wheelchair–to–La-Z-Boy lift in reverse and take him to bed. Before turning in myself, I'd send angry emails to my siblings about his treatment of the help. On one occasion, my brother wrote back, "Lay off the vitriol and the bourbon."

❧

I THOUGHT OUR FATHER might want to reconcile with Lizanne before he died. Surely he remembered the pain his own father caused by severing relations with him and never making up, which seemed to have left him locked in a Sisyphean struggle of always trying to prove himself to the old man, and endlessly coming up short. I felt I understood what that was like. Maybe I could help.

A therapist was out of the question, of course: Ernest Dichter was as close as Jack ever got to that racket. But although my father was completely agnostic, I thought that, given the family's long relationship with Deerfield Presbyterian, an emissary from the old man's church might carry some weight. Without telling Dad I was doing it (because I knew he would veto the idea), I arranged to fly the resident holy man down.

Pastor Ken Larter pulled up a chair on one side of the La-Z-Boy, and I sat on the other side. Within reach on a side table was an executive-model desktop phone that had Lizanne's name next to one of the speed dial buttons. He'd kept it there all these years and looked at it every day. What would it take for him to push that button? To lift a finger and touch it? Nope. He wouldn't budge. He closed his eyes, set his lips in a narrow line, and shook his head from side to side. When Pastor Ken suggested we pray over it together, Dad's eyes opened and looked daggers at me. Had he held on to one last whip from his collection?

CHAPTER 32

THE SESQUI AND THE SWISS BANKER

BOTH MY GRANDFATHER AND MY FATHER HAD SUR-vived grave threats to their livelihoods midway through their careers—setbacks that would have finished most men. C. F. lost his job and his investment when Alec White pulled the plug on his first vegetable factory in 1924, when he was forty-three. At forty-two, my father had lost his vocation, his home, and his father, when C. F. sold the company to Seeman's and evicted us. Both men had shown a cat-like agility to land on their feet after falls from great heights. Each had gone on to enjoy second and third acts in their American lives, defying whatever Scott Fitzgerald meant by that line. The overcoming of obstacles and setbacks is an essential aspect of the B. C. Forbes–Samuel Smiles capitalist hero, and both my grandfather and father seemed to check that box.

But knowing what I know now, I have come to view this inheritance in a different light—as a legacy of cheating.

❧

AFTER THE WHITES DISMISSED HIM from what became Del-Bay Farm in 1924, C. F. focused his energies on his contracting and engineer-ing work, which previously had been a side project. With the help of his corporate lawyer, New Jersey State Senator Albert R. McAllister, C. F. organized more than half a dozen contracting and construction concerns, concealing his own ownership through holding companies. He was already well connected in Trenton thanks to his term as high-way commissioner, and he promptly secured a big project grading the traffic circle on the Camden approach to the new suspension bridge, which would be the world's longest yet, and the first to span the lower Delaware River. It was scheduled to open July Fourth, 1926, on the same day as the grand exposition that Philadelphia was organizing to celebrate the 150th anniversary of the adoption and signing of the Declaration of Independence by the Second Continental Congress at the Pennsylvania State House, now Independence Hall. Belford was a gang boss on one of the work crews on the job, and his foot was seriously injured when it was run over by a tractor.

As he was completing that project, C. F. began to hear rumors about a crisis engulfing the Sesqui, as the exposition was known. The fair had been sold to the public as a world-class event to rival the Paris Exposition of 1890. But only a year before the opening date, the city's Republican political boss, William Vare, had persuaded Philadelphia Mayor W. Freeland Kendrick—a former pawn-shop owner who Vare kept in his pocket—to move the fairgrounds from Broad Street and the Beaux Arts center of the city to swampy South Philly, Boss Vare's political turf. According to *Sesqui!*, a history of the doomed expo by Thomas Keels, "This move alone guaranteed the fair's failure, since it added millions of dollars in development costs and delayed construction." As the July Fourth opening day approached, city planners started to panic that the project wouldn't be finished in time.

C. F. saw an opportunity. In a 1928 interview with *The Philadelphia Inquirer*, he explained the situation. "[In] the spring of 1926 . . . we got word that there was trouble at the Sesqui, that Mayor Kendrick wanted to open on the scheduled date and that it would take some extraordinary bustling to get the grounds in order. I went over to the Sesqui [and asked] if there was anything I could do to help." Plenty, as it turned out. His companies billed the city $85,000—almost $1.5 million in today's money—for the grading work on the Gladway, the entertainment and amusement center of the fair. In similarly adjusted dollars, he billed another $193,000 for roads and paths through it, and $819,000 for landscaping. (Later it was pointed out that the bushes Seabrook's men had planted around the fairground had no root systems; they had simply been scalped from the Koster Nursery in Deer-field and propped up with some dirt on the fairground, so of course they quickly turned brown and died.) By concealing his ownership interest in the different entities submitting these bills, and with the help of friends in City Hall, the wily Mr. Seabrook allegedly secured a full third of all the public works contracts for the Sesquicentennial. Altogether C. F.'s companies billed the Sesqui for almost $9 million.

In addition to widespread graft, the Sesqui was plagued with bad weather and poor attendance. City planners expected fifty million guests; fewer than five million came. The fair lost more than $300 million in today's money, and its organizing body went bankrupt in early 1927. Many of the contractors and subcontractors were never paid, but C. F. seems to have made out like a bandit. He hired Mayor Kendrick's former law partner, George Klauder, who also happened to be the head of the Sesqui-Centennial Creditors' Committee, to lobby for his interests, and collected all $9 million. Had he left matters there, no trouble might have ensued.

Klauder was part of William Vare's Organization, the political machine made up of corrupt politicians, city officials, and contractors that controlled public works in Philadelphia. With Klauder's help, C. F.'s various engineering and contracting firms sold fire-hose valves to the city at inflated prices. He sold the city a supposedly patented material called Multi Steel, which turned out to be ordinary steel with a 200 percent markup. By mid-1928, the scale of C. F.'s graft was too great even for Philadelphia. That summer, Philadelphia City Controller William Hadley and District Attorney Managhan accused C. F. Seabrook of being the "mastermind" behind a plot to monopolize all city contracts in Philadelphia, using Klauder's connections to the Organization.

"Seabrook Wanted in Phila Scandal" was the Vineland *Daily Journal's* headline for September 1, 1928. "Bridgeton's Midas Said to Be Implicated in Contract Grabbing Scandal." The story notes that "Seabrook was summoned to appear in the office of District Attorney Monaghan yesterday, but it is said that Seabrook has left Philadelphia."

Harry Mackey, who succeeded Kendrick as mayor in 1928, initially defended Bridgeton's Midas. *The Philadelphia Inquirer*, which published a series of front-page investigative articles on the scandal, wrote, "Mayor Mackey angrily pounded a table . . . [and] resoundingly denounced the Controller's probe into city contracts and his disclosures of the activities of the Mayor's friend and former law partner, George C. Klauder. 'They talk about C. F. Seabrook,' Mackey said. 'Seabrook was not a fly-by-night contractor. He was not a thief. . . . He is a big man, and everything he is connected with has real money of his own behind it!' " C. F. did eventually sit down with Managhan and told the district attorney that "a monopoly of city contracts in Philadelphia never occurred to me."

That seems to have been where the matter ended, as though it were all just a big misunderstanding, something to be settled quietly in a manner that was satisfactory to all parties, except the taxpayers. C. F. Seabrook was never charged with a crime, and the scandal didn't hinder his later career as a frozen-food magnate, or appear in any of his obituaries, including the one in the *Inquirer*. But he was banned forever from bidding again on public works for the city of Philadelphia.

My father was nine in 1926. He spoke often of his father's and Belford's involvement with the Sesqui, but he never mentioned the scandal or the stories in the *Inquirer*. I didn't know about any of this myself until after he was gone, so I didn't ask. Not that he would have told me. But I imagine that a bright boy like Jack Seabrook would have had at least an inkling of what his father was up to across the river.

❧

ONE DAY IN 1957, a Swiss banker with an interest in scientific farming named Carl Hirschmann visited Seabrook. Jack showed him around the plant and farm. During the tour, Jack questioned his guest closely about how the notoriously secretive Swiss banking system worked. Hirschmann, who was the owner of the Handelskredit Bank in Zurich, explained about the strict Swiss privacy laws that keep banking information anonymous and inaccessible, even to the U.S. government. As

Hirschmann later testified in a deposition, "Mr. Seabrook was having trouble at that time with the girls' mother, Anne," who was threatening to sue Jack for more child support. The earlier settlement had not been enough to support the lifestyle she imagined for herself in New York. Since his finances were entwined with the family business, Jack feared that an aggressive lawyer could extract a hefty chunk of the family's assets. He was also supporting Liz now, who he had been married to for less than a year. The Swiss banker explained that establishing an account in his bank would protect certain assets from Anne. For extra security, he might consider establishing two accounts.

After he returned from London with Liz in the summer of 1959 (where he made a quick side trip to Zurich, according to the diary), Jack began looking for work. He thought about moving to California. He had an offer from a major food company there. But instead, he decided to set himself up as an independent consultant, offering engineering and investment banking advice to his network of Philadelphia and New York business contacts, built up over twenty years at Seabrook Farms. Few men were better qualified to both assess the technical feasibility of a project and put together a deal to finance it than Jack Seabrook. He established a home office in nearby Woodstown, next door to the local opera company. Betty Gaunt, who left Seabrook Farms with her boss, worked there too.

Through Ben Sawin of the Provident Bank, my father became close to Howard Butcher III, a Philadelphia stockbroker who had inherited a fortune in Pennsylvania Railroad stock. Butcher was a generation older than Jack, and eventually took his place on his office wall of WASP superheroes as Jack's third surrogate father, after Thornthwaite and Sawin. Butcher was the major shareholder in a handful of utility companies, and he needed someone like Jack Seabrook to help him rationalize his holdings. He hired JMS as a consultant on several projects and paid him well for his advice. Eventually my father was able to consolidate Butcher's companies under a single corporate umbrella, called International Utilities, where he took a job in 1964, and became CEO and chairman by the early 1970s.

In 1961, Butcher had solicited the Washington, D.C., law firm of Goodwin, Rosenbaum, Meacham and White for investment advice. That was how Jack became acquainted with Joseph Rosenbaum, a Washington-based lawyer and lobbyist who was law partners with his younger brother, Francis. Both had worked for the OSS, the precursor to the CIA, during World War II (Joe had achieved the rank of colonel, which was how he subsequently styled himself) and had deep connections within government. Because Butcher owned utilities on both sides of the U.S.-Canadian border, there was a maze of regulations to work through, and well-connected lobbyists like the Rosenbaums were essential.

In early 1962, Colonel Joe approached Butcher about investing in a high-voltage direct-current line that would link the western U.S. with the Canadian province of Alberta. A company called Inergie would oversee the project, which would be the largest private electrical transmission program ever undertaken in the United States. The idea involved dizzying technical challenges, not least of which was converting AC to DC current on a massive scale. Jack Seabrook, with his twin talents for engineering and finance, took charge of evaluating the technical feasibility of the project and its worthiness as an investment. IU eventually sunk more than a million dollars ($10 million today), into feasibility studies for Inergie before determining the scheme was technically impossible. Much of that money wound up in a Swiss bank account controlled by Colonel Joe. A portion of it was then transferred to a Swiss bank account that belonged to John M. Seabrook. As for Inergie, government investigators later dubbed one of the feasibility studies that IU's investment paid for as "worthless," and another as "a piece of horseradish."

❧

LIZ MUST HAVE WONDERED where the money for four-in-hand coaching was coming from. Her husband was living far, far larger than whatever he was earning as a consultant. He had been all but cut out of his father's will, and yet he was playing at the sport of Rockefellers, DuPonts, and Wanamakers. By the mid-sixties, Jack Seabrook had raised his coaching game to the highest level. He won the elite driving competition at Richmond, England, in 1966, and drove around the track during Royal Ascot that year, when Queen Elizabeth and Philip, president of the Coaching Club, were in the Royal Box. A few years later, he took a borrowed team up the long drive at Windsor Castle, in a procession led by Philip. The costs of running a first-class coaching stable that could compete with the Royal Mews at coaching events had to be immense, including grooms, horse vans, the maintenance of his collection of coaches, carriages, and sleighs, and, of course, the horses themselves, which became progressively more royal through the years, until by the end he had a team of white Lipizzaners.

Money had to be found somewhere. Jack was spending a great deal of time with men who knew how to find it, wearing that *Sweet Smell of Success* suit that wound up in my closet in the eighties. Liz had met some of them socially, and didn't think Jack should be in business with these men. One struck her as particularly shady: Francis, the younger Rosenbaum. In 1965, Francis hatched a scheme with Andrew Stone, a Midwestern businessman, to defraud the U.S. government by overcharging the navy on an annual contract for rocket launchers. A shell corporation called Astco was created to own the rocket-launcher company, which was named Chromostat. In the complex financial maneuvers between Astco and Chromostat, there was the appearance of self-dealing and money laundering through secret Swiss bank accounts. Both Francis and Joseph eventually went to prison.

Jack was on the Astco board, and he was later sued in a class action that shareholders brought against the company's directors for fraud, resulting in years of litigation. But because the money had been routed through a Swiss bank account, it was impossible for investigators to trace it, unless the Swiss government and U.S. Justice Department were to negotiate a treaty allowing investigators to open the account. Still, in the eventual settlement, my father was hit with $520,333 in settlement costs, and another $453,700 in legal fees. The IU board, handpicked by my father, had voted to pay the settlement costs, as well as Jack's legal fees, since the litigation had occurred while he was running the company.

Jack hoped that resolving the Astco fraud case would close the book on his ill-advised relationship with the Rosenbaum brothers, but it did not. The Securities and Exchange Commission took renewed interest in the fact that IU had paid its CEO's penalty and legal fees. By the mid-1970s, the agency's investigation had expanded beyond the Astco settlement to Jack's alleged use of corporate perquisites, or "perks," a buzzword then in vogue, to pay for his princely lifestyle. The government also continued to seek access to the Swiss bank accounts that had been instrumental in the Astco-Chromostat rocket-launcher scheme.

ɔⱪc

SOMEONE IN THE GOVERNMENT leaked the SEC's investigation into John M. Seabrook to Jerry Landauer, a star *Wall Street Journal* investigative reporter. Landauer had emigrated to the U.S. from Germany with his parents in 1938 to escape the Nazis. He started off as a paperboy at *The New York Times* and eventually joined the staff of *The Wall Street Journal* in Washington. Driven by a righteous zeal to expose corruption, in 1973 Landauer broke the story that Spiro Agnew was under criminal indictment from the Justice Department, which ultimately forced the vice president to resign. After his Agnew scoop, Landauer began looking for a corrupt business leader to investigate. Our father, whose extravagant coach-and-four lifestyle was by then well known in Philadelphia and New York business circles, made juicy prey.

Up until Landauer took an interest in him, my father's relationship with journalists had been mutually satisfactory. He had long courted the press, going back to his Seabrook Farms days; he'd even married a reporter. Most journalists were happy to trade a sympathetic story for an insider's look into the aristocratic family behind the frozen commodity, and to get a coaching picnic out of the deal. The trip to Monaco that brought my parents together was in many ways a media junket designed to raise the company's profile—and Jack's.

Still, young Jack had lived through the 1934 strike, when his father and brothers had been portrayed unsympathetically in the left-wing press. He wasn't naïve about the fact that his rub-your-face-in-it, Slim

Aarons–style of living the good life had made him an inviting target for a takedown. But before the *Journal*'s investigation, the golden boy had always come out looking good in the press, mainly because of his potent personal charm. With Jerry Landauer, his luck ran out.

❧

THE FIRST FRONT-PAGE STORY appeared in the *Journal* on April 6, 1978. It began:

> John M. Seabrook, the silver-haired chairman of IU International Corp., likes to live stylishly. He belongs to fine clubs in Philadelphia, New York and London. He keeps seven handsome Oldenburg horses in the splendid stables near Salem, N.J., and he spends lavishly to acquire antique horse-drawn carriages. Right now, he owns 22, all lovingly maintained by a former British cavalryman. . . . In fact, Mr. Seabrook's substantial salary ($451,558 last year) at times seems insufficient to meet all his expenses.

IU was indeed picking up the tab for some of his coaching expenses, because when he appeared with his coach and horses at prominent events like the Royal Winter Fair in Toronto, he invited business associates from IU's portfolio of Canadian utility and mining companies to ride on top as he took the team around the arena. And because it was a sort of business meeting that he, the CEO and chairman, conducted from the box seat, whip in hand, it was a legitimate business expense. On one occasion, he FedExed his horses to Canada at an enormous cost and billed IU.

Not long after the first Landauer piece ran, IU's friendly board negotiated a deal with the SEC. A special counsel would be appointed to investigate the allegations of misusing company funds and determine whether criminal charges were warranted. The board chose Arthur Lane, a retired judge, to be the special counsel. Judge Lane was a Princeton man. That was "a win for our side," my father told me confidently.

That fall, on September 29, another front-page Landauer article appeared. The article reported that the SEC was seeking to reopen its investigation, in light of new evidence about payments from the IU treasury that wound up in a Swiss account belonging to John M. Seabrook in the early 1960s. Criminal charges were again a possibility. The article carried a dubious-sounding blind quote from an "experienced executive" who commented: "The fundamental issue raised by the information leading to the renewed investigation is whether the affairs of this major public corporation are being conducted solely in the interest of the corporation and its shareholders or for the primary benefit of John M. Seabrook." As the CEO of Seabrook Farms in the mid-fifties, Jack had attempted to curtail his father's practice of using the company as his "private piggybank." Now he stood accused of using IU's treasury in the same way.

One could argue, and our father frequently did, that he was being unfairly singled out by federal regulators, who were trying to impose a generational change on practices common to business executives in the 1950s and sixties, when men thought nothing of borrowing the company plane for a personal weekend, as Jack himself had often done at Seabrook Farms. But the reason he was singled out, as Lawrence Lederman, a high-profile New York attorney who dealt with Jack on several deals, once told me, was that my "father was sort of asking for it. With the horses and carriages. Those suits. That Duke of Windsor business. He made himself a target."

I did not discuss the Landauer articles in depth with my father. I'm sure he talked about them with Carol, who became partners with Jack's brilliant tax attorney, William Goldstein, at the white-shoe Philadelphia firm of Drinker, Biddle & Reath. I did speak to my mother about *The Wall Street Journal* and the SEC investigation. The notion that her husband might have done something illegal troubled her greatly. She had always tried to be a beacon of morality in the pea-soup fog of Seabrook situational ethics. But now she had to convince herself that if Jack had made "mistakes" when he became involved with the Rosenbaums in the early 1960s, it was because he'd lost his job and his inheritance, and he needed to provide for his family. His own father was really to blame for putting him in an impossible situation.

Of course, I wanted my father to be vindicated. No part of me wanted him punished, even if he had used money from IU to pay for his coaching. I worried that some of my Princeton contacts would notice the articles, but if they did no one mentioned them. At the same time, I was deeply impressed with the fact that a journalist, simply by asking questions, could uncover information that wreaked havoc on powerful men like Jack Seabrook.

❧

THE THIRD LANDAUER ARTICLE, which ran in May 1979, carried the headline: "Fee Paid to IU Chairman's Partner Leads U.S. to Look for Possible Plot to Loot Firm." The lede was a doozy.

> The executive perquisites at IU International Corp. aren't bad. For instance, until 1978, the diversified utility company paid its chairman "substantial" sums to transport and maintain his carriages and horses at the annual Royal Winter Fair in Toronto, where he exhibits them in the driving competition.
>
> That isn't all. Mr. Seabrook . . . has, among other things, an apartment in New York City, a chauffeur-driven automobile, and three staffed offices, including one near his home. Because the company believed it benefited as well from these perquisites, it pays for some or all of these expenses.

My father had grown up with his father's anti-Semitism. But he had known Jews at Princeton; like him, they were excluded from the elite clubs. Along with the Rosenbaum brothers, he had friends and business partners who were Jewish, such as Leon Schachter, the union leader, and Bill Goldstein, his attorney. Jack Seabrook was the epitome of the Wall Street trope about how to succeed in finance—dress British, think Yiddish. But after the third Landauer piece, C. F.'s attitudes reasserted themselves. Henry Ford's writings about the grand Jewish plot against "Nordics" had shaped C. F.'s thinking; now the ancient Roman mind virus was emerging in Jack. He ranted at a family gathering about how the SEC and Landauer were in it together. Their ultimate aim, he warned me, was to destroy our "way of life."

I listened in silence as my mother attempted to shush him. After all, she pointed out, the lawyers defending him were Jewish. But she could not prevent him from once again issuing his darkest curse: he promised to piss on Jerry Landauer's grave. And when Landauer did die unexpectedly two years later, of a heart attack at the age of forty-nine—a spooky coincidence that recalled the untimely death of Bob Sidur, whom Jack had similarly cursed—my father read aloud with grim satisfaction the obituary in the *Journal* at the breakfast table.

Judge Lane's decision was issued in May 1979. It was mostly good news for our father—there would be no criminal charges. He would have to pay back about $200,000 to IU. He would also have to step down as IU's president and CEO and could never serve in a management capacity at the company again. He was allowed to retain the title of chairman until he was sixty-five. At least the ordeal of the long investigation and the bad publicity it had generated was finally over. Except it wasn't.

It turned out that the SEC had continued negotiating with the Swiss High Court about accessing bank account number 192 at Handelskredit Bank. In early 1982, the court ruled that the SEC was entitled to John M. Seabrook's Swiss banking records, an almost unprecedented exception at the time. In explaining its decision, the Court said that since the records would show conclusively whether or not Seabrook himself had engaged in fraud, there was a public interest in granting this exception. This was very bad news indeed. If our father was guilty, now it was only a matter of time before the SEC obtained the evidence that would ruin him. And for what would he have thrown away his reputation, and possibly his freedom? So that he could fulfill his father's fantasy of a South Jersey dynasty that would last five hundred years.

The SEC opened the account that spring. Number 192 showed no unusual activity that might be associated with money laundering, self-dealing, or fraud. The government was forced to back down. Our way of life would endure.

CHAPTER 33

A CREDIBLE
ULTIMATUM

D AD MADE AN IRISH GOOD-BYE ON FEBRUARY 2, 2009.
He slipped away when no family happened to be visiting,
leaving by the side door, the way he came in. By the time Donnie went
to rouse him, he'd been gone for hours.

There was a viewing at a local funeral home. Jack met the last in a
lifetime of wardrobe gambits—what to wear to the grave—with typical aplomb, choosing a dark-blue pin-striped Huntsman suit and a
white shirt from Sulka with French cuffs, and a lighter-blue tie with
tiny white dots. Neither Bruce nor Carol wanted to look, but I stood
over his body for a long time. The face was made up with bright red
lips, horn-rimmed spectacles on. His lemony scent was missing; in
its place was a faint whiff of formaldehyde. I was angry and hun-
gover. I remembered how he had kicked me once when I was about
ten, the only time I recall him physically disciplining me. I had been
in the way as he and the coachman were rushing to harness the team,
and he kicked me in the butt to move me out of the way, but also to
express his general displeasure at my sullen attitude and sarcasm. He
never apologized, and I never said anything to my mother. I remembered the feel of his leather-booted foot.

Back in South Jersey, Pastor Ken presided over the funeral at the
Deerfield Presbyterian Church. My brother delivered the eulogy. He
ended his talk by quoting one of Jack's favorite equine double enten-
dres: "Ride 'em hard and put 'em away wet"—the first time that enter-
tainer Tennessee Ernie's Ford catchphrase had been spoken in the
sanctuary, I suspect.

To our surprise, Lizanne came to the service. I had not seen her in sixteen years. She had been driven down from the city by a tall man with his long hair in a ponytail, who wheeled her into the back of the church. I looked and waved, and she smiled and held up her hand. After the service ended, her attendant pushed her out to the gravesite, and I embraced her there, awkwardly bending over and putting my hands on her padded shoulders. That was the last time any of us saw her. She died in 2016.

Jack was laid to rest next to Liz, not far from Nana and at the feet of C. F., with Courtney and Mae nearby. (Belford is with Harriet at the Broad Street Methodist Church in Bridgeton, and Thelma is in Maplewood, the New York City suburb in Essex County that she had left Seabrook for years earlier.) We had a reception in the Pine Room in Salem, where the Nubians were still in residence; my brother later warehoused them in Miami. *The New York Times* did not run an editorial obituary. In the end it was Courtney, the Fredo of the three, whom the paper of record remembered. I wrote my father's obit myself, and it ran among the paid death notices in the weekend edition.

I tried to find a home for his wardrobe. The Costume Institute at the Smithsonian took some of his Coaching Club uniforms, as well as Bishop Sheen's overcoat, but there were still more than 130 bespoke suits, 500 handmade shirts, 50 pair of Edward Green shoes, perhaps 1,000 neckties, plus all the other separates—socks, sweaters, boxer shorts, handkerchiefs, shoehorns. Bruce had no use for the heavyweight woolen fabrics in Miami, and I had long ago taken whatever I wanted.

I called Gentlemen's Resale on East Eighty-First Street, a men's consignment shop, and spoke on the phone with the owner.

"Your *father's* suits?" he said. "See, right there is a red flag. We only work with stuff that's two, three years old."

"But they're in impeccable condition."

"I'm sure they are, but our customers are looking for something more contemporary. Did he have Prada, Helmut Lang, St. Laurent?" I could see where this was going.

"Some are Huntsman," I said hopefully.

"Who?"

I gave away what suits and shirts I could to my tall male friends, and I wrote a *Men's Vogue* piece about that for then editor in chief Jay Fielden, who covered the cost of the tailoring alterations; the photographer Max Vadukul took wonderful pictures. The rest of his wardrobe I slowly and sadly boxed up over long hours spent in the formerly magical closet. Without Jack's personality to animate the cloth, the fabric felt as heavy as a lead apron. Some of the clothes had been hanging there for decades, like his raccoon coat and his Princeton "beer suit" of white overalls. After calling around, I finally found a guy from New York who said he'd drive down and take "the collection" off my hands. He claimed to run a haberdashery, but I suspect he kept the wardrobe for himself.

As for the wine, thousands of bottles, many in unopened cases, remained in his cellar in Aiken after he died. Fortunately, my brother arranged to have everything auctioned off at Sotheby's. Had it been left up to me, I'd still be drinking them.

❧

AFTER MY FATHER WAS GONE, my drinking got worse. In a perverse act of alcoholic mourning, I decided to construct a small wine cellar of my own in our basement in Brooklyn and fill it with bottles I acquired at a bargain from my brother-in-law's former wine business. "An excellent foundation for a cellar!" I said out loud, recalling my father's words on my winning that case of Palmer, one of my greatest achievements as John Jr. After sneaking a couple of cocktails—I had promised Lisa I was cutting back—I would go down there, uncork a bottle, or maybe two, and spend the evening looking through the "Save for JMS Jr." papers Dad had left for me when he died. As with the Palmer, the wine was soon gone. After that I was back to buying a couple of bottles of ETS red at a time at the pricy place around the corner—something Jack never did.

Lisa scoffed at me when I acted innocent of any alcohol issues. She threatened an intervention. I agreed to try "moderate" drinking. But if I tried, my resolve soon faded, and I was drinking more than ever, reasoning that I needed to make up for lost time. I discovered what my grandfather found out: there is no worse feeling than lying to your family. In those dark moments of mendacity, I thought about the giant rat from *The Boy Who Drew Cats* that I had imagined escaping from my father's cellar on that first visit long ago.

Finally, Lisa delivered what's known in recovery as a credible ultimatum. She had found a family therapist, and we were either going to go to her and deal with my drinking, or we were going to a divorce lawyer. Take your pick. The only thing I feared more than losing alcohol was losing Lisa. That's what made the ultimatum credible.

So I came under the care of the extraordinary Lisa Spiegel, the second transformative Lisa in my life. Lisa Spiegel and Jean Kunhardt ran a small family therapy practice called Soho Parenting in lower Manhattan. My Lisa (if you think *you're* confused . . .) knew of their work through a parenting group. Lisa Spiegel, of the North Jersey Spiegels, practiced the Internal Family Systems model of psychotherapy that was created by Dr. Richard Schwartz in the early 1990s. IFS is premised on the idea that "the natural state of the human mind is to have many different personalities or selves that make up the whole of who we are."

All of us have an inner community of "parts," or subpersonalities. Some of those parts, which Schwartz labeled "exiles," are associated with painful, upsetting emotions: anger, fear, shame. Other parts, known as "protectors," keep the exiles in check. When protectors fail, a third class of parts, the "firefighters," step in and douse the exiles with emotional retardants to keep the pain from becoming overwhelming. Alcohol, drugs, and binge-eating are common firefighters. An IFS-trained therapist helps clients "go inside" to identify and map their parts and try to engage protectors in dialogue and persuade them to step back so that you can communicate directly with the exiles. The goal is to achieve a reconciliation of exiles, protectors, and firefights, and be led by what Schwartz calls the Wise Self, the compassionate essence that we all have inside.

When Lisa and I first started our work with Lisa Spiegel, we began talking about our issues as a couple. I was able for the first time to really hear how I hurt Lisa by checking out night after night, how lonely that had been for her, and how I had betrayed her trust by blurting out private things having to do with us or our family in public when I'd had a few drinks. As it became obvious my drinking was the real problem, we all agreed that doing solo sessions might be the best way for us to proceed. At first, I was completely on the defensive, and also scared. My unexamined, uptight, WASPy "way of life" was under threat by a brainy Jewish woman with suspiciously New Agey–sounding methods. But I couldn't deny that there was an emotional logic in the design of the system. IFS builds on the work of previous generation of systems-oriented psychologists, including Salvador Minuchin and Kenneth Kaye, who had brought insights into family-based therapy learned as a family business consultant. I felt like I knew where Schwartz was coming from. I was part of the family system that had built Seabrook Farms, but also destroyed it. The war over the business was still going on inside me, as a battle of parts.

For a long time I treated Lisa Spiegel like a hostile force, a threat to be managed weekly, as I tried to run out the clock on the endless sessions with trivial complaints about my marriage, when we both knew what the real problem was. Whenever my drinking came up, I would promise to try harder to practice moderation, even though I already knew moderation didn't work for me. IFS therapy does not preach sobriety; it guides the client to see that the "drinking part" is a protector, a pain reliever with a positive intention—to help the person manage what they believe is unmanageable pain. I insisted that I should be allowed to continue to drink because it was my birthright and my heritage. Alcohol, in the form of countless celebratory bottles opened on the occasion of this or that triumph, was the juice that sustained the promise of privilege, and the myth of Seabrook exceptionalism. Alcohol was both the transmitter of Seabrook family culture and the medicine I relied on to dull the pain of that inheritance: my favorite firefighter.

"You came by it honestly," Lisa Spiegel said of my drinking, after one session in which I had gone inside and ended up as a young boy on that first trip to the wine cellar with my father. Once we got there, we returned to the wine cellar frequently in our excursions inside. What was in there that my Wise Self kept coming back to?

Toward the end of one such incursion into my parts, Lisa asked, "What about that safe?"

"What about it?"

"It just seems odd to me that your father lost the combination. Given everything you've told me about him, there's no way he would do that. Come on! *This* guy?"

She was right, of course. The man who never misplaced anything was hardly likely to lose the combination to a safe. It says something about my father's powers of persuasion that this hadn't occurred to me before Lisa brought it up.

"You have to crack that Seabrook and Son safe!"

By then, Lisa Spiegel and I had spent several years working together. We'd been all through my father's anti-Semitic outburst over the Jerry Landauer articles, Aunt Thelma's enthusiasm over Hebrew-free Coral Gables ("Joke's on her," Lisa said), and C. F.'s conspiracy theories about Jewish bankers, which he got from Henry Ford himself. It hurt me to see how it hurt Lisa to hear these things. But it helped to tell her—to confess. Lisa pointed out that Seabrook Farms Creamed Spinach, now packed by Seabrook Brothers and Sons, is a key ingredient in Jewish family holiday feasts, which explains why that product sells more units in Miami Beach than anywhere else in the United States. "So, in other words," she said, "your family's most famous product was based on a recipe created by your grandfather's Black cook, and its most devoted customers are Jews."

If anyone knew the answer to what had been inside that safe, it would be Jack's faithful coachman since the 1980s, Chris Higgins, who had sat beside him on countless drives around the farm in Salem with the team, listening to his stories. Chris is a neighbor of mine in Vermont now, and one evening over dinner I asked him, "So what was really inside that safe?" Chris is generally the soul of discretion, but he likes a good Jack Seabrook story as much as I do, and this one was a peach. Yes, the SEC had managed to open Handelskredit Bank account 192 belonging to John M. Seabrook and found nothing unusual. But the government never knew about the second account that Jack had at Handelskredit Bank. Chris told me, "JMS said, 'They opened the wrong one.'" Even if the government had seized and searched Jack's files, investigators wouldn't have found any information about that second account. Those records were hidden behind a sliding bookcase and a hidden door, inside an old safe that could not be opened, because the combination had been lost.

ꕥ

ON EASTER WEEKEND, 2016, we spent Saturday night at Lisa's sister's house in Connecticut. Her family doesn't drink much, so I thought it prudent to bring along two extra bottles of ETS red, which I had packed in my suitcase, and then once we arrived, had stashed in the closet of our bedroom. I figured I could alternate between glasses I drank in front of Lisa and glasses I would drink in secret.

I was well into my first bottle when I made the mistake of engaging with my brother-in-law on his vile conspiracy theory that the Sandy Hook massacre, which had occurred only a few towns away, was a stunt pulled off by crisis actors, to weaken support for the Second Amendment. Lit by alcohol, I became furious and called him mentally ill, then stormed out of the house and sat in the car. Lisa eventually came out. She had found the bottles in the closet. She put it simply: "You have to stop drinking or I'm leaving." She drove me to the station, and I took the train back to Grand Central, a Cheeveresque figure facing a midlife crisis under the bleak interior lighting of Metro North.

The following week I took my last glass of wine on what would have been my father's ninety-ninth birthday, April 16, 2016, which is also the eve of his three-on-the-same-day procreational hat trick. Here's to you, Dad. I understand now why you had to be the man in the top hat, and why you wanted me to be that man too—not because you were so powerful, but because you were damaged, like I am damaged. I forgive you, and I hope you can forgive me.

Then I emptied the last of my final bottle of ETS red into the wrong glass and polished it off.

CHAPTER 34

THE HEART OF RECOVERY

W HEN I DRIVE DOWN TO SOUTH JERSEY, I PASS BY Bowery Farm, a twenty-first-century vegetable factory that occupies two former ten-story warehouses, in an industrial park outside Secaucus. Thanks to technologies that my grandfather was too early to use—LCD lighting, robotics, AI—cofounder Irving Fain has been able to build an indoor, hydroponic vertical farm to grow high-end leafy greens in an almost entirely automated setting: an indoor truck farm. The farmer is an AI. Machine-learning algorithms manage irrigation, cultivation, fertilizing, and harvesting. The Thornthwaite growth units system Seabrook farmers once used to calculate the lifespan of a crop has been fine-tuned down to the level of each individual plant. Sun, seasons, and weather don't exist at Bowery Farms: the farmer has at long last taken complete control of the elements. Labor isn't a problem: nimble and robotic "hands" work tirelessly. Human workers are mainly used for janitorial duties.

Down at the other end of the state, in Upper Deerfield Township it's still farm country, mostly. Driving into Seabrook along Route 77, you pass the shiny red Seabrook Fire Department engines outside the firehouse, and the Seabrook Buddhist Temple, where the membership has greatly declined. The school that my grandfather built, where my father was one of the first students, is now the Moore School. And in a karmic twist, my grandparents' house on Polk Lane is now Seabrook House, the headquarters of a successful and growing network of Seabrook House drug and alcohol rehab centers around New Jersey and Pennsylvania. Turnpike billboards proclaim "Seabrook: The

Heart of Recovery." The brand has certainly come a long way from the Keables' sodden cow pasture.

In the former solarium, where Nana used to play bridge, Seabrook House patients smoke, read, and watch daytime TV. My grandfather's magnificent gardens have been maintained in their former glory by Seabrook House gardeners. Drunks and addicts wander through follies and mazes, and down mossy brick pathways leading to secret arbors, trying to find their way back to sobriety. Sadly, the pool around which the family always gathered on July Fourth, and where Eva Gabor still swims naked in the collective memory of old Seabrookers, has been permanently covered over for safety reasons.

✲

IN 2019, I arranged for our crossing ancestor to have his own stone in the Deerfield Presbyterian churchyard, a good-sized hunk of pale granite that sits across the road from the Seabrook family monument, toward the back.

In Memory of SAMUEL SEABROOK
Born 1816
Stansfield, England
Died January 6, 1871
Interred in Strangers' Graves

Whatever Samuel did or didn't do to cause C. F. to retroactively disown his grandfather, without Samuel none of this would have happened, and all the destinies that led through Seabrook would have had different outcomes.

The house in Salem now belongs to a New York–based eye doctor who uses it as a weekend retreat. The wine cellar is a screening room, I'm told, and the Carriage House may become a whiskey distillery, if the state agrees to license it. I don't know what happened to the safe. Perhaps it will turn up one day on eBay, along with my father's wardrobe.

Jack Seabrook's final deal was, fittingly, with the state of New Jersey. In November 2008, Charles Kuperus, New Jersey's agriculture secretary, announced the state's purchase of the development rights to his two thousand acres of farmland: "This truly is a once-in-a-lifetime opportunity to be able to preserve such a sizable portion of Southern Jersey's agricultural land base." The price was a whopping $15 million, the most the state had ever paid for the rights to a single piece of land. When JMS died, he passed that money along to us and his six grandchildren, through a series of trusts. I am a trustee along with Bruce and Carol, who is as astute as our father was about tax and finance law. The Seabrook family business amounts to managing these investments for our children, though I'm not sure we are doing them any favors.

✺

IN THE FALL OF 2016, I joined the board of the Seabrook Educational and Cultural Center, the nonprofit that oversees the museum and cares for its archive of historical materials. I had an ambitious agenda of narrative reform. The museum still occupies a corner of the basement of the Upper Deerfield Township Municipal building, which was erected in the 1970s next to the foundations of the old plant. But the former workers' housing around the municipal building is now one of the poorest places in the most impoverished county in the state. According to a 2023 survey published on NJ.com, "Cumberland is New Jersey's poorest county. And it has long been considered the state's least healthy county. Its median household income is 35% lower than the state's and no county . . . has a higher percentage of people living below the federal poverty line." The article goes on to say: "In a state considered among the richest in America, Cumberland County is worse off than even some Appalachian counties in rural Georgia and Tennessee in key indicators for health and poverty."

In 1972, Mark Watson, a thirty-three-year-old attorney, and C. J. Achee, forty-five, a land developer from Bayville, New Jersey, paid

$9 million for the Seabrook Housing Corp. and the surrounding land, most of which went to the beneficiaries of C. F. Seabrook's estate. The new owners announced a grand plan to transform Seabrook into an "agri-city" that would have "all the modern conveniences of the large city with the rustic advantages of the small American town," according to an interview they gave to *The New York Times*. The scheme never got off the ground.

In 1987, the Department of Housing and Urban Development designated 326 units of Seabrook worker housing for its Moderate Housing Rehabilitation Program, known as "Section 8" housing for people living below the poverty line. The Washington lobbying firm of Manafort, Kelly, and Stone received a $326,000 consulting fee for bringing these units to HUD's attention. One of the principals in the firm, Paul Manafort, then thirty-eight, also had a concealed ownership interest in a property development company, the CDC Financial Group of Hartford, Connecticut, that had, with remarkably fortunate timing, purchased the Seabrook units not long before the HUD contract. Manafort's ownership stake became much more valuable thanks to the contract, which was worth $11 million in tax credits, $30 million in rent subsidies, and another $5 million in renovation costs, when it would have been more economical to raze the crumbling cinderblock barracks-style buildings.

HUD also awarded CDC the contract to manage the rentals, which allowed the company to raise the rents as high as $750 per unit. The federal government was paying the rent, so it didn't matter that the units were wildly over market price, unless you happened to be one of the by then elderly Japanese or Estonian former Seabrook workers who didn't quality for Section 8 housing. These former Seabrookers, unable to afford the inflated rent, were booted from their homes. Altogether, taxpayers spent $47 million in Seabrook for a project the community never wanted, and one that disrupted the lives of its residents. Like many grifters who take advantage of government largesse—which is how C. F. had built a good deal of Seabrook in the first place—Paul Manafort did very well.

IN 2017, I became president of the Seabrook cultural center's board. A few good things happened during my tenure. I was fortunate to get to know Andrew Urban, a labor historian at Rutgers University, who was researching a book about Seabrook's role in mid-century East Coast migratory labor. Andy became an invaluable ally. The two of us spent a lot of time together down Jersey way. I also commissioned a New York–based architecture and design firm, Partner + Partner, to create a new website that opened the Seabrook story to critical interpretations centering on race, workers' rights, and semicaptive labor. The board didn't approve it.

In 2019, we secured funding from the New Jersey Council on the Humanities to investigate the expanded role that the museum and the SECC could play in the community and the culture at large. An executive committee was formed, led by me; including Andy; Penny Watson, who is a local architect; Janet Sheridan, a cultural heritage specialist; and Mas Nakawatase, who had come to Seabrook as a child during the war and had been emcee at the "Seabrook: A New Beginning" event where my father spoke in 1994. We used the grant money to organize two public hearings, to which we invited a wide variety of possible stakeholders. The pandemic hit the week the hearings were scheduled, so we held two Zoom sessions instead.

Among the attendees was Gloria Kates, an African American Seabrooker whose family migrated from Georgia to South Jersey during World War II. Kates spoke about her experience of walking into the museum and looking at the pictures on the walls. "I didn't see *us* there," she told the group. Following those meetings, Andy and I began collecting oral histories from African American Seabrookers, beginning with Gloria, her friend Betty Brown-Pitts, Jeanna Rogers, Jimmy Lane, and others in their family and peer group. We developed additional sources of funding from the state and from private donors to expand the work of communal remembering and to mount a future special exhibition devoted to the African American experience at Seabrook Farms. Gloria Kates became an SECC board member, and the museum now has a permanent display of photographs and text that recognizes the contributions made by Black Seabrookers, under a banner that says "We made money for that man!"

But my efforts to reform the narrative mostly failed. An SECC stalwart from the Japanese American community told a reporter anonymously that I was "biting the hand that feeds me" in being critical of my grandfather. People whose own life stories incorporate the notion of C. F. Seabrook as a humanitarian capitalist who helped them in their hour of need—"a head for business, a heart for people" as one mythologizer put it—weren't interested in changing their views because the great man's privileged grandson, a New York liberal who drove down now and then, told them that the old man was a corrupt demagogue and an abuser who only ever cared about power, control, and himself. Social justice is a fine thing, but the truth wasn't going to set anyone free. C. F. had given his workers something more compelling than truth. Their lives had meaning. C. F. made them feel like they mattered. And people want to matter. When it became clear that my version of the family story conflicted with the institutional interests of the SECC, I resigned, and Mas took over as president.

❧

ON ONE OF OUR ORAL-HISTORY-GATHERING TRIPS, Andy and I were early for our appointment in the museum, so we went across Route 77 to Franco's, a convenience store and grill, for breakfast sandwiches and coffee. As we sat outside at a picnic table, an elderly Black man pulled into the parking lot and went into the store, then came out and put his coffee on the table next to ours. When we told him we were there for Seabrook Farms research, he immediately offered an opinion about the demise of the company, although we hadn't asked.

"The old man could have run this place," he said. "IF the boys had let him," he added, with a vocal all-caps. He added, "But the boys wanted it for themselves."

I had been going to introduce myself as C. F.'s grandson, but I held back. It was always interesting to hear what local people actually thought of my family, and not what they said to me just to be respectful.

"They said the old man was an alcoholic," he went on. "And they were right, he was an alcoholic. But just because you are an alcoholic doesn't mean you can't run a company."

❧

My life as a husband and a dad got immensely better after I stood up in a meeting and said out loud, "Hi, I'm John, and I'm an alcoholic." Getting on my feet in front of a peerage of misfits and fuckups in the basement of a church in Park Slope, and trying to say how I came to be there, was about as close to a religious experience as I've had. I apologized for having no grisly rock-bottom moments to share, explaining that I started by defiling the Jag, and that "after that, I learned how to manage my drinking better." I quoted my therapist about how I came by my drinking "honestly," and why that mattered so much. "Even if it led to a lot of dishonesty" I said, "there was a kind of honesty, or at least a sincerity, in my relationship with alcohol." By the time I sat down, my old life was over.

JMS Jr. with Lisa, Rose, and Harry. Vermont 2021.

A NEW FATHER

"THE CHILD IS THE FATHER OF THE MAN" IS A LINE from a Wordsworth poem that I had never fully understood before a morning in February 2010, when I was in the back of an SUV with a child on my lap, parked next to a highway in Haiti. The driver had pulled over and stepped out to talk to a group of men standing in the shade of some palm trees. In the front passenger's seat was a social worker from Holt Fontana, an international adoption agency. Next to me in the back was a sixteen-year-old girl named Ayida, who held a toddler, Fredeline, on her lap. I held fifteen-month-old Rose Mirlande, my daughter, whom I had met the day before. Under ordinary circumstances, a three- or four-year process of bureaucracy and red tape would have been in our future, before getting to bring Rose home. But these weren't ordinary circumstances.

The Haitian earthquake had occurred less than three weeks earlier. As many as three hundred thousand people had been killed. Rose was in the Holt Fontana orphanage, about forty miles outside the epicenter of the quake. The children were unharmed, but the building in the capitol where the adoption records were kept—in our case almost two years of FBI and Homeland Security background checks, along with a social worker's home study, proving we weren't child traffickers and could provide a stable home for a child—had collapsed, killing the judge who presided over adoptions.

The U.S. State Department had hastily worked out a deal with the Haitian government whereby families like ours, who were legally vetted, could take their children home and finish the paperwork back in the States, under the U.N. policy of Humanitarian Parole. Almost a thousand children were granted HP status, including the younger of the two adopted children of Justice Amy Coney Barrett. Like her, many of our cohort of adoptive parents were Evangelical Christians. We are not, which is why, when one of the adoptive parents we met the next day in Miami asked us, "When did you get the call?" we thought she was talking about a call from the government about the HP policy.

Before the policy became official, I had managed to get into Haiti as a journalist; the airport was still closed to commercial flights. Holt's Haiti coordinator, Mike Noah, met me in Port-au-Prince. I was carrying a bright blue rabbit I'd bought from a rack of plush toys at the gift shop at the Miami International Airport, which I presented to Rose when we met for the first time at the orphanage later that day.

The next day, back at the U.S. Embassy, I learned Rose was among the seventeen kids at the orphanage who had been granted Humanitarian Parole, texting Lisa the news with shaking hands. The ensuing hours had been a rush of preparations with the caregivers back at the orphanage. The seventeen children, who ranged in age from seven months to fifteen years, were mostly headed for places much colder than Haiti, especially in February. One child was bound for Alaska, and Kansas and Minnesota were also on the list. Their adoptive parents needed to know their children's shoe and coat sizes so that they would have something warm to wear when they got to their new American homes. The children who hadn't made the list watched these preparations with sad faces. They would hopefully make the next list, or the one after that. Eventually all did leave for adoptive families in the United States.

Earlier that morning, there were heartbreaking goodbyes with the "mommas" who had cared for the children, in some cases for years, including Rose's momma, whose name was MyWorld. They sang a few Haitian songs together, all gathered in a big semicircle. Rose, seated on her caregiver's lap for the last time, was smiling. The blue rabbit was gone. Perhaps it was headed for Alaska too. I recorded the singing, while behind my phone I wept. But if Rose felt sad to be leaving her caregivers, her country, her culture, and her biological mother behind, she showed no sign of it. What we would come to think of as "grief-howls" would come, but not for years.

"*I'm a new father,*" I whispered into the back of Rose's neck, as we waited in the SUV. She screamed with pleasure; evidently, everything this big white father-man did was hilarious. I thought of the day when our son, Harry, was born. There was some of the same wild joy and hope at the miracle of a new human in your intimate circle of family— even though Rose had arrived by diplomatic rather than biological means, three years premature. But the joy came wrapped in tragedy. On the drive out to the orphanage from Port-au-Prince the day before, the driver had pointed out the site of a mass grave where earthquake victims were being buried by bulldozer.

❧

IT WAS HOT IN THE CAR. Rose was a warm squirmy bundle, grabbing at my iPhone as I texted Lisa that we were on our way to the airport, where a military transport plane would fly us to Miami. Lisa and Harry, now ten, were flying out of JFK to greet Harry's new sister.

Sitting there with Rose on my lap, the enormous consequences of what we were embarking on—the radical experiment in human kinship that is transracial adoption in America—pressed in on me like the tropical heat. I knew that I was drastically altering Rose's prospects and her future, but I had no idea that she was going to change my past, or at least how I make sense of my past. My narrative.

In the beginning of my story I had a grandfather, C. F. Seabrook, who in addition to his extraordinary gifts as a farmer and an engineer, was a champion of white supremacy—not just some ignorant South Jersey redneck, but a true believer in the superiority of the Nordic Christian male—who designed a whole caste system based on race, a white man's wonderland where your home and your job had everything to do with the color of your skin, all in mid-twentieth-century New Jersey. Our family continues to honor him as our patriarch. The unpleasant part we don't talk about.

Now, at the other end of my story, was my Black daughter. What was I going to tell Rose of the community of African Americans who began journeying to Seabrook to escape the Jim Crow South as far back as 1920? What will I say to this girl if she asks me why the Black people at Seabrook had to live in tents and shacks, and work outside, while lighter-skinned workers got much nicer houses and better indoor jobs? Should I say, as gently as possible, "I'm sorry to tell you this, sweet-heart, but the patriarch of your adoptive family was a racist"? Should I add that we directly benefited as a family from these racist policies, and that we owe some of our privileges to them?

And what if she asks then, "What did you do about it, Dad?"

~✿~

AYIDA, THE FIFTEEN-YEAR-OLD, was being adopted by a family in Brick, New Jersey. Ayida already looked like an American teenager, but the prospect of becoming one seemed to terrify her. She was sullen and unresponsive when I tried to engage in conversation.

I searched for a map of Brick on my iPhone to show her that it was close to the Jersey Shore. Rose kept lunging for the phone, knowing instinctively that this magical device was the portal to the world where she was headed. She had already figured out from watching me that touching the screen made things happen. By the time we had reached the airport, she knew how to use it.

"Near the sea!" I exclaimed to Ayida, as I showed her a map of the Jersey Shore. "That's good, right?" Ayida said nothing. She turned her head and looked out the window at the men talking in the shade.

At the embassy, we were processed by exhausted Marines and then transferred to a minivan driven by two soldiers, which would take us to the airport. The one riding shotgun had a bandage on his hand. "My sergeant told me two things—don't drink the water and don't pet the dogs," the wounded man said to his comrade. "So what do I do? I pet the dog."

We waited in the vehicle on the runway for several hours. Some of the children had to get out and pee on the tarmac. Finally, the van rolled up behind a C-5 military transport plane. We climbed out and I walked up the ramp at the back with the other children. There was no interior cladding in the plane. The seats were made of canvas straps, and the only windows were too high to see out of. For young children who had never been on an airplane before, the C-5 was a dreadful prospect. I remembered a picture taken by a Seabrook Farms photographer of young college women from the South being flown up for summer jobs in the plant in the 1950s. The plane they were sitting in looked a lot like this one.

The children climbed into the canvas seats and got buckled in. Then the ramp was raised with a loud screeching sound, encasing us in semidarkness. The children calmed each other, except for Lucsenda, the seven-year-old next to me, who clung to my leg fiercely. Rose fell asleep on my lap. I dozed off too. When I woke, I felt like my destiny had shifted.

The plane landed in Miami three hours later. The ramp at the back opened and let the purple evening light into the hold. Ayida picked up Fredeline. I held Rose in one arm and took Lucsenda's hand. We walked down the ramp together.

ACKNOWLEDGMENTS

Like C. F. Seabrook's vegetable factory, *The Spinach King* needed many hands to make it work. In addition to the cultivating of rows of weedy sentences by some of the most skilled word gardeners in the field, I gained crucial insights from friends who read earlier, dreadful drafts of the manuscript, and was also aided in ways small and large by research assistants, fact checkers, copy editors, and family members.

Tom Mayer, the editorial padrone on the project, believed in the book when I wasn't sure I did, and patiently read through years of drafts as I blindly moled my way forward through the loamy material. Tom is that rare editor who is equally good at structure and line editing, and he was the one essential man in making this book what it is. Jane Cavolina fine-tuned the manuscript. Deborah Garrison edited the original *New Yorker* article, commissioned by Tina Brown, and Aaron Retica fact-checked it, a delicate task that involved going over the piece with my parents. Cressida Leyshon worked on other prequels published during David Remnick's tenure at the helm of the magazine.

Helen Handelman assisted with the book in many ways. She imposed order on the chaos of my filing "system"; she researched and discovered countless pieces of Seabrook history and lore that I never knew; she introduced me to Microsoft Word Online; she handled photo permissions and did the endnotes. I will never forget the day we realized that the Meyer Handelman in the text was in fact Helen's great-great-uncle. Before Helen, Alexandra Kelly Wainwright worked with me, and we made several fact-finding trips to Deep South Jersey.

My agent, Joy Harris, expected to see the book-length version of the 1995 *New Yorker* article in another year or two. It took thirty, which is three fewer than building the Panama Canal required.

For early reads and suggestions, thanks to Jeanne McColloch, Phil "Stick Figure" Weiss, Rob Buchanan, Markley Boyer, Peter Grigg, Helga Merits, Chris Woodside, Cynthia Zarin, Lisa Spiegel, Colleen Lawrie, Alexander Henry, Tom Beller, Eric Schlosser, Katrina vanden Heuvel, and Andy Urban. Andy and I made numerous trips to Seabrook, New Jersey, and he generously shared discoveries he made while researching his own book, including the Ernest Dichter papers covering his work for Seabrook Farms. Jonathan Montgomery and Alex Henry were my guides to the history of the illustrious White family. Henry Breed shared correspondence—now in NYU's Bobst Library—that his grandparents carried on from Moscow about Seabrook Engineering's disastrous road-building project. Sonia Melnikova-Raich helped me with research in Moscow, and also kindly provided me with lunch at her home in San Francisco. Sonia's published works on Saul Bron and Amtorg were valuable background for C. F.'s Seabrook's Russian Adventure. Olga Dubitskaya, at the Garage Museum, also helped in Moscow. Beverly Carr did research in the Gloucester County Historical Society. Jim Bergmann generously shared his research on the South Jersey KKK with me, as well as his unpublished biography of George Agnew Chamberlain. Bruce Peterson told me of Paul Manafort's role in the corrupt dealings surrounding Seabrook housing.

Interviews with former Seabrookers took place over many years. I recorded Jonas McGailliard, C. F.'s longtime employee, in 1982, when—fresh out of college—I first began to think of writing the Seabrook story. Mas Nakawatase, Theodora Yoshikami, Stephanie Pierce, Sharon Yoshida, Evii Truumees, and Mari Ferentinos contributed information about the Japanese American and Estonian communities. Helga Merits was researching her 2024 film about Seabrook's Estonian community, *The Paradox of Seabrook Farms*, while I was researching my book, and I learned a great deal from our numerous conversations.

I am grateful to Donna Pearson, Gloria Kates, Betty Brown-Pitts, Sharon Walker Brown, James and Lionel Woodley, and Jimmy Lane, for sharing their migration stories with me, and for their commitment to remembering Seabrook Farms' African American workers and their families. I missed getting to meet Mack Bradwell, but I was very fortunate to speak to his sons, Mack and Ernest Bradwell, in 2021; both died the following year. I also spoke to his daughter, Margy Bradwell-Gonsalves, who is ninety-five as I write, and Mack's granddaughter, Jeanna Rogers. The Bradwells and the Seabrooks go back more than one hundred years. My grandfather brought Mack up North to work for him in 1920. Uncle Courtney ran him over with a truck in 1934. And yet it was Mack Bradwell who remained loyal to the old man until the very end, and—even after C. F. was gone—Mack continued to maintain the grounds, the master of the riding lawn mower.

My cousins Jim, Wes, Brian, and Ivin Seabrook (who is Charles F. Seabrook III) are the owners and managers of Seabrook Brothers & Sons. They kindly hosted me at the plant and gave me a tour of the quick-freezing operation and cold-storage facility. Thanks to them and Seabrook Brothers' five hundred workers, Seabrook Farms Frozen Creamed Spinach—sold in the Mylar Miracle-Pack—is still widely available throughout the New York metro area and North Jersey. I guarantee you won't find a better comparable product on the market. We grow our own, so . . .

My father could have thrown away the "JMS Jr." papers he left to me, but he didn't. My mother's habit of making carbon copies of her marvelous "Dearest Family" letters allowed me to hear the story of her career and how it led to the Seabrooks of South Jersey, told in her own voice as it was happening. I didn't ask my siblings, Carol S. Boulanger and Bruce Seabrook, to participate in the book, in order to allow them plausible deniability. They have processed some of these events differently, as siblings do. I am grateful to them for tolerating my version of the Seabrook story.

Lisa has lived with this book almost as long as she's lived with me, and without her support it couldn't have been written. Harry and Rose have never known life without Dad's "family book." I'm so thankful to have kids with a social conscience and a strong belief in equality and fairness. You do the Seabrooks proud.

NOTES

I did not witness the rise or the fall of Seabrook Farms. In researching and reconstructing the story of how Arthur Seabrook's sixty-acre truck farm became "the biggest vegetable factory on earth," as *Life* called Seabrook Farms in 1955, and how a succession battle between father and son brought the company down, I relied on—in addition to interviews with former Seabrookers—a wide variety of published and unpublished sources. The latter includes family letters, diaries, timelines, and memoirs by the principal players in the family drama.

It helped that the Seabrooks were litigious; their lawsuits left lengthy paper trails. C. F. Seabrook brought actions against numerous people and entities, including the U.S. government, and his sons had legal crusades of their own. In 1964, the sons sued their father's estate, arguing that the old man had not been of sound mind when he disinherited them in 1959. In preparation for trial, the sons' lawyer conducted interviews with some forty Seabrook personnel. Jack, Courtney, Belford, and Norma also prepared timelines of their own, charting the patriarch's decline. The proceedings got as far as depositions: Jack Seabrook, Leo P. Dorsey, and Judge Samuel Orlando were all deposed, among others. The parties eventually reached a settlement before the trial began.

I also benefited from coverage of Seabrook Farms in general and of the Seabrook strike in particular in the many regional newspapers that once existed in South Jersey, including the Vineland *Daily Journal*, the

Millville Daily, and the *Bridgeton Evening News*, all now digitized and searchable on newspapers.com. The Cumberland Historical Society preserves printed versions of old journals as well as microfilm in its comfy Greenwich (GREEN-wich), New Jersey, digs.

The Seabrook Education and Cultural Center, located in Upper Deerfield Township, is both a public museum and an archive. The main focus of the collection is the Japanese American experience at Seabrook during the war and after. The postwar Estonian community is also well documented. The archive is a valuable resource for researchers studying mid-Atlantic migratory labor, Big Ag in the East, and farmworkers' rights.

The exhibition space presents a version of Seabrook Farms history that is derived from the company's own PR in the late 1950s. The museum is more like a diorama depicting a mythical "bootstrap village" of Seabrook than a reality-based institution. Still, the SECC's collection of materials was helpful to me in many ways. The oral histories of the workers who came during World War II and in its aftermath were an important resource, as were bound volumes of *The Seabrooker*, the company newsletter. The SECC's many extraordinary photographs of Seabrook Farms and its workers, taken over four decades, were tremendously useful in helping me to visualize the now-vanished plant, the farm machinery, and the indoor and outdoor workers. The staff photographers working for *The Seabrooker* in the early 1920s, and again on the newsletter's revival in the '50s, left behind a rich visual record that can be viewed on the New Jersey Digital Highway, a Rutgers University–funded public memory project, as well as in SECC's archives.

The 1934 farmworkers strike, a significant event in the history of organized farm labor, was extraordinarily well documented by photographer Walter Ranzini of the *New York Post*, among others. During the 1930s and '40s, members of the elite group of photojournalists assembled by the Farm Security Administration under the direction of Roy Stryker, who included Dorothea Lange, Arthur Rothstein, Walker

Evans, and Ben Shahn, also captured working and living conditions at Seabrook Farms in photographs now in the National Archives.

My father also conducted a long love affair with the camera that is preserved in bound volumes of family photographs.

Introduction: BOOTSTRAP VILLAGE

1   **the largest farm:** States of Incarceration, "New Jersey: Seabrook Farms and 'Free' Labor," exhibit overview.

1   **photo essay:** Yale Joel, "Biggest Vegetable Factory on Earth," *Life*, January 3, 1955.

1   **print ad blared:** Seabrook Farms, Miracle-Pack advertisement, *Oakland Tribune*, June 24, 1959, 79.

3   **two thousand Japanese American:** George G. Olshausen, "Experiment at Seabrook Farms." *Far Eastern Survey* 16, no. 17, September 24, 1947, 200–201; Tom Infield, "Their Lives Uprooted, in Name of Security," *Philadelphia Inquirer*, February 19, 1992.

3   **seven hundred Estonians:** Helga Merits, director, *The Paradox of Seabrook Farms*, (The Netherlands: Merits Productions, 2024).

4   **de facto Jim Crow segregation:** David Brinkley's Journal, "Election Year in Averagetown," NBC, June 18, 1964.

Chapter 1: A CEO OF HIS OWN PAIN

12   **western incarceration camps:** Ed Kee, *Saving Our Harvest: The Story of the Mid-Atlantic Region's Canning and Freezing Industry* (Baltimore: CTI Publications, 2006), 218.

13   **a eulogy:** "Charles F. Seabrook Dies at 83; Pioneer in Quick-Frozen Foods," *New York Times*, October 21, 1964.

14   **front-page coverage:** "Farm Strike Ends; Reds Leader Ousted," *New York Times*, July 11, 1934.

15   **the Protestant elite of Philadelphia:** Janny Scott, *The Beneficiary: Fortune, Misfortune, and the Story of My Father* (New York: Riverhead Books, 2019).

16   **"Little Joe" Cione:** Chanize Thorpe, "Joseph Cione Haircutters," *New York Magazine*, n.d.

17   **I had written:** John Seabrook, "Eighty Thousand Bottles of Wine on the Wall," *GQ*, September 1, 1986.

Chapter 2: DEEP SOUTH JERSEY

21   **golf game:** John Seabrook, "Why Dan Quayle's Life Is Like His Golf Game," *Manhattan, inc.*, November 1988, 94.

22   **famous phrase:** "Origins of the Nickname," NJ.gov.

23   **notorious scandals as Bridgegate:** Kate Zernike, "Christie Faces Scandal on Traffic Jam Aides Ordered," *New York Times*, January 8, 2014.

23 **FBI informants:** Michael Ray, "Abscam," Encyclopedia Britannica.
26 **Palladian window:** Guy Roop, *Villas & Palaces of Andrea Palladio, 1508–1580* (Milan: Arte Grafiche Francesco Ghezzi, 1968).
37 **etymological cataclysm:** "Nimrod: 'great hunter," 1712, a reference to the biblical son of Cush, referred to (Genesis x.8-9) as 'a mighty hunter before the Lord.' . . . The word came to mean 'geek, klutz' by 1983 in teenager slang, for unknown reasons. (Amateur theories include its occasional use in 'Bugs Bunny' cartoon episodes featuring rabbit-hunting Elmer Fudd as a foil; its alleged ironic use, among hunters, for a clumsy member of their fraternity; or a stereotype of deer hunters by the non-hunting population in the U.S.)," Online Etymology Dictionary.

Chapter 3: MY FATHER'S CLOSET

40 **garment originally made for:** "Biography of Fulton J. Sheen." Catholic University of America.
40 **celebrities, socialites, and movie stars:** Slim Aarons, *Bernard Weatherill's*, photograph, 1964.
42 **Rolodex 3500-T:** For more, see Anna Jane Grossman, "The Life and Death of the Rolodex," Gizmodo, March 20, 2010.
42 **swashbuckling novelist:** Jack Hummel, "George Agnew Chamberlain's Secretary Reflects on Quinton's International Author," NJ.com, February 15, 2015.
43 **"a momentous turning point":** John M. Seabrook, *The Henry Ford of Agriculture* (New Jersey: Seabrook Educational and Cultural Center, Inc., 1995), 33.
44 **"We got the money":** Seabrook, *The Henry Ford of Agriculture*.
44 **"On October 3, 1941":** Seabrook, *The Henry Ford of Agriculture*.

Chapter 4: IT COULDN'T BE HELPED

46 **"return home" and "pain":** "Nostalgia," Online Etymological Dictionary.
47 **torn down in 1979:** James P. Quaranta, "Dynamite Blast Razes Seabrook Farms Stack," *Daily Journal* (Vineland, NJ), July 24, 1979.
47 **Ritter shut its:** "The World's Largest Catsup Bottle, PJ Ritter Photo Collection."
47 **Ardagh Glass moved away:** Al Stinger, "Remains of Ardagh Glass (Formerly Anchor Glass) in Salem NJ," *YouTube*; Bill Gallo Jr., "Ardagh Glass to Close 150-Year-Old Salem City Plant," NJ.com, July 16, 2014.
48 **"OK, life is unfair":** Richard Ikeda, interview with author.
48 **"You could never talk":** Theodora Yoshikami, interview with author.
49 **One of the speakers:** Michi Nishiura Weglyn, *Years of Infamy: The Untold Story of America's Concentration Camps* (Seattle: University of Washington Press, 1996).
49 **"Oh my God":** Michi Nishiura Weglyn, interview with author.
49 **"We were required":** Seiichi Higashide, *Adios to Tears: The Memoirs of a Japanese-Peruvian Internee in U.S. Concentration Camps* (Seattle: University of Washington Press, 2000).
50 **"was never close":** John M. Seabrook, *The Henry Ford of Agriculture* (New Jersey: Seabrook Educational and Cultural Center, Inc., 1995), 16.
51 **"I sometimes wonder":** Seabrook, *The Henry Ford of Agriculture*, 53.

Act II: THE HENRY FORD OF AGRICULTURE, 1859–1924

55   "This is the age of the engineer": "Carnegie on Kings: Talks to Engineers," *New York Tribune*, December 10, 1907.

Chapter 5: STRANGERS' GRAVES

57   Little Seabrook: Building Record, "Little Seabrook Farmhouse," Buckinghamshire Council: Heritage Portal.

57   I collected DNA: John Seabrook, "The Tree of Me," *New Yorker*, March 26, 2001.

58   death notice: Wickhambrook, "Obituaries," *Bury and Norwich Post*, February 11, 1873.

59   Landis named the place: "Charles K. Landis Founder of Vineland Was Considered Dreamer in 1861," *Daily Journal* (Vineland, NJ), July 1, 1952; Vince Farinaccio, *Before the Wind: Charles K. Landis and Early Vineland* (New York: Lulu.com, 2018).

59   Thomas Bramwell Welch: "Corporations: Almost Like Wine," *Time*, September 3, 1956.

60   "Dear Sir": Samuel Seabrook Letter to Charles K. Landis, September 18, 1867, Vineland Historical Society Archives.

Chapter 6: TRUCKERS

62   *bouwerie*, for "farm": "Bowery," Online Etymology Dictionary.

62   began to favor salads: Laura Shapiro, *Perfection Salad: Women and Cooking at the Turn of the Century* (Berkeley: University of California Press, 1986).

62   the archaic meaning of "truck": "Truck," Online Etymological Dictionary.

63   "Garden State": Maxine N. Lurie and Richard Veit, eds., *New Jersey: A History of the Garden State* (New Brunswick, NJ: Rutgers University Press, 2012).

64   "Hadrosaurus": Ria Sarkar, "The Story of New Jersey's State Fossil: Hadrosaurus foulkii," Rutgers Geology Museum.

65   more than 90 percent: "Farm Owner Operator Demographics and Statistics in the U.S.," Zippia.

66   "He soon wearied": "The Boy Returned," *Bridgeton Pioneer*, March 3, 1908.

67   Truck farming was: Deborah Kay Fitzgerald, *Every Farm a Factory: The Industrial Ideal in American Agriculture* (New Haven, CT: Yale University Press, 2010); Robert Winslow, *In the Blood: Understanding America's Farm Families* (Princeton, NJ: Princeton University Press, 2015).

Chapter 7: THE SKINNER SYSTEM

69   "most disastrous drought": *Evening Journal* (Vineland, NJ), May 29, 1903.

69   "In the main": "Value of Overhead Irrigation Demonstrated on a New Jersey Farm, Where High Priced Crops Are Produced with Certainty in Spite of Droughts— Labor Problems Also Solved," *The Sun* (New York), June 3, 1917.

70   Assyrian god Ninurta: K. van der Toorn and P. W. van der Horst, "Nimrod Before and After the Bible," *Harvard Theological Review* 83, no. 1 (1990); Terry Fenton, "Nimrod's Cities: An Item from the Rolling Corpus," in K. J. Dell, G. Davis, and Y. V. Koh, eds., *Genesis, Isaiah and Psalms* (Leiden, The Netherlands: Brill, 2010).

70   "A System of Irrigation": Charles W. Skinner, "System of Irrigation," U.S. Patent No. 614,507 (Washington, DC: U.S. Patent and Trademark Office, November 22, 1898).

73   shows ten hired men: Thirteenth Census of the United States: 1910—Population, Cumberland County, New Jersey, National Archives.

73   reporter from the *Bridgeton Evening News*: "Famous Truck Farm of This County," *Bridgeton Evening News*, August 2, 1920.

74   "One of the prettiest productive sights": Cora Shepherd, "An Irrigation Farm," *Rural New-Yorker*, March 4, 1911.

Chapter 8: THE VEGETABLE FACTORY

76   The family made: Jonathan Montgomery, private correspondence with author.

78   "famous truck farmer": *Dollar Weekly News* (Bridgeton, NJ), January 24, 1913.

78   "My first recollection": The JMS Jr. Papers, Seabrook Family Archive.

79   1917 interview: "Value of Overhead Irrigation Demonstrated on a New Jersey Farm, Where High Priced Crops Are Produced with Certainty in Spite of Droughts— Labor Problems Also Solved," *The Sun* (New York), June 3, 1917.

79   Food prices, already rising: James H. Shideler, *The Farm Crisis, 1919–1923* (Berkeley, CA: University of California Press, 1957).

79   "world's wheat king": Hiram Drache, "Thomas D. Campbell: The Plower of the Plains," *Agricultural History* 51, no. 1 (1977): 78–91.

80   Campbell, seeking capital: "The Biggest Wheat Farm in the World," *Country Gentleman*, October 26, 1918, 7.

Chapter 9: "NEW YORK TALKING, MR. SEABROOK!"

83   "We believe growth": Marc Andreessen, "The Techno-Optimist Manifesto," a16z.com, October 16, 2023.

84   biographical sketches: B. C. Forbes, *Men Who Are Making America* (New York, B.C. Forbes Publishing Co., 1917).

85   Forbes's method derived: Samuel Smiles, *Lives of the Engineers* (London: John Murray, 1879).

85   put him on its cover: Carl Snyder, "Doubling the Yield of Farms: Some Startling Results of Intensive Cultivation," *Collier's*, July 1917.

85   profiled the farmer-industrialist: Bruce Barton, "You Don't Altogether Like Your Job?," *American Magazine*, May 1921.

85   *The Dearborn Independent* story: Joseph Jefferson O'Neill, "'The Farm Should Be a Food Factory' – and This Big One Is!," *Dearborn Independent*, December 27, 1919.

86   A second article: "Farming an Occupation? No—a Business!," *Dearborn Independent*, January 3, 1920, 12, Henry Ford Motor Company Archives.

86 **"Four inches around"**: Seabrook Farms, Honey Heart Strawberries Advertisement, *New York Times,* June 2, 1916, 6.

87 **The Bradwells arrived:** Bradwell Family, interview with author and Andrew Urban.

88 **Ernest Liebold:** E. G. Liebold, Letter to Gus C. Wescott, February 21, 1922, Henry Ford Motor Company Archives: Acc. 380 Box 24 Invitations.

88 **two articles:** see above O'Neill, "'The Farm Should Be a Food Factory,'" and "Farming an Occupation? No—a Business!"

88 **Later that year:** "The International Jew: The World's Foremost Problem (Volume 1)," *Dearborn Independent*, 1920.

89 **"The strongman's trick"**: Ruth Ben-Ghiat, *Strongmen: Mussolini to the Present* (New York: W. W. Norton, 2021).

89 *The Seabrooker*: Bound editions of *The Seabrooker* are archived at the Seabrook Educational and Cultural Center in New Jersey, https://seabrookeducation.org.

89 **"Every employee pays"**: C. F. Seabrook, "Are You Paying Someone To Think For You?," *The Seabrooker* 2, no. 7, August 1922.

90 **Rockwell was a noted:** Frederick Frye Rockwell, *Around the Year in the Garden* (New York: Macmillan Company, 1917).

90 **"The greenhouses loom up"**: "Horizons: Sometimes the Nearer You Are to a Thing the Smaller It Looks," *The Seabrooker* 2, no. 6, December 1921.

91 **day-to-day life:** "Who Doesn't Know 'Tommy?,'" *The Seabrooker* 2, no. 6, December 1921.

91 **The Seabrook Farms Planting:** The Seabrook Farms Planting and Harvesting Schedule, compiled from editions of *The Seabrooker*, 1920–1921.

94 **"Many who have"**: O'Neill, "'The Farm Should Be a Food Factory.'"

Chapter 10: THE HIGHWAY COMMISSIONER

97 **In fact, farmers:** Dan McNichol, *Paving the Way: Asphalt in America* (Washington, DC: National Asphalt Pavement Association, 2005).

98 **C. F.'s contracting:** "Seabrook Tells About Big Contracts in Which He Has Been Involved," *Bridgeton Evening News*, September 4, 1928; C. L. McIlvaine, "Bridgeton Man Will Rank High in Russian Internal Improvements, *Bridgeton Evening News*, November 2, 1929.

98 **the Engineers Club:** "Palatial Home and Workshops for New York Engineers," *New York Times*, September 4, 1904.

100 **"I just threw"**: James H. Shideler, *The Farm Crisis, 1919–1923* (Berkeley, CA: University of California Press, 1957).

101 **C. F. had merely "retired"**: "Seabrook to Remain Here: Will Not Leave Bridgeton But Intends to Develop Other Interests," *Bridgeton Evening News*, October 2, 1924.

Act III: BLOODY HARVEST, 1929–1934

103 **"The day of the great promoter"**: Samuel I. Rosenman and William D. Hassett, eds., *The Public Papers and Addresses of Franklin D. Roosevelt, Volume One: The Genesis of the New Deal* (New York: Random House, 1938), 742–55.

Chapter 11: SHIRTSLEEVES

109 account of a farmworkers' strike: Colston E. Warne and Leo Huberman, "Your Government Is a Strike-Breaker," *The Nation*, August 15, 1934, 188–90.

Chapter 12: SUSPENDED ANIMATION

113 "Until I was 13": John M. Seabrook, *The Henry Ford of Agriculture* (New Jersey: Seabrook Educational and Cultural Center, Inc., 1995), 12.

114 "C. F. was probably pleased": Seabrook, *The Henry Ford of Agriculture*, 16.

114 the *International Herald Tribune* reported: "$150,000,000 Roads Contract Signed for Soviet System," *New York Herald*, July 19, 1929, *International Herald Tribune* Historical Archive 1887–2013.

115 rosy picture: "Seabrook, Bridgeton Financial Wizard, Talks of Soviet Before Sailing Again for Russia," *Daily Journal* (Vineland, NJ), August 2, 1930.

115 photographs of crumbling roads: *Za Rulem*, no. 22, November 1930, 20–23.

117 "He told Belford and Courtney": Seabrook, *The Henry Ford of Agriculture*, 15.

118 Quick-freezing: Mark Kurlansky, *Birdseye: The Adventures of a Curious Man* (New York: Anchor Books, 2013).

118 happened to sample a frozen goose: "Mrs. Marjorie Merriweather Post Is Dead at 86," *New York Times*, September 13, 1973.

121 secured a large loan: Seabrook, *The Henry Ford of Agriculture*, 18.

121 a windfall: Seabrook, *The Henry Ford of Agriculture*, 18.

122 a viable "cold chain": Nicola Twilley, *Frostbite: How Refrigeration Changed Our Food, Our Planet, and Ourselves* (New York: Penguin Press, 2024).

Chapter 13: "THE NEGRO JOINS THE PICKET LINE"

123 "The workers are divided": Colston E. Warne and Leo Huberman, "Your Government Is a Strike-Breaker," *The Nation*, August 15, 1934, 188–90.

124 "Half-clothed, half-starved": Lester B. Granger, "The Negro Joins the Picket Line," *Opportunity: A Journal of Negro Life*, August 1934.

125 "Only fanatics are willing": George P. West, "Communists Tried Under I.W.W. Law," *New York Times*, January 20, 1935.

126 "Hunger pulls people together": William W. Dusinberre, "Strikes in 1934, with a Case Study of New Jersey Farm Workers" (master's essay, Columbia University, 1953).

127 "'Jerry,' said Seabrook": Granger, "The Negro Joins the Picket Line."

127 "Mr. Seabrook explained": "Other Farm Employees Join Seabrook Strike When Mediation Fails," *Bridgeton Evening News*, April 9, 1934.

128 McKeen quit: "Farm Strike Arbiter Quits; Declares 'Reds' Have Control," *Morning Post* (Camden, NJ), April 9, 1934.

Chapter 14: REDS

129 the Hendersons: "Jersey Reds Asked About Faith in God," *New York Times*, August 23, 1934; "Police Halt Protests of 30 in Harlem Court," *New York Times*, September 3, 1932.

129   **living with their son:** The Hendersons' oldest son, Curtis (1926–2009), later achieved renown as a pioneer in the field of "cryonics," the pseudoscience of preserving people in suspended animation through quick-freezing, a practice that reaches back to Birdseye's early experiments among the Inuit in attempting to reanimate frozen fish, and the Seabrooks work with lima beans. In Curtis's only published remarks about his parents, he says they were both great believers in causes, which, he surmised, might partly explain his commitment to the cause of cryonics. Was cryonics inspired by young Curtis listening to his parents' talk about the Seabrooks' quick-freezing operation while mimeographing strike literature with the Dahls in their Vineland residence? Curtis is himself quick-frozen and stored in liquid nitrogen at the Cryonics Institute in Michigan, so perhaps he will return one day to enlighten us. "Curtis Henderson," *Cryonics* 303 (2009).

129   **Eleanor ran unsuccessfully:** "10-Day Term Given to Mrs. Henderson," *New York Times*, October 23, 1932.

129   **Henderson's firing:** "Columbia to Drop Donald Henderson," *New York Times*, April 5, 1933.

130   **became the headquarters:** "Probe Dynamite Found in Garage of Strike Leaders," *Daily Journal* (Vineland, NJ), June 28, 1934.

131   **"We wanted more money":** Bradwell family interview, with author and Andrew Urban.

131   **someone had alerted:** Colston E. Warne and Leo Huberman, "Your Government Is a Strike-Breaker," *The Nation*, August 15, 1934, 188–90.

131   **"Sheriff Brown took the party":** "Strike Settled at Seabrook's," *Bridgeton Evening News*, April 9, 1934.

131   **burned a cross:** T. R. Poston, "Strike: Betrayal Laid to Government in New Jersey Farm Disorder," *New York Amsterdam News*, July 21, 1934; "4 Injured, 4 Seized in Series of Riots," *Morning Post* (Camden, NJ), June 30, 1934.

131   **the largest KKK gathering:** "Klan Plans Great Seashore Outing," *Asbury Park Press*, July 2, 1924; "Eight Thousand in New Jersey's Klan Parade," *Bayonne Times*, July 5, 1924; "Big Klan Gathering at Elkwood Park," *Keyport Weekly*, July 11, 1924.

131   **clambake:** "Ku Klux Klan at the Park," *Bridgeton Evening News*, July 28, 1924.

131   **Bridgeton Mayor:** *Bridgeton Evening News*, July 28, 1924.

132   **"Packaging its noxious":** Joshua D. Rothman, "When Bigotry Paraded Through the Streets," *The Atlantic*, December 4, 2016.

132   **"Rumor has it that":** "Cumberland Country Club Buys Tumbling Dam Park for $30,000," *Bridgeton Evening News*, May 1925.

132   **"Klan Day":** "Klan Day at the Park," *Bridgeton Evening News*, July 20, 1925.

132   **ad for a KKK show:** "K.K.K. Attention," *Bridgeton Evening News*, August 22, 1925.

133   **"Vigilantism strengthened the Klan":** Linda Gordon, *The Second Coming of the KKK* (New York: W. W. Norton, 2017).

134   **Record Vault:** Public Land Records, Cumberland County New Jersey Clerk's Office.

135   **cuts were necessary:** "Armed Farmers Band to Rout Reds in Strike," *Daily News* (New York), July 2, 1934.

135   **"Officials of the farm":** "4 Injured, 4 Seized in Series of Riots," *Morning Post* (Camden, NJ), June 30, 1934.

135   **Shots were fired:** "Seabrook Farm Strike Continues, But Police Keep Peace and Order," *Bridgeton Evening News*, June 26, 1934.

135   **"A mass-meeting:"** "Seabrook Farm Remains Idle," *Bridgeton Evening News*, June 27, 1934.

136 **not to treat them:** "Violence Flares at Nearby Farm; Ask for Militia," *Daily Journal* (Vineland, NJ), June 29, 1934.

136 **had named Uncle Courtney:** "Extra Police Called for Seabrook Strike to Prevent Violence," *Bridgeton Evening News*, June 29, 1934.

136 **"This was the signal":** "4 Injured, 4 Seized," *Morning Post* (Camden, NJ), June 30, 1934.

137 **"Warrants were issued":** "Extra Police Called For Seabrook Strike."

137 **"the farm was a vital part":** "Extra Police Called for Seabrook Strike."

137 **dynamite and some blasting caps:** "Probe Dynamite Found in Garage," *Daily Journal* (Vineland, NJ), June 28, 1934.

137 **"Big Jack Saunders":** William W. Dusinberre, "Strikes in 1934, with a Case Study of New Jersey Farm Workers" (master's essay, Columbia University, 1953).

138 **Among those following:** Esther Peterson, *Restless: The Memoirs of Labor and Consumer Activist Esther Peterson* (Rancho Palos Verdes: CA: Caring Publishing, 1997).

138 **The summer school:** Suzanne Bauman and Rita Heller, *The Women of Summer: Part 1 and Part 2* (New York: Filmakers Library, Inc, 1985).

138 **"to be damned nuisances":** Rita Heller's interview with Colston Warne, Bryn Mawr College Library Archives: The Rita Heller Papers, box 2, folder 24.

138 **"I decided to join":** Peterson, *Restless*.

139 **"press room":** "Peace Agreed On in Farm Walkout," *New York Sun*, July 10, 1934 (ACLU Clippings-Cases By State: New York, Volume 727).

139 **"Communist agitator":** Warne and Huberman, "Your Government Is a Strike-Breaker."

140 **"I DO NOT INTEND":** C. F. Seabrook, "Attention! Citizens of Cumberland County: Insincerity of Communist Leaders," *Bridgeton Evening News*, July 6, 1934.

140 **"BLACK JACKS":** "Mass-Meeting Tonight," *Bridgeton Evening News*, July 8, 1934.

140 **"AS A TRUE AMERICAN":** C. F. Seabrook, "Attention! Citizens of Cumberland County: Police, Not Rioters Injured," *Bridgeton Evening News*, July 7, 1934.

140 **"The White Legion":** Seabrook, "Attention! Citizens of Cumberland County: Police, Not Rioters Injured."

141 **Matthew Williams was lynched:** "Lynchers in Salisbury Had Right-of-Way," *Afro American*, December 12, 1931; Daniel Hardin, "The 1937 Phillips Packinghouse Strike—Promise & Defeat," Washington Area Spark, September 18, 2014.

141 **"five carloads" of Klansmen:** "Klan Directs Terror Reign After Strike," *New York Amsterdam News*, July 28, 1934.

Chapter 15: BLOODY HARVEST

143 **Seabrook strike didn't come up:** "Seabrook Farm Strike Conference Today May Ease Labor Situation," *Bridgeton Evening News*, July 5, 1934.

143 **"Italian immigrants smashed":** "Arrest of 22 Klan Members at Jersey Home Foils Group's Plans for Rally," *New York Times*, November 25, 1979.

143 **the Klan held a meeting:** "Klan Guards Farm Workers In Red Strike," *The News*, July 6, 1934 (ACLU Correspondence-Cases By State: New Jersey, Volume 749).

143 **another fifteen-foot fiery cross:** "Klan Guards Farm Workers In Red Strike."

144 the rocks struck Gouldy: "Four More Are Injured in Seabrook Farm Strike," *Mill-ville Daily*, July 6, 1934.

144 "charged the building": "Eighteen Striking Farmers Arrested for Inciting Riot; Judge Loder May Arbitrate," *Daily Journal* (Vineland, NJ), July 7, 1934.

144 "If they aren't satisfied": Colston E. Warne and Leo Huberman, "Your Government Is a Strike-Breaker," *The Nation*, August 15, 1934, 188–90.

145 "Mr. Seabrook said": Frances Warne, Notarized Affidavit, American Civil Liberties Union: Case Correspondence, July 30, 1934; William W. Dusinberre, "Strikes in 1934, with a Case Study of New Jersey Farm Workers" (master's essay, Columbia University, 1953), 69.

146 "As the strikers": "Twenty-Seven Jailed in Seabrook Farm Rioting," *Millville Daily*, July 10, 1934.

146 "hand to hand battle": "Women Lead 300 Strikers in Battling Police," *Delaware News Journal*, July 10, 1934.

146 In 16mm footage: "1934—Depression, USA: Waterfront Strike; Seabrook Farms Agricultural Workers Strike. Jul34," Footage Farm (News Reel Number 220461-26).

146 choke hold: "Gas Balks Rioters on Jersey Farm," *New York Times*, July 10, 1934.

147 "A beet truck": Vivian Dahl, "Them Women Sure Are Scrappers," *Working Woman*, August 1934.

147 "I had supposed": Mildred Fairchild, *Letter to Lem Harris*, American Civil Liberties Union: Case Correspondence, July 29, 1934; Dusinberre, "Strikes in 1934," 68.

147 unventilated icebox: T. R. Poston, "Strike: Betrayal Laid to Government in New Jersey Farm Disorder," *New York Amsterdam News*, July 21, 1934.

148 a federal mediator: "Farm Strike Ends; Red Leader Ousted," *New York Times*, July 11, 1934.

148 "I have done all I can": "Farm Strike Ends; Red Leader Ousted,"

148 Henderson "leaped on the soapbox": "Farm Strike Ends; Red Leader Ousted."

149 only three were rehired: "Klan Continues Terrorism Against Jersey Negroes: KLAN DIRECTS TERROR REIGN AFTER STRIKE, Seeks Destruction of Union by Attacks on Negro Workers," *New York Amsterdam News*, July 28, 1934.

149 Lester Granger returned to: Lester B. Granger, "The Negro Joins the Picket Line," *Opportunity: A Journal of Negro Life*, August 1934.

150 "issued an ultimatum": "Seabrook Farm Strike Ended, Agitator's Leave," *The Daily News* (Lebanon, PA), July 11, 1934.

150 hunger strike: "Wife Spends Day with Hunger Striker to Mark 20th Wedding Anniversary," *Evening Courier* (Camden, NJ), November 27, 1934.

150 mock trial: "Mock Trial in Seabrook Case," *Millville Daily*, July 14, 1934; "Mock Trial Ends with 'Indictments," *Daily Journal* (Vineland, NJ), July 16, 1934; Sasha Small, "Open Hearing in Jersey Farm Town Reveals Low Pay, Terror," *Daily Worker*, July 20, 1934; "New Strike Looms; Negroes are Barred," *New York Amsterdam News*, July 21, 1934.

151 "You didn't work *with*": Donald H. Grubbs, *Cry from the Cotton: The Southern Tenant Farmers Union and the New Deal* (Chapel Hill: University of North Carolina Press, 1971); Lowell K. Dyson, "The Southern Tenant Farmers Union and Depression Politics," *Political Science Quarterly* 88, no. 2 (1973), https://doi.org/10.2307/2149109.

151 poison by accident: "Ex Educator's Wife Dies: Mrs. Donald Henderson Is Victim of Poison in Chicago," *New York Times*, June 12, 1941.

151 **took the Fifth:** Testimony of Donald Henderson, National Secretary Treasurer, Distributive, Processing and Office Workers Union of America, Subversive Control of Distributive, Processing, and Office Workers of America: Hearings before the United States Senate Committee on the Judiciary (Eighty-Second Congress, second session), February 14, 1952.

151 **final appearance:** C. P. Trussell, "Educator Is Asked to Head the 'Voice,'" *New York Times*, February 23, 1953.

Chapter 16: REVENGE OF THE NUBIANS

155 **I wrote the piece:** John Seabrook, "The Spinach King," *New Yorker*, February 20 & 27, 1995.

155 **"Belford Seabrook, son":** Colston E. Warne and Leo Huberman, "Your Government Is a Strike-Breaker," *The Nation*, August 15, 1934, 188–90.

157 **"Every journalist":** Janet Malcolm, *The Journalist and the Murderer* (New York: Vintage, 1990).

157 **"writers are always":** Joan Didion, *Slouching Towards Bethlehem* (New York: Farrar, Straus & Giroux, 1968).

Chapter 17: GROWTH UNITS

166 **"C. F. didn't want":** John M. Seabrook, *The Henry Ford of Agriculture* (New Jersey: Seabrook Educational and Cultural Center, Inc., 1995), 28.

167 **climate classification:** C. W. Thornthwaite and John Leighly, "Status and Prospects of Climatology," *Scientific Monthly* 57, no. 5 (November 1943), 457–65; John M. Seabrook, "Applied Climatology at Seabrook Farms," *Weatherwise* 6, April 1953, 36–37, 59.

168 **called "cropmeters":** C. W. Thornthwaite, "Operations Research in Agriculture," *Journal of the Operations Research Society of America* 1, no. 2 (February 1953); "Science at Seabrook," *Johns Hopkins Magazine*, October 1951, 4.

168 **tribute to organized crime:** Seabrook, *The Henry Ford of Agriculture*, 19–20.

169 **"the Seabrook family":** "H.R. 4769: Extension of NLRA to Agricultural Employees," Hearings Before the Special Subcommittee on Labor of the Committee on Education and Labor House of Representatives (Ninetieth Congress, First Session), May 1967, 32.

169 **Jack told a reporter:** *Farm Labor Organizing 1905–1967: A Brief History* (New York: National Advisory Committee on Farm Labor, 1967), 40.

169 **first farm on the East Coast:** "Seabrook Farms Workers Ratify AFL Unionization," *Daily Journal* (Vineland, NJ), March 14, 1941.

169 **The old man later grudgingly:** *Farm Labor Organizing 1905-1967*, 40.

Chapter 18: THE "STROKE"

171 **my father wrote:** John M. Seabrook, *The Henry Ford of Agriculture* (New Jersey: Seabrook Educational and Cultural Center, Inc., 1995), 34.

172 **The old man returned:** Belford Seabrook, unpublished memoir (December 1966), 25.

173 **Belford riding a bike:** "Bicycles Replace Autos at Seabrook Farm," *Bridgeton Evening News,* January 31, 1942.

175 **"I admit I have been":** Edwin Kemp, "Racial Discrimination Barred at 13,000-Acre Seabrook Farms," *Courier-Post* (Camden, NJ), April 29, 1943.

Chapter 19: SEABROOKS AT WAR

176 **Wartime propaganda:** "Food Will Win the War!," *Prologue Magazine* 49, no. 4 (Winter 2017), National Archives; "Food Will Win the War, 1917," Gilder Lehrman Institute of American History, History Resources.

176 **increase in production:** Lania Davis Gavin, "Food Dehydration—New Field for Workers: Unbiased Seabrook Farms in Step with Vast War-Time Program," *Pittsburgh Courier,* December 19, 1942.

176 **writer from *Coronet*:** Mona Gardner, "Assembly-Line Farmer," *Coronet,* November 1943.

177 **three enormous dehydrators:** "Food Is Studied by Army Aide at Seabrook Farms," *Courier-Post* (Camden, NJ), May 25, 1942; *Seabrook Farms Co. v. Army,* Proceedings Nos. 307 and 312," *Decisions of the Appeal Board: Office of Contract Settlement,* vol. 5 (Washington, DC: U.S. Government Printing Office, 1953), 63–75.

178 **1,250,000 pounds of dehydrated beets:** *Seabrook Farms Co. v. Army,* 65.

178 **turned bloodred:** "Rempfer Awarded $20,000 from Seabrook Farm," *Daily Journal Post* (New Jersey), April 29, 1949.

179 **camps around Cumberland County:** *New Jersey: A Guide to Its Present and Past,* compiled and written by the Federal Writers' Project of the Works Progress Administration in the State of New Jersey (New York: Viking Press, 1939).

180 **A PhD student:** Margaret Hermenia, Gordon, "A Study of Migratory Labor at Seabrook Farms 1941–1945" (master's thesis, Atlanta University School of Social Work, June 1947), 37–39.

181 **seventy-two hours to report:** *Seabrook at War,* Radio documentary, narrated by Kurt Vonnegut Jr., New Jersey Historical Commission, 1995.

181 **told to head east:** Ed Kee, *Saving Our Harvest* (Baltimore: CTI Publications, 2006), 218.

182 **"we were questioned":** George Sakamoto interview with Wes Yokoyama (Seabrook Educational and Cultural Center Oral History, 1991), 11.

182 **"The dozen or so American-born":** "West Coast Japs Enjoy Working on Jersey Farm," *Courier-Post* (Camden, NJ), January 26, 1944.

183 **"loyalty questionnaire":** Natasha Varner, "The 'Loyalty Questionnaire' of 1943 Opened a Wound that has Yet to Heal," Densho.org, July 19, 2019.

184 **dibs on the government housing:** Gordon, "A Study of Migratory Labor at Seabrook Farms 1941–1945," 42.

Chapter 20: THE MIRACLE-PACK

187 **form of publicity even more effective:** John M. Seabrook, *The Henry Ford of Agriculture* (New Jersey: Seabrook Educational and Cultural Center, Inc., 1995), 39.

187 **The consumer society:** Andrew Urban, *Processing History: Labor, Capitalism, and Memory at Seabrook Farms* (forthcoming, 2026).

188 "Belford was never again": Seabrook, *The Henry Ford of Agriculture*, 34–35.

189 print ad: Seabrook Farms Miracle Pack Ad, "Fearfully, I Served It," *New York Daily News*, November 17, 1960, 11.

190 Mylar Miracle-Pack: Joseph W. Barclay, "Seabrook's 'Miracle-Pack' Prepared Foods," *The Seabrooker*, August 1959.

190 "At most family parties": Seabrook, *The Henry Ford of Agriculture*, 16.

Chapter 21: KILL YOUR DAH-LINKS

192 Russian-born gossip writer: "Eager Igor," *Time*, November 5, 1945.

192 Noel Coward was: Philip Hoare, *Noel Coward: A Biography* (Chicago: University of Chicago Press, 1998).

193 Ian Fleming was: David G. Allan, "Ian Fleming's Jamaica," *New York Times*, November 6, 2008; *The Letters of Ann Fleming* (London: Harvill Press, 1985).

193 newspaper baron Lord Beaverbrook: Anne Chisolm and Michael Davie, *Lord Beaverbrook: A Life* (New York: Knopf, 1993).

193 Princess Margaret holidayed there: Christopher Warwick, *Princess Margaret: A Life of Contrasts* (London: Andrew Deutsch, 2003).

194 "It was as if": Merv Griffin, *Merv: An Autobiography* (New York: Simon & Schuster, 1980).

194 The sisters were: Dawn Porter, *Those Glamorous Gabors: Bombshells from Budapest* (Staten Island, NY: Blood Moon Productions, 2013).

194 "Like Sally Field": Bruce Handy, "Glamour and Goulash," *Vanity Fair*, July 2001.

196 "Eva Gabor's current favorite": Walter Winchell, "Gossip of the Nation," *Philadelphia Inquirer*, December 10, 1951.

196 "Eva Gabor's intended third husband": Danton Walker, "Gossip of the Nation," *Philadelphia Inquirer*, August 19, 1952.

Chapter 22: BOY SCOUTS

200 "swathed in a Turkish towel": "Dentist Denies Indiscretions Charged by Prominent Wife; Judge to Inspect Mansion," *Daily Journal* (Vineland, NJ), June 12, 1952.

201 asking for $2 million: "Dentist Sues His Estranged Wife For $2 Million," *Daily Journal* (Vineland, NJ), June 5, 1952.

201 "Saunders is alleged": "Seabrook Employee Held After Dr. Harry Barber Suffers Cut in Skirmish," *Daily Journal* (Vineland, NJ), July 23, 1952.

Chapter 23: "A MARKED PLAYBOY"

205 "Jack Seabrook, the wealthy young": Dorothy Kilgallen, "The Voice of Broadway," *News-Herald* (Franklin, Pennsylvania), April 21, 1953.

205 "The once-flourishing romance": Dorothy Kilgallen, "The Voice of Broadway," *New York Journal-American*, April 30, 1953.

205 "Eva Gabor's romance": Hedda Hopper, "Hollywood," *Daily News* (New York), May 19, 1953.

205 "Eva Gabor has iced": Edith Gwynn, "Hollywood," *Los Angeles Mirror*, May 28, 1953.

Chapter 24: HURRICANE HAZEL

213 **dynamics of American family businesses:** Kenneth Kaye, *The Dynamics of Family Business: Building Trust and Resolving Conflict* (N.p.: IUniverse Publishing, 2005).
213 **"Like an addictive drug":** Kenneth Kaye, "When the Family Business Is a Sickness," *Family Business Review* 9, no. 4 (December 1996): 347–68.

Chapter 25: THE INVITATION

214 **4-page photo essay:** Yale Joel, "Biggest Vegetable Factory on Earth," *Life*, January 3, 1955.

Chapter 26: "DEAREST FAMILY"

222 **"One theory of the accident":** "Further Details of the Death of Maude Toomey," *Daily Deadwood Pioneer-Times*, January 18, 1920.
225 **Sadie Hawkins Day story:** Elizabeth Toomey, "Recommends Direct Approach in Learning Leap Year Reactions," *Terre Haute Tribune*, January 25, 1948.

Chapter 27: THE PRINCE AND THE REPORTER

234 **read about his exploits:** Earl Wilson, "Ann Miller and Jack Seabrook, the Frozen Foods Fella, Are a New Duo," *Daily News* (New York) November 18, 1953.
235 **high-caliber male journalists:** Donald Edgar, *Express '56: A Year in the Life of a Beaverbrook Journalist* (London: John Clare, 1981).
237 **"One of the most serious":** Art Buchwald, "Diplomatic Tempest Rages Over Wedding Attire," *Oakland Tribune*, April 19, 1956.
237 **The cathedral wedding:** Judith Balaban Quine, *Bridesmaids: Grace Kelly, Princess of Monaco, and Six Intimate Friends* (New York: Grove Press, 1989).

Chapter 28: MARRIAGE OF THE CENTURY

244 **the lead item:** Dorothy Kilgallen, "Gossip In Gotham," *Times-Tribune* (Scranton, Pennsylvania), September 8, 1956.
247 **the bride wore:** "New Jersey Man Weds Miss Elizabeth Toomey," *Columbia Missourian*, October 8, 1956.

Chapter 29: "MODERN FOOD DREAMS"

248 **"The Effete East":** Roger Angell, "The Effete East," *Holiday*, March 1958.
248 **Aarons's collection:** Slim Aarons, *A Wonderful Time: An Intimate Portrait of the Good Life* (New York: Harper and Row, 1974).
248 **the marketing consultant:** Stefan Schwarzkopf and Rainer Gries, *Ernest Dichter and Motivation Research: New Perspectives on the Making of Post-War Consumer Culture* (New York: Palgrave Macmillan, 2010).

249 "If the desire for freedom": Daniel Horowitz, "The Birth of a Salesman: Ernest Dichter and the Objects of Desire," 1986.

249 "After the privations": Barbara Ehrenreich, *The Hearts of Men: American Dreams and the Flight from Commitment* (New York: Anchor Books, 1982).

249 criticized his work: Vance Packard, *The Hidden Persuaders* (London: Longmans, Green and Company, 1957).

250 Dichter recommended the company: Ernest Dichter, "A Creative Problem Analysis and Proposal for the First Two Phases of a Motivational Research Program for Seabrook Farms Company," Hagley Museum and Library Manuscript and Archives Repository: The Ernest Dichter Collection (1907–1991), 1957.

250 "Elizabeth Seabrook" brand: Dichter, "A Creative Problem Analysis and Proposal for the First Two Phases of a Motivational Research Program for Seabrook Farms Company."

251 The Luchow's dishes: John M. Seabrook, *The Henry Ford of Agriculture* (New Jersey: Seabrook Educational and Cultural Center, Inc., 1995), 64.

252 Walker's daughter Sharon: Sharon Walker Brown, interview with the author.

255 famous hoarder: Corey Kilgannon, "Buried by His Past," *New York Times*, March 7, 2014.

Chapter 30: "A MESS OF POTTAGE"

264 "We were a public company": John M. Seabrook, *The Henry Ford of Agriculture* (New Jersey: Seabrook Educational and Cultural Center, Inc., 1995), 35.

264 "During the past four years": Seabrook, *The Henry Ford of Agriculture*, 57–59.

266 "ultimate enabler": Tom Hubler, *The Soul of Family Business: A Practical Guide to Family Business Success and a Loving Family* (Minneapolis, MN: Lilja Press, 2018).

267 Jack was clearly behind everything: "Seabrook Asks for Release," *Evening Bulletin* (Philadelphia, PA), March 30, 1959; "Family Seeks Guardian for C. F. Seabrook," *Bridgeton Evening News*, April 22, 1959; Rowland T. Moriarty, "The Seabrook Struggle: Overalls to Success," *Evening Bulletin* (Philadelphia, PA), June 14, 1959; "Seabrook Family Ends Dispute," *Bridgeton Evening News*, June 15, 1959.

Epilogue: SEABROOK & SON

277 "If *guilt* is the psychoanalytic word": Adam Phillips, "On Getting Away with It," *Psychoanalytic Dialogues* 19, no. 1 (2009): 98–103.

Chapter 31: THE COTTON PLANT

279 "Samson Air": Patrick McGeehan, "David Samson, a Christie Ally, Is Sentenced to Home Confinement," *New York Times*, March 6, 2017.

280 For the catalogue: Tom Ryder, *Half a Century of Coaching: The Driving Career and Carriages of John M. Seabrook* (Hanover, PA: Sheridan Press, 2001).

283 Confederate flag: Aaron Blake, "The Story of Nikki Haley and the Confederate Flag," *Washington Post*, February 15, 2023.

284 keeping slaves in stocks: Whitemarsh B. Seabrook, "A Memoir on the Origin, Cultivation and Uses of Cotton, from the Earliest Ages to the Present Time" (Charleston,

SC: Miller & Browne, 1844); "Gov. Whitemarsh Benjamin Seabrook," National Governor's Association.

285 **When Courtney died:** Eric Pace, "Charles Courtney Seabrook, 94, Pioneer in Frozen Vegetables," *New York Times*, October 10, 2003.

Chapter 32: THE SESQUI AND THE SWISS BANKER

289 **"This move alone":** Thomas H. Keels, *Sesqui!: Greed, Graft, and the Forgotten World's Fair of 1926* (Philadelphia: Temple University Press, 2017).

289 **a 1928 interview:** "Selected Klauder as Mackey Link," *Philadelphia Inquirer*, September 4, 1928.

290 **"Seabrook was summoned to appear":** "Seabrook Wanted in Phila. Scandal," *Daily Journal* (Vineland, NJ), September 1, 1928.

291 **"Mayor Mackey angrily":** Harold J. Wiegand, "Mackey Denounces Attack on Klauder as 'Pack of Lies,'" *Philadelphia Inquirer*, September 1, 1928.

291 **"a monopoly of city":** "Seabrook Charges Political Attack on Contract Deals," *Courier-Post* (Camden, NJ), September 4, 1928.

295 **broke the story:** Jerry Landauer, "Agnew Is Investigated in Md. Extortion Case," *Wall Street Journal*, August 7, 1972.

296 **"John M. Seabrook":** Jerry Landauer, "Beyond the Fringe? SEC Probes Payment by IU International of Chief's Legal Costs,'" *Wall Street Journal*, April 6, 1978.

296 **another front-page Landauer article:** Jerry Landauer, "IU International and Its Chairman Cited as SEC Reopens Payments Investigation," *Wall Street Journal*, September 29, 1978.

298 **"The executive perquisites":** Jerry Landauer, "Fee Paid to IU Chairman's Partner Leads U.S. to Look for Possible Plot to Loot Firm," *Wall Street Journal*, May 17, 1979.

299 **the court ruled:** Kenneth B. Noble, "Swiss Bankers Expected to Relax Secrecy on U.S. Stock Violations," *New York Times*, September 1, 1982; "Swiss to Tell Some Bank Secrets," *Chicago Tribune*, September 1, 1982.

Chapter 33: A CREDIBLE ULTIMATUM

301 **my father's obit:** Deaths, "Seabrook, John Martin," *New York Times*, February 15, 2009.

302 **I gave away:** John Seabrook, "Hand Me Down Blues," *Men's Vogue*, November 2007.

303 **An IFS-trained therapist:** For further reading on IFS Systems, see Lisa Spiegel, *Internal Family Systems Therapy with Children* (New York: Routledge, 2017).

Chapter 34: THE HEART OF RECOVERY

308 **The farmer is an AI:** John Seabrook, "The Age of Robot Farmers," *New Yorker*, April 8, 2019.

308 **"Seabrook: The Heart of Recovery":** "History," Seabrook, https://seabrook.org/history/.

310 **"Cumberland is New Jersey's poorest county":** Susan K. Livio, "Crisis in Cumberland," NJ.com, July 27, 2023.

---

311   **grand plan:** "An 'Agri-City' Is Planned on State's Largest Farm," *New York Times*, March 26, 1972.

311   **Paul Manafort:** "Abuses, Favoritism, and Mismanagement in HUD Programs (Part 4)," Hearings Before the Employment and Housing Subcommittee of the Committee on Government Operations (One Hundred First Congress, First Session), October 2, 1989.

IMAGE CREDITS

C. F. broke the 1934 strike: SECC
The company first froze vegetables: SECC
Jack Seabrook: SECC
Under Jack and his brother: Seabrook Farms Archive
The logo on the water tower: SECC
Jack was eight inches taller: Arthur Rothstein/Library of Congress, Prints & Photographs Division, Farm Security Administration/Office of War Information Black-and-White Negatives
JMS invited New York pals: Seabrook family photograph
My father's horsedrawn family picnics: Seabrook family photograph
After the war: Seabrook family photograph
No one knew more: SECC
Thanks to lobbying by JMS: Yale Joel/The LIFE Picture Collection/Shutterstock
Starlet Eva Gabor: Seabrook Farms Archive
Hints of Eva's later role: Seabrook family photograph
Eva and Jack: Seabrook family photograph
The Gabor sisters: Seabrook family photograph
E. A. Toomey: Seabrook family photograph
On joining United Press: *Photoplay*, April 1955
The Stork Club: Seabrook family photograph
Toomey: Seabrook family photograph
One chilly day: Seabrook family photograph
Elizabeth Toomey: Walter Carone/Getty Images
Liz shared a stateroom: Bettmann/Getty Images
Jack was also on the ship: Seabrook family photograph
Liz first visited Seabrook: Seabrook family photograph
Liz wasn't sure: Seabrook family photograph
But Jack persisted: Seabrook family photograph
As a woman: Seabrook family photograph
Coaching afforded Jack Seabrook: Seabrook family photograph
Titled "We Know Our Place": Slim Aarons/Getty Images
Liz traded her hard-earned independence: Seabrook family photograph
Aaron Shikler's 1969 portrait: Seabrook Family Collection
Inside Bernard Weatherill, Civic and Sporting Tailors: Slim Aarons/Getty Images